Hugh Mackay is a social researcher and the author of seventeen books – eleven in the field of social analysis and ethics, and six novels. He is a Fellow of the Australian Psychological Society and has been awarded honorary doctorates by Charles Sturt, Macquarie, New South Wales and Western Sydney universities. In 2015, he was appointed an Officer of the Order of Australia. He lives in the Southern Highlands of New South Wales.

www.hughmackay.net.au

Other books by Hugh Mackay

NON-FICTION

Reinventing Australia

Why Don't People Listen?

Generations

Turning Point

Media Mania

Right & Wrong

Advance Australia . . . Where?

What Makes Us Tick?

The Good Life

The Art of Belonging

FICTION

Little Lies

House Guest

The Spin

Winter Close

Ways of Escape

Infidelity

To Mick & Diana
Welcome to Australia!
Best wishes
Hugh Mackay

Beyond Belief

Hugh Mackay

Pan Macmillan Australia

First published 2016 in Macmillan by Pan Macmillan Australia Pty Limited
1 Market Street, Sydney, New South Wales, Australia, 2000

Reprinted 2016 (twice)

Cataloguing-in-Publication entry is available
from the National Library of Australia:
http://catalogue.nla.gov.au

Typeset in Bembo 12.5/16pt by Midland Typesetters, Australia
Printed by McPherson's Printing Group

Text acknowledgements appear on pages 267–9.
The author and the publisher have made every effort to contact copyright holders for material used in this book. Any person or organisation that may have been overlooked should contact the publisher.

The paper in this book is FSC® certified.
FSC® promotes environmentally responsible, socially beneficial and economically viable management of the world's forests.

Human life 'means' nothing. But that is not to say that it is not worth living. What does a Debussy Arabesque 'mean', or a rainbow or a rose? A man delights in all of these, knowing himself to be no more – a wisp of music and a haze of dreams dissolving against the sun.

Peter De Vries, *The Blood of the Lamb* (1961)

To Sheila

Contents

What this book is about

What do people actually mean when they say 'God'?

Considering how much harm it causes, why does religion continue to prosper in the world?

Were Bible stories ever intended to be taken literally?

Can we be both rational and spiritual – and what might 'spiritual' mean, anyway?

If, like most Westerners, you think of yourself as basically Christian in your attitudes, values, ideals and way of life, but you can't bring yourself to embrace all the beliefs and doctrines of the institutional church, you may well recognise yourself in the following pages. *Beyond Belief* is a book about people's quest for meaning in a society that has lost its appetite for conventional religion. It is written from a broadly Christian perspective because our culture has been heavily influenced by Christianity, through churches serving as places of worship and community hubs, through the influence of church schools, and through the cultural ubiquity of Bible stories and biblical references.

But this is not a book for committed Christians. Nor is it likely to appeal to committed atheists – certainly not to anti-theists – or anyone else whose mind is closed to new ways of thinking about God. It is a book for doubters, sceptics, heretics, agnostics and religious fringe-dwellers, including some who may attend church but feel uncomfortable doing so, as if they don't quite fit, can't quite bring themselves to believe what everyone else seems to believe, or sometimes feel as if they are expected to leave their brains at the church door.

If any of that sounds like you, and you're still open to the idea of faith in 'something greater than ourselves', then *Beyond Belief* may offer you some clarification, some comfort and some encouragement.

Throughout the book, you'll encounter verbatim quotations from a series of personal interviews I have conducted with people representing many different points on the spectrum of faith. They are acknowledged at the end of the book, though all their names have been changed in the text, and their stories have been edited, where necessary, to preserve their anonymity. I have also created several vignettes, loosely based on real people and real events, drawn from the personal stories I have been privileged to listen to during my career as a social researcher.

Why did I write the book? Over the past twenty-five years, our yearning for 'something to believe in' has become increasingly obvious, as people look for ways to fill the gap left by the mass retreat from traditional religious faith and practice. *Beyond Belief* explores some of the ways we might satisfy that yearning.

INTRODUCTION

Religion goes marching on

Globally, religion is on the rise.

You might not think so if you lived in Scandinavia, some parts of Western Europe, or countries like Canada, Australia and New Zealand that have drawn much of their cultural heritage from Europe; in those places, although most people continue to identify with Christianity, church attendance has been steadily waning for fifty years and some commentators now refer to this as the West's 'post-Christian era'.

Not elsewhere, though. According to John Micklethwait and Adrian Wooldridge in *God is Back* (2009), 'the proportion of people attached to the world's four biggest religions – Christianity, Islam, Buddhism and Hinduism – rose from 67 percent in 1900 to 73 percent in 2003 and may reach 80 percent by 2050'.

Although accurate global figures on religious practice (let alone religious belief) are notoriously difficult to come by, it does appear that in the very countries where the most vigorous attempts have been made to stamp out religion – Russia under Stalin, India under Nehru and China under Mao Zedong – there has been a massive subsequent upswing in religious interest and observance. Micklethwait and Wooldridge report that Russia's president, Vladimir Putin, maintains a private chapel and sometimes wears a baptismal cross, the Russian security organisation (successor to the KGB) has its own Orthodox church just across the road from its Moscow headquarters, and former president Mikhail Gorbachev has prayed at the tomb of St Francis of Assisi, claiming that, for him, St Francis is 'the other Christ'.

In China, the post-Mao rise of religion has been extraordinary. Though Mao is still revered as a national hero and the majority of the population remains unresponsive to the appeal of religion, the widely respected Pew Research Center's 2006 Global Attitudes Project reported that 31 percent of Chinese people regard religion as either somewhat or very important in their lives. Religious affiliation in China is mostly with Buddhism, Taoism or Confucianism; there are over 100 million Buddhists, for instance. But Christianity has been present in China since the seventh century and there are now many more Christians than members of the Communist Party: official Chinese government statistics put the number of Christians at 21 million in 2007 – up from 14 million in 1997. Writing in the *Financial Times* in November 2014, Jamil Anderlini estimates the current figure as closer to 100 million, many of them worshipping 'under the radar' in informal house churches. Islam is also on the rise in China; again quoting Pew Research data, Micklethwait and Wooldridge predict that, by 2050, 'China could well be the world's biggest Muslim nation as well as its biggest Christian one'. They also note that the Virgin Mary has growing appeal in China, with many fishermen now dedicating their boats to her and an annual celebration of her 1900 'appearance' in the village of Donglu attracting thousands of Roman Catholics.

If Anderlini's figures are even roughly correct, things are changing more rapidly than Micklethwait and Wooldridge predicted.

Anderlini quotes projections by Fenggang Yang, director of Purdue University's Center on Religion and Chinese Studies, confirming that, by 2030, there will be more Christians in China than in any other country on earth. By then, on present trends, Chinese churchgoers will outnumber US churchgoers.

The resurgence of religion in countries once avowedly opposed to it seems remarkable – but not surprising. Prohibition and persecution inevitably stimulate and reinforce the very attitudes, beliefs and practices they seek to suppress.

By contrast, religion has long been an integral part of the culture of most of the countries of Latin America, Africa and the Middle East, where religious observance continues to be accepted as a normal part of daily life, as it once was throughout Europe. Although the global rise of religion is popularly associated with Islam, Christianity is also extending its reach: more than half the population of Africa, for example, is at least nominally Christian. Though the figures are unreliable, Nigeria may well have the world's highest rate of both belief in God and church attendance (while also having among the world's highest rates of illiteracy, poverty, infant mortality, political and corporate corruption, ethnic tensions and religious conflicts).

While overall church attendance in the UK is continuing to decline, a report in the *Economist* ('Resurrection?' 9 January, 2016) notes that there are pockets of modest revival, especially in London. Weekly participation in Christian services in London has grown by 16 percent since 2005, partly as a result of the influx of immigrants who favour Pentecostal – or more broadly evangelical – forms of worship. But attendance at cathedrals across Britain has also been growing – up by 35 percent in the period from 2002 to 2012.

Nowhere has the place of Christianity traditionally seemed more secure than in the US, where the enduring religious heritage of the Pilgrim Fathers and the power of assorted religious lobby groups have made religion a central issue in many political, legal and educational controversies, ranging from abortion law to the teaching of 'creationism' in schools. The widely perceived association between religion and success in American life has sometimes cast US-style Christianity as the handmaiden of capitalism – an impression reinforced by the popularity of so-called 'prosperity theology', where personal wealth is interpreted as a sign of God's blessing. US-style Christianity has also placed heavy emphasis on those quintessential American virtues, freedom and choice, resulting in an endless proliferation of denominations and independent churches.

And yet, according to 2014 Pew Research data, only about 70 percent of Americans now identify themselves as Christian – down by 8 percent in the past seven years. About 40 percent claim to attend church regularly, though some anecdotal evidence suggests the actual attendance figure is well below that. While only 3.1 percent of Americans formally identify themselves as atheists, the number has increased from 1.6 percent in 2007, and those classifying themselves as 'nothing in particular' has also risen from 12.1 to 15.8 percent in the same seven-year period.

In Western countries, regular churchgoers tend to be older than the average age of the population, predominantly female and mostly from families where there has been a tradition of church attendance. Religious observance also appears to be associated with less affluence; church attendance in Ireland, for example, fell sharply when Ireland was briefly a 'tiger economy' but has revived recently, in spite of the sexual-abuse scandals rocking the Catholic Church, as the economy flags. Weekly church attendance in Ireland now stands at 41 percent – the highest in Europe.

Religious observance in Australia and New Zealand, as in many of the countries of Europe, presents a very different picture from the global trend. Although 61 percent of Australians and almost 50 percent of New Zealanders still tick 'Christian' in the national census, only about 15 percent attend church once a month or more often, and regular weekly attenders are down to about 8 percent of the population – a very similar picture to that of the UK, Germany, France and Belgium, higher than in Scandinavian countries and lower than in Italy, Greece, Spain and Ireland. Those figures need to be put in the context of a steady rise in the number of people reporting 'no religion' in the census, now standing at 22 percent of Australians and 42 percent of New Zealanders.

Yet there are mini-booms in church attendance occurring in both countries – mainly, as in many other parts of the world, led by Pentecostalists operating under such banners as Hillsong, Christian City Church, Assemblies of God and Metro. The Pentecostalists' so-called megachurches attract many thousands of people to their Sunday services, though this may be as much about the 'bandwagon' effect of belonging to a thriving, supportive community as about embracing specific doctrinal beliefs.

In spite of the overall decline in religious practice, Australians and New Zealanders like to think of theirs as Christian countries, built on Christian values – especially when they are confronted by the appearance of a Muslim mosque or Hindu temple in their midst – and nothing comes anywhere near Christianity when Australians declare their identification with a religion. The most numerically popular non-Christian religion in Australia is Buddhism, accounting for a mere 2.5 percent of the population, though its influence is more widespread than that: Buddhism-based meditation, 'mindfulness' training and Happiness conferences attract many people who would not describe themselves as Buddhists. In the same way, most of the people who embrace the various Hindu disciplines of yoga would not describe themselves as Hindus, though they will often refer to the spiritual dimension of yoga as well as its more obvious physical benefits. Hinduism is actually the fastest-growing religion in Australia (though still comprising only 1.3 percent of the population), largely driven by immigration from the Indian sub-continent. Islam accounts for 2.2 percent of the Australian population, and Judaism 0.5 percent. In New Zealand, the most popular non-Christian religion is Hinduism (2.1 percent), followed by Buddhism (1.5 percent) and Islam (1.1 percent).

Though atheism has experienced a burst of popularity around the Western world that has made it seem positively fashionable, religion appears to be returning to the public conversation in ways unimaginable even twenty years ago. In Australia, two factors may be contributing to a more sympathetic attitude towards the idea of nurturing the spiritual dimension of our lives – whether via religion or some other strategy. First, there have been some signs of a pulling-back from the rampant consumerism of the past thirty years, as Australians realise they may have been too dependent on the mining industry for a sense of economic invincibility that has, ironically, translated into record levels of household debt. At the same time, new research coming from the field of positive psychology is challenging the wisdom of our obsession with the pursuit of personal happiness and restoring some common sense to the debate about the sources of life's deepest satisfactions. (It turns out they do not include holiday houses, swimming pools, renovated kitchens or new cars, though any of these things might make us happy, at least for a while.)

None of this would lead anyone to predict a resurgence of religion in Australia on the scale of some other parts of the world – especially less-prosperous nations, where religion has always carried the implied promise of a better life, at least in the hereafter. But, if the swinging pendulum of history is any guide, it does suggest that some forms of religion – or possibly a more generic 'spirituality' – will make a modest comeback, and new forms of faith will continue to emerge. It also suggests that much-maligned agnosticism – the position that reserves judgement about the existence of a supreme being in whatever form – may gain ground. After all, scepticism is a well-established principle of honest philosophical and scientific enquiry and the leap to doubt-free atheism is at least as bold as the leap to doubt-free theism.

Already, the spirituality movement has captured the imagination of many people – especially young people – who vehemently deny any interest in religion but still want to explore the non-material values and concepts, and the meditative practices, traditionally associated with religion. Indeed, many people are now seeking ways of making sense of religious ideas, including the idea of Christian faith, without relying on traditional notions of a supreme being, and without surrendering themselves to a conventional framework of doctrines and beliefs.

Beyond Belief is a response to that kind of quest. While it rejects superstition and resists any suggestion of the supernatural, it acknowledges that life, and faith, are full of mysteries. To find all the answers to those mysteries would be to strip away too much of the pleasing sense of wonder we gain from our encounters with them. Answers close off the question; sometimes – in the spiritual life and, indeed, in personal relationships – it's better to stay with the question. Why pretend to know the unknowable?

1

Born to believe

Nature abhors a vacuum, and so does the human mind in its endless quest for answers. The trouble is that the universe is a mysterious place that raises all sorts of questions whose answers seem to lie beyond our reach: *How did it all happen? Was there ever a beginning? How did we get here? Is there a reason we're here? Is anyone else out there? What's it all about? Is it 'about' anything at all?* Though they sound like scientific questions, these are intensely subjective questions designed to give some focus to the meaning and purpose of our own life. That's why the lack of definitive answers bothers us, and why we are desperate to find something we can hang on to. Science tries to address some of those questions, but even the Big Bang theory is vague about what was going on before the Bang, and the mysteries of dark energy, dark matter and quantum foam remain just that – mysteries.

All this is complicated by the fact that any view of space and time that includes the idea of infinity or eternity obviously excludes any possibility of 'creation'; you can't try to break into a loop of infinite existence by claiming to have found a starting point or a 'cause' that set it all in motion, even though particular cataclysms might, from time to time, profoundly alter the nature of the universe (or, at least, *this* universe).

So, cosmically speaking, no beginning; no end; no inherent meaning.

This sense of an impenetrable mystery at the heart of our existence explains our 'existential angst' – a permanent, underlying rumble of anxiety about the fact that we don't seem able to answer the very questions that most intrigue us. Our responses to this angst, through the millennia of human existence and right up to the present day, have been many and varied. Some of our forebears created myths to explain the inexplicable, and some of those myths morphed into folk religions and then into something more formal and institutionalised. Others hared off to witchdoctors, shamans, priests, poets – or, more recently, psychotherapists – to help cope with the darkness. Some learnt how to master therapeutic techniques ranging from meditation to chanting, designed to distract us from our angst (but also from more mundane concerns, like 'Did I turn off the gas?' or 'Are the children getting on with their homework?') through disciplined focus on the present moment. Some have taken to strong drink or other mind-altering substances to dull the pain of unknowing. Some lose themselves in creativity. Some have trained and exercised themselves into an oblivion of body-fixation. Some have become perpetual-motion machines driven by an unnamed restlessness that leads them to travel constantly, to be always working on the next sexual conquest, or to pursue their ambitions as if the only way to attach meaning to life would be through the relentless pursuit of wealth, power and status. Some have sought refuge in the pursuit of personal happiness, as if that might work like a giant poultice on their angst, smothering it with joy. However we try to deal with it, the Big Question always lurks: *Why?* Why this kind of life and not some other – or none at all? To say nothing of the other big one: *Is this all there is?*

We demand answers!

This is a deeply unsettling state of affairs for creatures like us who strive to make sense of everything. We are by nature great interpreters: we like to feel as if we know what's going on and, if possible, why. We instinctively try to solve puzzles; to penetrate mysteries; to get to the heart of the matter; to discover 'the truth'. If the bus is running late, we feel there must be a reason, as we do if one of our kids goes off the rails or a tsunami wipes out an entire village. Surely things can't 'just happen', we say to ourselves as we search fruitlessly for rational explanations.

When we can't actually *know* what's going on, we may construct a set of beliefs that seem to have explanatory power – just as scientists construct a theory they can work with until more definitive data comes along. Beliefs are the way we fill in the gaps in our knowledge. In our quest for answers and insights, we seize on anything. That's why gossip is so irresistible, rumours so unstoppable and conspiracy theories so tantalising: they promise 'the inside story'.

We may variously conceive of life on earth as a cosmic accident, the implementation of a divine purpose or the inevitable consequence of processes we will one day understand better than we do now. We may conceive of it as a mystery destined to remain beyond our comprehension but suitable as a subject for contemplation and awe. Or we may try to set the whole thing aside – put it in the 'too hard' basket – in the hope that incomprehensible and uncontrollable forces won't interfere too much with our daily life.

One way or another, most of us choose to believe *something* about human existence, partly because such beliefs imbue us not only with a sense of understanding, but also of control. Any system of belief, even if based on the blindest of blind faith, makes us feel as if we have cracked some code or acquired a reference point for making sense of the world around us. Once you have a theory, you feel as if you know what's *really* going on: 'Ah, now I get it – it's all about the class struggle', or 'The world government people are behind this', or 'It's the collective unconscious doing its thing', or 'This is how God works'.

We may place our faith in boffins, via the deification of science. We may worship the free market and decide that economic growth is what really matters. Or we may look to the stars for guidance: a large minority of the citizens of most Western countries – 40 percent in Australia, according to a 2009 Fairfax/Nielsen poll – claim to believe in astrology, precisely because they experience such belief as a key that can unlock some of the mysteries of life, especially the mystery of why people behave as they do. (Maybe we can't know why we're here, but at least we can know why the boss is such a tyrant – it's down to her star sign.)

The embrace of superstition, even if only half-serious, is another popular way of trying to connect with 'mysterious forces' by appearing to make sense of coincidence and happenstance. People will tell you that if they go through a particular routine, they can always find a parking spot, as if they have some mystical power, some special access to the celestial department that manages earth-bound parking arrangements. If you do manage to find a dream parking spot on three or four consecutive occasions when you had a particular handbag with you, or were playing a particular song on your car's audio system, that old black magic gets you in its spell: *Play the song! Clutch the handbag! Sure enough, there's my parking spot!*

Actors have their own preparatory rituals, and most are gripped by – or at least go along with – superstitions that have a long history in the theatre: never mention *Macbeth* inside a theatre (it must be referred to only as 'the Scottish play') and, if you do let the word slip, go outside, turn around three times, spit, curse, and knock before re-entering. In the traditions of the stage and concert platform, saying 'good luck' brings bad luck and should therefore be replaced by 'break a leg'.

Many sports people have rigid routines they must go through before a match or particular pieces of clothing or equipment they can't do without. The tennis champion Rafael Nadal's routine before every point is almost a caricature of the practice, and most cricketers go through a series of repetitive gestures before they settle over the bat. Some racing drivers obsessively don one glove before the other; some footballers always wear a particular pair of underpants.

How Adrian helps his team win

Spectators can be gripped by unshakeable faith in their ability to influence the outcome of a game. Adrian McGuigan, a longtime supporter of his local football team, is convinced the team can only win if he sits in a particular seat, wears a particular shirt and drinks a certain quantity of beer before half-time.

'You might think I'm nuts, but I have experience on my side, mate,' he says to the sceptics.

Experience? It's true that after a run of spectacular losses several years ago, Adrian's team won convincingly on a day when he sat in a particular part of the grandstand at the team's home ground, wore a particularly lurid shirt under his pullover and drank three plastic beakers of beer during the first half of the match. He was sitting with two of his close friends – similar devotees – and was also wearing a wig in the team colours. The following week was another at-home game, so Adrian dressed in the same way and sat in the same place, with the same two friends, and drank the same amount of beer at the same rate. The team won again. On that occasion, Adrian had forgotten to wear his wig, so he decided the seat-shirt-beer-friends combination was the winning one, and the wig was optional.

The next week, at an away game, Adrian couldn't find a seat that equated exactly to the one at his home ground, so he settled for the closest thing, based on a complex formula worked out by one of his friends who happened to be a mathematician with a side interest in numerology. It worked.

Adrian was now locked into this pattern of behaviour, declaring that, by some magical means, it was feeding directly into his team's performance.

Did he really believe it?

'Look at the evidence, mate. Who's going to argue with that?' Adrian says with a wink. However much his friends may mock him, and however much Adrian may laugh at his own harmless obsession, his faith is sufficiently strong that he never deviates from the established pattern of behaviour, just in case. On one occasion when Adrian was too sick with a cold to venture out on a wet Saturday afternoon, he dispatched Carla, his wife, to take his place: same shirt (well hidden under a jumper and jacket), same seat, same beer consumption (though it was not her preferred drop), flanked by the same two friends who could hardly believe what a good sport she was. The team won again.

Occasional losses don't faze Adrian. 'Look at it this way,' he says, 'the shirt-seat-beer-friends combo is no guarantee of success, but you have to give the team their best chance. I'm improving the odds for them. They'd be grateful if they knew.'

Superstition permeates our culture, simply because we can't give up the quest to make sense of what's happening to us, to find some thread of connection between us and life's mysteries, and to avoid putting ourselves in harm's way. We are determined to see patterns where there might actually be no more than coincidence. 'It was meant to be,' people say – including people of no discernible religious faith – as if a particular event had been preordained by someone or something beyond our ken. If you were to ask (as I'm often rather churlishly tempted to do), 'Meant *by whom*?', you would most likely be met with a frosty stare. People like to cling to the vague idea that there must be a pattern, a reason, an intention lying behind apparently random or inexplicable events.

We are particularly good at interpreting events through the prism of our prejudices and then finding, to our great joy, that the prejudices have been further reinforced by those events. (What a surprise!) The process is circular and internal, but it *feels* more significant than that; it feels as if we're on to something, especially where superstition is involved: 'I always knew the Apollo 13 space mission would be a disaster – they should have skipped that number'; 'I read where an asylum-seeker assaulted someone – I told you that's what would happen if we let these people in.'

Lucky numbers, obsessive personal rituals, rigorous adherence to the principles of feng shui in furnishing your office or home (did you know, for instance, that an outside waterfall may create more cash flow?), plus the standard superstitions about umbrellas raised indoors, fingers crossed for luck, not walking under ladders ... all rather silly when viewed rationally, but all signs of some residual faith in the idea that there are mysterious forces loose in the world that should be treated with caution and respect.

Some of us believe that we shouldn't mention a possible negative outcome lest the mere mention of it might jinx us. Others believe that only good things will happen to us if we behave in a certain way (in spite of the evidence that bad things happen to everyone). Some people react to the appearance of a black cat in their path, as if it signifies something, though the 'something' varies between different cultures: good luck in some places, bad luck in others. Even a run of good luck – the flight was on time, there was a vacant taxi just when I needed it, I arrived at the meeting with five minutes to spare – can tempt us into a little fantasy where it seems the universe is on our side, for once.

Many superstitions begin with persuasive events – usually a coincidence that feels like a causal link – but all of them are evidence of our disposition to believe. In *What Makes Us Tick?* (2010), I identified 'something to believe in' as one of the ten most basic desires that drive human behaviour. When you look at the evidence, it's hard to argue with the great British mathematician and philosopher Bertrand Russell, who wrote in 'An Outline of Intellectual Rubbish' (1960): 'Man is a credulous animal and must believe *something*; in the absence of good grounds for belief, he will settle for bad ones.'

When it comes to explanations, we'll even clutch at straws. Some of the beliefs we have constructed on the long journey towards an explanation of life on earth are merely fanciful. The world was once thought to be flat and to be resting on the back of a giant turtle (that turtle, in turn, was resting on the back of another, and another . . . at least you could say that was a stab at the concept of infinity). Another legend had the earth being supported by the god Atlas (an early version of the idea that humanity was at the mercy of a god).

Most beliefs are serious attempts to make sense of whatever evidence is available. For example, people who regard the 'design' of the world as evidence of a designer will feel that their belief in a creator-god is eminently reasonable, and they will be unmoved by evidence of flawed design (in human anatomy, for instance), by nature's grotesque mutations, birth defects, or by the suggestion that we are an insignificant little evolutionary subplot in the eternal saga of the cosmos.

In *The Interpretation of Cultures* (1973), the cultural anthropologist Clifford Geertz wrote that 'the existence of bafflement, pain and moral paradox – the Problem of Meaning – is one of the things that drives men towards belief in gods, devils, spirits, totemic principles'. So there's the first driver of our tendency to believe: life's mysteries perplex us and, in response, we try to fill in the gaps with explanations that seem plausible, or at least reasonable enough to justify our faith in them. We need *something* to believe.

Believing is easier than not believing

A second reason for our apparent gullibility is that we find it cognitively easier to believe something we're told than to remain sceptical about it. Believing is just a matter of 'going along with it', provided your credulity isn't unduly strained. We are believers by default. Our natural tendency is to accept what we're told.

And once we believe something, it's an effort for most of us to change our minds.

Political spin doctors know this only too well: they know that most of us can't tell the difference between information and misinformation, especially if it's a subject we don't yet know much about. One of the world's arch-propagandists, Nazi Germany's Joseph Goebbels, cynically (but accurately) remarked: 'He who tells the world first is believed.' In other words, tell us something – more or less anything – and because we are by nature credulous, we'll tend to believe it, provided the information doesn't directly contradict our own experience or conflict with something we already know or believe.

What happens next gives us an insight into one of the most significant tendencies of the human mind. That new piece of information is incorporated into our framework of knowledge, attitudes and beliefs, and becomes part of the filter through which we subsequently observe the world. We impose our own values, preconceptions and expectations on what we see and interpret it accordingly: the viewer is always part of the view. From then on, we will tend to process any relevant information *selectively*, being especially attentive to messages that confirm the information we have previously taken on board. Conversely, we'll be less inclined to attend to messages that challenge or contradict it: prejudices and preconceptions are the greatest of all barriers to listening. (I have described this process in detail in my 1994 book, *Why Don't People Listen?*)

You can see how the process of selective perception works, and observe the quest for reinforcement, whenever people argue. If someone attacks our existing point of view, we are most unlikely to suspend our own beliefs just in case this person's views turn out to be more sensible, rational or plausible than our own. No; our instinctive tendency is to dismiss the challenging material, defend our existing viewpoint and, as a result, come to feel even more strongly about our position *simply because we have been called on to defend it.* That's why arguments are more likely to confirm people's opinions than change their minds, and it's why the persecution of minorities generally leads to an even stronger assertion of their religious, ethnic or cultural identity. In large part, we are defined by our beliefs, so it's no wonder we tend to be defensive about them.

Most parents aren't professional spin doctors, and yet, from an early age, they feed us stories we later realise couldn't possibly be true – Santa Claus, the tooth fairy, the Easter bunny, the bogeyman, plus the usual assortment of superstitions and prejudices. Because they expected us to believe what we were being told – and we obligingly did so – it's almost as if our parents were conditioning us to be believers and to rein in our scepticism. (But let's not be too hard on them; they might have been unconsciously training us to live with the mysterious, the unpredictable and the irrational.)

The famous Jesuit claim attributed to Francis Xavier – 'Give me a child until he is seven and I will give you the man' – is often quoted as if it's true, because it is very close to being true. If you indoctrinate a child, you might not capture his or her loyalty and devotion forever, but you will certainly affect his or her point of view forever. It is said of Gustav Mahler that every one of his symphonies contains a march because, as a child, he lived in a military barracks and was constantly exposed to marching music.

When it comes to Bible stories, most children will readily accept that Noah really did load two of every species into his ark to save them from the flood, that Moses really did part the waters of the Red Sea and that Joshua (one of the Bible's grisliest genocidal murderers) really did make the walls of Jericho tumble in response to a trumpet blast. They might later reflect on all this and decide it was all myths and legends, but sometimes the beliefs stick and scepticism never takes over. Even when children reach the point of realising that such stories couldn't be literally true, the influence of their underlying metaphorical messages may be permanent.

Our disposition to believe is easily accounted for by the combination of our desire to fill in the gaps in our understanding of why we're here and what it's all about, and our natural tendency to go along with whatever we're told. Our credulity is not the result of some inherent weak-mindedness; yes, it's cognitively easier than scepticism, but it's also because we have been trained from the beginning to be acquiescent in the face of confident-sounding assertions, especially if they come from an authority figure like a parent, teacher or priest.

But not everyone is satisfied with that account. Since the rise of neuroscience and the increasingly sophisticated understanding of the human genome, scientists have inevitably set out on the hunt for the 'religion' gene, or the 'belief' gene, in an attempt to discover whether religious faith and the tendency to believe are genetically imprinted in us, as our cooperative nature apparently is. So far, the closest they seem to have come is in locating a 'hypnotisability' gene and assuming that the same kind of susceptibility might be involved in religious belief.

If there turned out to be a gene for religion, what would we do with that information? I suppose if some zealous proselytiser stopped you in the street to enquire whether you were 'saved', you might be able to respond with a regretful frown: 'Sorry, I lack the gene for it.' And some predestinationists who believe that a person's capacity for faith was predetermined at the beginning of time might welcome the idea that their doctrine has been confirmed by science. Otherwise, it's hard to see how the discovery of a genetic basis for religious faith is going to get us far.

In any case, we already know what will happen when the scientific hunt either finds or fails to find its quarry. The conclusion will be drawn – as it is always drawn – that our genes create predispositions, but do not determine outcomes. In the case of our beliefs and values, there's always 'nurture' to be taken into account, just as, in the case of disease, you have to acknowledge the contribution of diet and exercise.

In any case, the long-term evidence suggests that cultural transmission is so effective, we scarcely need an additional explanation. The UK biologist Richard Dawkins has come up with the idea of 'memes' that transmit cultural material just as genes transmit biological material, though I'm not sure how that helps. An entire theory of 'memetics' – the study of replication, both genetic and cultural – has been developed by the British parapsychologist Susan Blackmore in *The Meme Machine* (1999), but in the case of cultural (including religious) transmission, it's hard to see how this improves our understanding of such well-known cultural transmitters as myths, legends, music, art, rituals, games, language, jokes, inventions, heroism and other forms of personal influence.

For the time being, at least, it seems safe to settle for those two rather simpler and more obvious explanations of our disposition to believe: we want answers, and we're conditioned to believe what we're told.

2

Why religion will survive and prosper

Throughout history, religion based on faith in a 'supreme being' or 'higher power' has supplied humans with the most popular way of addressing our existential angst. And because religious traditions have been deeply embedded in the culture of every society, religious stories and precepts have also been an integral part of the education and formation of young children. Those are powerful reasons why religion has survived all attempts to legislate or argue it out of existence, but there are other equally powerful factors at work.

The power of faith

'Faith can move mountains.' Well, not literally. But the power of faith to motivate people to do good works, to express religious ideals in practical charity and to translate dreams into reality is legendary. In the case of Christianity, the examples of William Wilberforce (anti-slavery), Martin Luther King (anti-racial segregation), the founders and members of assorted teaching and nursing orders, and the work of faith-based charities in addressing injustice, deprivation and suffering all suggest that social activism wedded to religious faith can be a formidable combination.

Faith has also been a powerful motivator and source of inspiration for many writers, composers, painters and poets. Every note of J.S. Bach's prodigious output was dedicated by him 'to the glory of God', since God was regarded by Bach as the source of his inspiration. The same was true of the English composer and patriot Edward Elgar, and of such poets as John Donne, Gerard Manley Hopkins and T.S. Eliot, all of whom were motivated by their relationship with – or their yearning for – God. In *Real Presences* (1989), literary critic George Steiner quotes D.H. Lawrence: 'I always feel as if I stood naked for the fire of Almighty God to go through me – and it's rather an awful feeling. One has to be so terribly religious to be an artist.' And W.B. Yeats: 'No man can create as did Shakespeare, Homer, Sophocles, who does not believe with all his blood and nerve, that man's soul is immortal.' Many creative artists describe the experience of being a mere vehicle, or vessel, for material that seems to have come through them rather than from them. Some attribute that process to divine inspiration; others simply accept that creativity can be a mysterious, unpredictable business.

It's not only religious faith that is powerful; faith in *anything* can move mountains, both constructively and destructively. Faith in political ideas has created monsters as well as heroes: Hitler, like Alexander the Great, had unshakeable faith in his dream of world domination, and many leaders of modern Western democracies are so wedded to their faith in democracy that they have felt justified in trying to impose it on societies that might not have been willing or able to accept it. Faith has inspired leaders to wage just and unjust wars. Faith in their capacity to go higher, faster, further has driven athletes to record-breaking performances. Faith in their ability to outrun the law has motivated criminals. Faith in a relationship or a family or an organisation has produced acts of amazing courage, sacrifice and loyalty. In fact, you'd be tempted to say that the very best of human behaviour (and, occasionally, the very worst) relies on faith in some kind of ideal that people will often describe as being 'beyond ourselves'; faith in the idea that we can do better, or *be* better, than we might otherwise have thought possible. Faith is always experienced as an enlargement or enhancement of the self. That may be why faith also seems to imbue us with a sense of personal power.

If you doubt the power of faith, consider the well-documented placebo effect in medical research. When medical researchers want to conduct a clinical trial of a new drug, they will recruit two matched samples of willing subjects. One sample will receive the drug being investigated; the other will receive a placebo (that is, an inert substance with no known therapeutic properties). The subjects are all aware of the fact that they are taking part in the trial of a new drug, and they all know there's a 50 percent chance they will be given a placebo instead of the drug. Not even the researchers administering the study know which subjects get which.

What happens? Time after time, trial after trial, published paper after published paper, a pretty reliable 30 percent of those taking the placebo will report the health benefits they would have expected to receive from taking the drug. In the case of menopausal symptoms such as hot flushes, night sweats and mood swings, the so-called placebo effect sometimes rises as high as 50 percent, which accounts for the fact that many clinically unproven products sold to relieve such symptoms appear to work, simply because of the faith of the consumer in the efficacy of the product (aided by the fact that most menopausal symptoms ease naturally with time).

'Your faith has made you whole,' Jesus of Nazareth was reported to have said to a woman healed of persistent bleeding. You'd better believe it: the modern drug trial sits within the long history of faith healing, providing yet more evidence for the proposition that if we *really* believe it, our faith may indeed make us whole, though I wouldn't personally recommend using faith as a do-it-yourself substitute for more conventional therapies when they are available.

The 70 percent of placebo-takers who experience *no* therapeutic effects presumably had no expectations one way or another; they knew they would either get the drug or the placebo and were prepared to wait and see what happened. But how do we explain the 30 percent without acknowledging the power of faith, especially in cases where you'd reasonably think faith alone could not possibly do the trick, as in my personal favourite: arthroscopic surgery designed to relieve the effects of osteoarthritis of the knee, where 'fake' surgery (an incision that was simply sewn up) produced essentially the same result as the real thing, at least in the short term.

Hypnosis provides another fascinating example of the power of faith. It's well accepted among people who use hypnosis for therapeutic purposes, or even to entertain an audience, that not everyone is susceptible to the process; the essential prerequisite is that you must have faith in the idea that it will work. But here's a surprising twist in the tale: it seems the hypnotist must also have faith, according to a 1994 study by Dr A.A. Mason, an anaesthetist who subsequently became a psychoanalyst. He cites a compelling example in which, using hypnosis, he cured what he believed to be a patient's viral warts, only to discover later that the warts were caused by a congenital skin condition. In the light of this information, Mason came to think of the cure as having been virtually impossible, and found that he was unable to replicate his success with other patients who came to him with the same condition. Mason's conclusion was that hypnosis is a collaborative process in which hypnotist and patient must both be believers.

Faith in something beyond ourselves also has the power to comfort and console, to aid in recovery from illness and to carry us through the most testing periods of our lives. There's mounting evidence that religious faith may well be good for your health in all sorts of ways – sounder sleep, healthier heart, longer life – though such effects are also strongly associated with stable marriages, a generally healthy lifestyle and the proven benefits of belonging to a cohesive social group, all factors likely to be present among members of a faith community.

In *Handbook of Religion and Health* (2012), H.G. Koenig and his co-authors reported that 'in the majority of studies, religious involvement is correlated with well-being, happiness and life-satisfaction; hope and optimism; purpose and meaning in life; higher self-esteem; better adaptation to bereavement; greater social support and less loneliness; lower rates of depression and faster recovery from depression; less anxiety'. Though we should be wary of drawing too many conclusions from statistical correlations, Koenig's findings are consistent with some of the work of the positive psychologist Martin Seligman, whose research led him and his colleagues to the conclusion that one necessary condition for a sense of meaning in life is to feel attached to something larger than the self.

US philosopher Daniel Dennett acknowledges that religion can bring out the best in a person. In spite of his personal wish to eradicate religion from society, Dennett notes in *Breaking the Spell* (2006) that 'for day-in, day-out lifelong bracing, there is probably nothing so effective as religion: it makes powerful and talented people more humble and patient, it makes average people rise above themselves, it provides sturdy support for many people who desperately need help staying away from drink or drugs or crime'. He also suggests that religious faith gives people a perspective on life that helps them 'make the hard decisions we would all be proud to make'. At the same time, Dennett reminds us that there are many wise, engaged, morally committed atheists and agnostics, and that we have no sufficiently solid research to permit generalisations to be made about the social attitudes or values of believers versus sceptics.

The relationship between faith and wellbeing is not as simple as it sounds; such apparently causal relationships never are. The alleged benefits of religious faith are generally studied within the supportive environment of a stable community of fellow believers, and many of the therapeutic effects – particularly for *mental* health – claimed for religious faith and practice are also claimed for many other activities, such as choral and instrumental music-making, engagement with a local community and the practice of meditation, especially so-called loving-kindness meditation. Indeed, researchers at Stanford University (Hutcherson, 2008) have shown that the practice of loving-kindness meditation – an ancient Buddhist technique for inducing positive feelings towards others and transforming anger into compassion – can have a positive effect on a person's sense of social connectedness and reduce their feelings of social isolation, with obvious benefits for their sense of general wellbeing.

Similar research by a team from the universities of North Carolina and Michigan (Fredrickson, 2008) has shown that loving-kindness meditation can make a significant contribution to the development of personal resources such as mindfulness, sense of purpose and social support. This disciplined focus on compassion was also associated with an improved sense of life satisfaction and reduced symptoms of illness, including depression, and has even been shown to produce significant reduction in pain and psychological distress among sufferers from chronic low-back pain (Carson, 2005). More broadly, the work of Jon Kabat-Zinn at the University of Massachusetts Medical School (author of the 1994 bestseller, *Wherever You Go, There You Are*) has shown that mindfulness-based stress-reduction programs can have a beneficial effect on psoriasis, pain, anxiety, brain function and the body's immune systems.

You might well adopt mindfulness meditation – particularly loving-kindness meditation – as a pathway to social and emotional health, or even for the relief of back pain, but only the most ruthlessly pragmatic churchgoer would suggest that positive health effects are a sufficient reason to embrace religious faith and practice. The apparent health benefits of religion – or, more precisely, the combined benefits of religious faith and the rewarding sense of belonging to a religious community – have nothing to tell us about the *truth* of a person's beliefs. In religion, as in medicine, there are plenty of placebos out there.

There is one area of life, however, where faith is clearly power*less*, and that's the faith we invest in political leaders. Too many voters in too many elections have placed excessive, unrealistic faith in a leader to cure a country's woes – balance its budget, ward off its enemies, restore social harmony, promote economic growth – only to be disappointed by the discovery that this leader, like all the others, had feet of clay.

The power of myth

In our culture, the word 'myth' has been devalued. Whereas its origins lie in the idea that there are ancient stories and legends that endure through endless retelling because of the rich and powerful ideas embedded in them, these days the word is commonly used to convey the idea of a lie or a deliberate misrepresentation: 'Oh, that's just a myth,' sneer politicians defending themselves against charges of misrepresentation or other mischief.

This is a great pity, since myths and legends are often the most eloquent transmitters of truth and wisdom. Our current lack of respect for myths – or even our contempt for them as irrelevant, unscientific tosh – helps to explain why so many people abandon their connection with formal religion: when they discover that they can no longer sustain beliefs based on the literal, historical truth of religious stories, they may come to feel the whole thing was a hoax. This represents a failure to grasp the power of myths to educate, enlighten and inspire us.

In fact, the power of myths does not rely on historical truth at all: a myth is a particular kind of story that derives its power from some universal truth it conveys – psychological, moral, cultural or spiritual. We do not, for instance, regard the stories of King Arthur and the Knights of the Round Table as being historically 'true', yet we acknowledge the many truths they have to teach us about the value of courage, bravery, loyalty, fidelity and the destructive power of their opposites.

We don't have to believe that Robin Hood existed as an historical figure to appreciate the underlying lessons from the tales of derring-do in Sherwood Forest and Nottingham. Those tales have acquired mythical power in our culture because they present stories of a campaign against injustice and a desire to remove the social inequities that arise from gross inequalities of wealth attached to class and privilege (Robin Hood's strategy of 'robbing the rich to pay the poor' being the way some rich people characterise income tax).

The 'dreamtime' myths of Australian Aboriginal culture don't rely on historical accuracy for their power to inspire or their ability to transmit important cultural truths. And who would profess literal belief in the stories from ancient Greek mythology about the exploits of the gods on Mount Olympus and their interventions in human affairs? Yet, as Luke Slattery writes in *Dating Aphrodite* (2005): 'Myth has dressed nature in the colours of narrative, and made something beautiful from the universal desire to name nature's workings and to banish fear. Knowing the old stories, one lives with an extra light source, an added store of nourishment, a vitamin supplement.' Slattery notes that 'the ancients were consoled by a death and resurrection fantasy enacted many centuries before the coming of Christ'. Detached from its later religious significance, he says, it remains 'a beautiful story about the turning of the seasons and the regeneration of nature which hints at the conquest of death'. (In the Christian tradition, as we shall see, the resurrection story has yet more layers of potential meaning to offer us.)

In spite of our contemporary disdain for the grand narratives of ancient myths, we embrace the minutiae of modern, so-called urban myths with zeal. Heard the one about the man who bought a new Winnebago campervan and went for his first drive, put the van on cruise control, left the driver's seat and went into the kitchen to make a cup of coffee? The van crashed. The owner then sued the company for misleading him into thinking cruise control was something like autopilot.

It's all rubbish, needless to say. It never happened. But even when you tell people that it never happened, *they still want to repeat the story as if it's true.* Why? Because it so perfectly illustrates a popular concern about the rise of the nanny state, about people's reluctance to take responsibility for their own actions and about the fact that Western society is becoming more litigious. (Oh, and it's sometimes used to illustrate how stupid men are.) So it works beautifully as a myth: it's not about the truth *of* the story, but the truth *in* the story.

Australians are no strangers to the process of making myths out of history. The Anzac legend is based on a disastrously callous miscalculation of the risks involved in trying to invade Turkey by landing troops on a beach at Gallipoli overlooked by a huge force of heavily armed Turks. But the myth no longer bears much relation to the historical facts. The exercise was futile from the start and although 100,000 Turks were killed, they decisively won the battle and some Australian troops behaved as badly as any troops would under such horrendous conditions. A mere one hundred years later, the inglorious has become glorious: the Anzac legend now portrays Gallipoli as the crucible of nationhood. The new story has become central as the historical detail recedes, and we *like* the new story: we celebrate it annually with increasing solemnity, devotion and patriotism, as if it somehow showed us at our best.

Karen Armstrong argues strongly for renewed attention to be paid to the value of myths in our lives. In *A Short History of Myth* (2005), she bemoans the paucity of a culture that narrows the focus of 'truth' to mean either historical veracity or scientifically provable facts. Noting that enduring myths are generally associated either with death or extreme events, she writes that 'mythology is an art form that points beyond history to what is timeless in human existence, helping us to get beyond the chaotic flux of random events, and glimpse the core of reality'. Although you can't reasonably apply the same tests of veracity to myths as you might to accounts of alleged historical events, they acquire mythical status precisely because they *contain* truths about the human condition and the aspirations of the human spirit.

In *Creating the Future School* (2001), Australian educationalist Hedley Beare described mythology as 'the most widely used explanatory device known to the human race ... it means to take the ineffable and to make it intersect with what we deem to be real'. Mythology, for Beare, 'touches us at the outer limits of our understanding and gives us a method to cope'. In other words, myths are an accessible and effective way of helping us make sense of what *is*, both cosmically and personally.

US scholar Joseph Campbell was widely regarded as the world's foremost authority on mythology. Best known for *The Hero with a Thousand Faces*, Campbell was not orientated towards religion in his work; his goal was to offer psychological and cultural interpretations of myths that would enhance our appreciation of their enduring power. In *The Power of Myth* (1988) he wrote: 'People say that what we're all seeking is a meaning for life. I don't think that's what we're really seeking. I think that what we're seeking is an experience of being alive, so that our life's experiences on the purely physical plane will have resonances within our innermost being and reality, so that we actually feel the rapture of being alive.'

Campbell's interpretation of Christianity's virgin-birth myth is a good example of how he worked. Widely regarded as the most challenging, puzzling or unreasonable of all Christian doctrines, the virgin birth is cast in a new light by Campbell's insistence that it should not be thought of as an actual birth of an actual person, but as a symbolic representation of the idea of a spiritual birth – an awakening spirituality – that transcends our animal nature. Noting that virgin births are relatively common in mythology (there's Persephone, Leda and Isis as well as Mary, the mother of Jesus), Campbell interprets this myth, like all myths, as being about *us*, not about the characters portrayed in the story. For Campbell, the virgin birth has no literal meaning at all: it is about 'the birth of compassion in the heart'. So the challenge of the virgin birth, when read as myth, is not to decide whether or not you can believe it, Campbell says, but to grasp the meaning of the question it poses: 'Have you [yet] come to life as a human incarnation of compassion?' Consistent with this line of interpretation, Campbell goes further and asserts that anyone who is 'spiritually reborn' is a god – an idea that depends entirely on what you mean by 'god' (and we'll revisit that question in chapter 6).

You don't have to buy Joseph Campbell's specific line of interpretation on this or any other myth to find his underlying argument interesting. Through human history, the same mythical themes emerge time and time again – as do the same jokes – and we would do well to work out why this is so, what those themes might be saying to us, and how their inner truth might be understood and applied.

The metaphorical meaning we attach to myths unlocks their power. Our understanding of that process can work as a defence against the argument that religious faith depends on accepting the literal truth of improbable or even inconceivable stories embedded in a particular religious tradition. A clearer view of the value of myth can save us from jettisoning stories that are obviously 'untrue' simply on the basis of a modern test of truth/falsity, when they may still have valuable truths to teach us.

Indeed, when the central myths of the Christian tradition – virgin birth, resurrection, miracles – are presented as historical rather than metaphorical truths, Christian apologists tie themselves in all kinds of knots. If you're going to argue that such things actually happened, you will run into a wall of scientific and other resistance. On the other hand, if you embrace such stories as seminal myths, rich with meaning and redolent with wisdom, the resistance crumbles; who's going to argue with the underlying truth, the inner meaning, of a myth? It would be as absurd to deny the value to our culture of the Christian myths as it would be to try to defend them as historical fact.

Nevertheless, many religious believers *do* regard some of the seminal stories of their faith tradition as being literally, historically true: the physical resurrection of Jesus three days after his crucifixion, for instance, is treated as the absolute lynchpin of Christianity by some – but by no means all – Christians. If your faith depends on such stories being regarded as historical facts, what will you say when they are challenged by the application of reason or revealed to be untenable in the light of modern scholarship? Should faith be dependent on belief in the historicity of certain stories, no matter how improbable? By harnessing the power of myth, an unreasonable faith in the truth *of* the story can be transformed into a more reasonable faith in the truth *in* the story.

Many of our most enduring myths are enshrined in religious traditions and practices that have proved themselves over the millennia to be highly effective cultural transmitters. Churches don't just retell the myths: they wrap the faithful in them through liturgical rituals, music and prayer, and blend them with history. No wonder religion survives!

The power of the tribe

To say that humans are tribal creatures is to say the single most culturally significant thing about us. Our sense of ourselves as social beings, grounded and shaped by our social context, is more psychologically important than our personal identity. As I argued in *The Art of Belonging* (2014), 'Who am I?' is never the real question for us; the real question – the most interesting and significant question – is: 'Who are *we*?'

Yes, we need a sense of our individuality as well; to be reassured that I am who I am and no one else. But even our sense of personal identity is essentially social: if you want to find yourself, don't gaze into a mirror or at your own navel; gaze instead into the faces of family, friends, neighbours and colleagues – the people who love you or at least are prepared to rub along with you. We discover who we are by discovering where we belong.

Like many other species on earth, we really do need each other to survive. We must congregate; we must cooperate; we must establish and maintain the communities that sustain us. A great deal of behaviour that might otherwise seem puzzling – our eagerness to conform to the social norms of a group, for instance – can be explained by that deep need to connect, to belong, to be taken seriously by others and accepted by them.

Some of our social identity derives from our membership of small, herd-sized groups – typically six to eight people – that satisfy our need for social intimacy. Herds can range from nuclear families to friendship circles, work groups, sporting teams, book clubs, musical ensembles and special interest groups of all kinds. But we also need to belong to larger and more muscular groupings: in addition to the emotional comfort of small groups, we need the strength, power and protection of the tribe.

Traditionally, extended families satisfied our tribal urge, and they still do for many people on the planet. But the stability and cohesiveness of extended families in Western society is breaking down in the wake of high divorce rates, low birthrates, an increasingly mobile population and a culture of rampant individualism. (There's a potential counterrevolution in the new cyber-tribes of the internet, but we have yet to see whether digital connectedness will encourage the same kind of moral sensitivity and responsiveness as occurs in communities that rely on face-to-face encounters.)

Modern tribes take many forms. Some organisations generate a strong sense of tribalism – esprit de corps – among their employees, while also fostering strong links between the members of smaller work-group herds. Professional people such as doctors, dentists, lawyers and psychotherapists, who often work in isolation or in company with just one or two others, need the collegiality of professional associations and tribal gatherings (euphemistically called 'conferences'). Political parties operate like tribes – though there are often several factional sub-tribes within each party. Schools and, to a lesser extent, universities generate strong tribal identities fuelled by 'school spirit'. There are socio-economic tribes in the various regions of our major cities; commercial tribes of people who strongly identify with particular brands; and cultural tribes based on shared tastes in the arts, shared convictions about social justice or a shared inclination to hang out in certain places.

Religion is one of history's most obvious examples of how we satisfy our tribal yearnings, even potentially transcending ethnicity. Because religious faith and religious convictions run so deep, they foster intense feelings of belonging among groups of like-minded people, and that can work in both positive and negative ways.

The 'in-group' effect has a generally positive psychological impact, boosting people's confidence and reinforcing their conviction that they are on the right side. 'I'm a Christian' or 'I'm a Muslim' or 'I'm a Jew' are statements that link people to vast global movements rich with cultural tradition. Within each of those tribes, though, there are sub-groups that sharpen people's sense of identity and further strengthen their tribal bonds: 'monolithic' religions turn out, on closer inspection, to be far less monolithic than they may appear to outsiders. 'I'm Catholic/Sunni/Orthodox' carries even more emotional and cultural freight than 'I'm a Christian/Muslim/Jew'.

While intense feelings of tribalism imbue us with a feeling of social and emotional strength, the downside is obvious: 'in-groups' beget prejudice against 'out-groups', often questioning their legitimacy and mocking their beliefs. The consequences of those divisions for social cohesiveness can be disastrous. As the satirical novelist Jonathan Swift put it, 'We have just enough religion to make us hate, but not enough to make us love one another.' Some of history's most bitter religious hatreds have been between people who seem to outsiders to be closest to each other on the spectrum of faith: Protestant/Catholic and Sunni/Shiah struggles over hundreds of years testify to the destructive power of divisions between tribes-within-a-tribe. The fact that Anglicanism incorporates both Catholic and Protestant traditions almost guarantees that it will be riven by tribal conflict within its own walls. The broader the church, the less likely it is to remain cohesive.

Because we are by nature tribal beings, conformity comes naturally to us, but it doesn't always bring out the best in us. People desperate to belong to a particular tribe may suppress their own convictions and their own sense of integrity in order to meet the expectations, mores, conventions and style of the tribe, and that can be psychologically damaging for them. Part of the appeal of extreme or marginal sects and cults lies in their intensely tribal character: the former members of such groups often reflect on how much they felt they had had to give up to be accepted by the group and, in turn, how much they lost, emotionally and socially, when they decided to leave. (*People in Glass Houses,* Tanya Levin's 2007 account of leaving Hillsong, is a graphic case in point.)

Nothing is more intense than the hatred directed at people who switch tribes: 'turncoats', 'traitors' and 'backsliders' are the kind of derogatory terms we reserve for those who have turned their back on our tribe.

Christian chameleons

Another reason why Christianity will survive and prosper, even in Western societies where it currently appears to be in the doldrums, is that Christians are constantly evolving new ways of expressing and sharing their faith. In the words of Karen Armstrong, 'As our circumstances change, we need to tell our stories differently in order to bring out their timeless truth.'

Traditional formal liturgies are still conducted in many churches, but innovative and informal variations are booming. You can see the range of variations in the contrast between the traditional Anglican liturgies of the major metropolitan cathedrals, and the amplified music and highly experiential services of a Pentecostal church like Hillsong. In all kinds of settings between those two extremes, modern songs are being integrated with traditional hymns, guitars are replacing or augmenting organs and pianos, the dress of clergy varies from ecclesiastical robes to casual garb that would not be out of place at a backyard barbecue. 'We must adapt or die' is a popular cry, though it mostly seems to refer to style, not substance, and is rarely accompanied by an embrace of contemporary theological scholarship. Indeed, there's a curious paradox here, too: some of the most radical sermons are preached in the most conservative liturgical settings, and some of the most conservative theology is dished up in the most contemporary services.

The steady growth of the house-church movement (evidently huge in China, as mentioned in the introduction) is a sign of the desire to bypass institutional forms altogether, with, as the name implies, small groups of Christians gathering in private homes for intimate, informal discussion, Bible study, prayer and singing. Some of these groups see themselves as reverting to the mode of the early Christians, when gatherings of the members of the new Jesus movement were held in secret and there were no bricks-and-mortar churches.

Christian meditation groups are also on the rise, offering a way to adapt the growing interest in Buddhist-inspired meditation and 'mindfulness' to the Christian context. Some people who attend such groups treat them as an alternative to conventional church services, finding that they offer a simpler, more 'authentic' and more 'spiritual' experience.

Every year, 100,000 Christians, most of them young people, make a pilgrimage to the ecumenical monastery at Taizé, in the Burgundy region of France. The Taizé monastery was the origin – and has become the symbolic heart – of a new Christian approach to prayer, meditative chanting, study and community service. The radically simple Taizé-style service is now being replicated in many churches around the world, as a supplement to more conventional, traditional liturgical programs.

The *Economist* of 9 January 2016 reports that the Anglican Church in the UK is experimenting with many non-traditional models, in an attempt to attract new congregations. One initiative, called Fresh Expressions, includes Messy Church for children and Cafe Church for adults. Many of these new forms have lay leaders, eschewing the traditional model of the parish church presided over by an ordained priest. So-called 'network' churches, similarly, meet in pubs and offices, right outside the traditional parish system.

'How can religious people believe something so *irrational*?'

Attacks on religion that focus on its alleged irrationality appear to be based on the idea that we humans are essentially rational creatures – an idea that is itself ludicrously out of touch with the evidence. Just look at us: we say one thing and do another; we do the very things we criticise other people for doing; we are often at a loss to explain something we've done that, on reflection, seems reckless or stupid. 'Why did I do that?' we plaintively ask ourselves, and usually fail to come up with a satisfactory answer. In everything from falling in love to throwing a punch, most of us are textbook examples of how the heart rules the head. Our biggest life choices – where to live, what job to do, whether and who to marry, whether or not to have children and how many – often feel more like accidents than decisions. (Even in these days of enlightened attitudes towards birth control, almost 50 percent of first pregnancies are unintended, according to family-planning experts.) In fact, if you think of life as a series of accidents that happen to essentially non-rational creatures, the human condition might make more sense to you.

Our superstitions, our obsessions, our addictions, our unshakeable prejudices, our convictions based on the flimsiest evidence or none at all, our fierce loyalty to sporting teams or even to commercial brands – from cosmetics to cars – that are virtually indistinguishable from their marketplace competitors ... this is *rational*? It's not rational to nurse grudges or to carry wounds from childhood trauma throughout our lives, but many of us do it, because we can't help ourselves. It's not rational to try to persuade people to change their minds – to see things our way – yet we do that all the time, too. 'Why can't you be more rational?' is one of the unkindest things spouses ever say to each other. (The correct answer is: 'Because I'm human. Would you really prefer to be married to a robot?')

It's true that we are capable of rational behaviour, but it usually requires sustained instruction and guidance – whether it's learning how to cross the road safely, to work our way patiently through a page of prose or to build a bridge that won't fall down. In fact, twelve long years of formal education is the standard minimum for teaching us how to curb our impulsiveness, our recklessness, our irrationality to a point where we can be relied on to behave rationally in the interests of public health and safety, raising a family or earning a living.

Attempts to analyse human behaviour should therefore start with the assumption that the behaviour we're analysing is the work of a species to whom rationality comes neither easily nor naturally.

The second assumption we should always make is that human behaviour is never driven by one motivation (rational or otherwise), but is always the outcome of a dynamic interaction between several desires or motivations that are often in competition, and sometimes in direct conflict, with each other. Who has not felt, for instance, the tension between the desire for love and the desire for control in a personal relationship, or between the desire to belong to a social group and the desire to 'do your own thing'?

The list of basic human desires capable of being satisfied by the various forms of religious experience is very impressive. In *What Makes Us Tick?*, I described the ten most basic desires driving human behaviour, and in the postscript to the second edition of that book (2013), I suggested that religion ticks most of those boxes for a believer.

We have already seen how religion can most obviously satisfy two of the ten: *The desire for something to believe in* and *The desire to belong.* Let's briefly look at the other eight on the list.

> *The desire to be taken seriously.* Whatever else we may want, we all want to be noticed, to be heard, to be appreciated, to be recognised. *Not* being taken seriously is one of the great frustrations of life. So if your religion promises that you will be taken seriously as an individual by God, no less, the occasional setback in personal relationships – being ignored, unappreciated or even mocked – pales into insignificance.

And a church community is also likely to take you seriously if you share its beliefs and conform to its standards of behaviour.

The desire for 'my place'. A church, for the churchgoer, is a place like no other; the sense of being 'part of the place' is impossible for an outsider to comprehend. For non-churchgoers, there is no obvious equivalent. For the faithful, 'my church' stands as a symbol of the faith, a refuge from everyday life, a haven, a sacred site.

The desire to connect. We desire to connect with ourselves through self-knowledge, with each other through communication and community, and with the natural world or, more grandly, the cosmos, the universe or God. Religion offers the believer pathways to the satisfaction of all three facets of the desire to connect.

The desire for control. This is one of the most hazardous of all the desires that drive us, mostly because we keep falling into error of believing that we can control the uncontrollable – other people, for example, or random events. (It takes most of us some time to work out that all we can control is ourselves and our reactions to those people and events.) Eventually, we realise that finding meaning and purpose in life is one way to satisfy that desire for control. The overarching narratives of religion, whether viewed as myth, parable, legend or historical fact, imbue the faithful with the conviction that they understand the way the world works, and why it works like that.

The desire to be useful. Acts of generosity and compassion come quite naturally to people whose religious training has emphasised loving-kindness, self-sacrifice and service to others as a form of service to God. Local congregations also provide many opportunities for people to do volunteer work within both the church and the local community.

The desire for more. We are, by nature, an insatiable species: we always want more of whatever we enjoy having or doing. While there's life, there's demand! The ultimate greed is our lust for life, life and more life. If possible, we'd like to prolong it forever. Most religions offer their believers some version of 'eternal life', and what other attempts to satisfy the desire for more can compete with that?

The desire for something to happen. The life of religious faith and practice is full of rituals, festivals and other experiences associated with services of worship and private devotions. Most churchgoers look forward to their services for both social and spiritual refreshment, and the major festivals of Christmas and Easter are religious as well as cultural highlights of their year.

The desire for love. Uniquely among the desires that drive us, the desire for love is satisfied only by the combination of giving and receiving. Christianity, with its emphasis on charity, kindness and compassion, encourages the faithful to interact with the world through the prism of a loving disposition. To love God is typically seen as part of the duty of the believer (indeed, it's the first of the Ten Commandments), but for the believer to be loved *by* God is to feel truly, unconditionally loved.

How irrational is any of that? The question seems no more relevant to religion than to any other human activity that brings us emotional satisfaction. When it comes to religious faith and practice, satisfying seven or eight of those ten desires would be an easy stretch.

The English author, literary critic, journalist and uncompromising rationalist Christopher Hitchens asserted that 'religion poisons everything' (the subtitle to his 2007 book, *God Is Not Great*).

Needless to say, that's not the way religious believers experience it, and it's not even the way most members of so-called Christian societies see it either. In spite of all their reservations about the institutional church, 88 percent of *non*-churchgoing Australians believe the presence of a church is good for a local community, according to McCrindle Research. When a participant in one of my research projects said, 'I like to see people standing around on the footpath outside a church on Sunday mornings', it was clear he had no intention of joining them, but the remark seemed to reflect a generally benign attitude towards other people's profession of their Christian faith and an expectation that a church would make a positive contribution to the life of a local community.

Naturally, your attitude to religion rather depends on what you mean by religion. In *Breaking the Spell*, Daniel Dennett defines religions as 'social systems whose participants avow belief in a supernatural agent or agents whose approval is to be sought'. That definition puts Dennett out of step with the branch of contemporary theological scholarship that reinterprets Christianity without recourse to a supernatural being. (The same phenomenon can be seen in the emergence of the Humanistic Judaism movement.) Dennett is scathing about such attempts and, indeed, about theology itself: 'This earnest intellectual exercise scratches the skeptical itch of those few people who are uncomfortable with the creeds they were taught as children, and is ignored by everyone else.' Amusingly provocative, perhaps, but Dennett's dismissive assessment overlooks the spate of books in contemporary theology that have sold in their millions to people around the world who mistrust traditional interpretations of Christianity but don't want to throw the baby (faith) out with the bathwater (dogma).

The father of psychoanalysis, Sigmund Freud, thought religion was a neurosis and religious faith an illusion, though his one-time colleague and collaborator, Carl Jung, a Christian, believed Freud, who was raised in the Jewish faith, had simply replaced God with sexuality as the object of his worship. The poet Matthew Arnold wrote that 'the true meaning of religion is . . . not simply morality, but morality touched by emotion'. The anthropologist Clifford Geertz saw it as a cultural system of symbols and practices that describe a particular 'order of existence' and motivate people to try to achieve that order. That definition fits with Geertz's rather poetic view that 'man is an animal suspended in webs of significance he himself has spun'.

In everyday language, we use the word 'religion' in two quite different ways: institutional and personal. When we refer to institutional religion – powerful corporate enterprises like the Roman Catholic and Anglican churches – the connotations are often negative: arrogance, financial corruption, undue political influence, sexual abuse of children and women (especially by allegedly 'celibate' priests), relentless self-interest, rigidly hierarchical and mostly male-dominated structures that both exploit and protect their own power.

But that's not the whole story. Religious institutions have supplied the cultural frameworks, the words, the rituals for marking life's most significant passages – births, deaths and marriages. As we have already acknowledged, they have spawned most of the charities devoted to the alleviation of the world's poverty and suffering, founded some of our best schools and finest hospitals. Representatives of the Christian churches were highly influential in the formation of the United Nations and in the creation of its Universal Declaration of Human Rights. Occasionally, a figure like Pope Francis captures the public's imagination and challenges the prejudice against institutional religion. But, at least in Western societies, it remains true that when you say 'institutional religion', many people's first response is to recoil.

On the other hand, when we hear the word 'religion' used in reference to the simple faith of a humble believer, our responses are rather different. As we have already seen, there's strong evidence to suggest that religious faith and practice is psychologically beneficial, at the very least. And the popular assertion that religion exists only in response to people's fear seems hard to support, unless you count 'existential angst' as fear, in which case a great deal of human behaviour – from alcohol abuse to philosophical enquiry – could be interpreted as a response to fear.

No doubt some preachers still try to promote fear via the threat that, if we sin, we might spend eternity in hell (though talk of hell seems to have diminished; the concept may have gone out of fashion in a society increasingly obsessed with 'positive outcomes'). But, mostly, religion is about the desire to harness the power of faith; to be part of a tribe with a clear purpose; to have one's nobler impulses nurtured. For many believers, religious faith is a kind of super-charged morality, born not of fear but of the desire to be a better person.

The times could suit religion (or 'spirituality')

Look around the world at all the factors contributing to our rising levels of anxiety: civil wars, the threat of international terrorism, climate change, global economic fragility (the most powerful country on earth – the US – is in debt to the tune of trillions of dollars, with its major creditor, China, regarded as a geopolitical rival). And all this is accompanied, in many Western countries, by a recurring complaint about a lack of vision among political leaders whose courage and integrity seem compromised by their short-term obsession with re-election.

Meanwhile, social, cultural, economic and technological change proceeds at a gallop. Changing patterns of marriage and divorce are reshaping our families and communities. A low birthrate is helping to accelerate the phenomenon of an ageing population (while also producing a generation of kids at some risk of being both overprotected and, paradoxically, under-parented).

Shrinking households have increased the risk of loneliness and social isolation. The gap between high-income and low-income earners is widening. The sense of job insecurity is rising in response to a steady increase in casual and part-time work and the growing problem of underemployment. The rise of consumerism puts pressure on middle-class households to go more deeply into debt. The local neighbourhood is less stable and cohesive than it used to be, and there's a temptation to compensate by engagement with online communities, courtesy of an IT revolution that seems to bring us closer together yet makes it easier than ever to stay apart. We are more restless than ever, partly because the IT revolution has revved up our demand for stimulation.

The good news is that many people have already sensed the danger in all this to our mental health and social wellbeing, and are doing something about it. Community redevelopment is happening; neighbourhoods are rediscovering their soul; the herd instinct is asserting itself in new ways. And, on a larger scale, social activists are emerging to fill the vacuum created by the lack of visionary political leadership that might otherwise have addressed the question: *What kind of society do we want to become?*

Nevertheless, the Age of Anxiety is still with us, as it has been since the English poet W.H. Auden gave it that label in the period immediately after World War II. We are anxious about the rate of change. We are concerned about the ecology of the planet and the impact of global warming. We are worried about our physical safety and our emotional security. We fear for the state of the world, geopolitically as well as economically. We wonder what cataclysms might lie ahead of us. Even when we are not focused on a specific issue, we experience a background rumble of anxiety. For many of us, stress has become a constant companion.

We'd like it to be different. We'd like to believe that stronger leadership could 'save' us. We'd like to think that humans will eventually come to their senses; that war will become a thing of the past; that religious and ethnic tensions will ease, as peaceful and respectful coexistence becomes our way of life; that territorial contests could be settled through diplomacy and respectful negotiation. But we're not holding our breath waiting for any of that to happen. Our anxieties get the better of us, and politicians seem shameless in their exploitation of our fears (in Australia, for example, by hammering the notion of 'border protection' until we lapse into a dulled acquiescence, even in the face of our unconscionable and reprehensible treatment of asylum-seekers, and by the exaggerated threat of terrorism, the modern bogey that has replaced Cold War communism). We are regulation-happy. We yearn for anything that might create order out of the chaos, reduce our level of anxiety and restore our confidence.

We are ripe, therefore, for the consolations of the spiritual life. We are in need of stories that will help us to make sense of what's happening to us or to recognise the causes of our underlying angst. Even in a determinedly secular society like Australia, all those non-churchgoing people who still choose to identify themselves as 'Christian' are presumably saying something about the values they still aspire to, the kind of cultural heritage they still respect, and possibly the kind of institutions they still want to preserve.

Not that traditional, institutional religion is in for a revival – there's no sign of that, though it's true that the social conditions I have just described have been favourable to the rise of black-and-white fundamentalism, not only in religion, but in politics and cultural life more generally. One response to anxiety is to retreat to the comfort and safety of conservative and inflexible opinions.

But fundamentalism is not the long-term solution for most people. Simplicity is unlikely to be the best answer to authentic complexity. A yearning for certainty may be understandable, but it is incompatible with the uncertainty that is inherent to human life. As one of my respondents put it, 'The Christianity of St Paul removes uncertainty, and if you remove uncertainty, you remove humanity.'

The post-fundamentalist phase of our response to the Age of Anxiety is likely to see a growing number of people being prepared to take another look at Christianity, or 'spirituality' more broadly, in an attempt to find some deeper, richer, more nuanced approach to life than social-media chatter or the slogans of a glib fundamentalism can provide.

As long as we must live with uncertainty – and we must – and as long as our confidence is sapped by the anxiety provoked by the social and economic upheavals reshaping our society, we are bound to return, eventually, to some of those ancient questions: *Why are we here? How should we live? Does it all mean anything?* We might also decide that some ancient answers – including religious answers – might have something to offer, even if the truth and wisdom embedded in them has become clouded by dogma and distorted by the pressure of institutional power.

If that's the case, words like 'religion', 'faith', 'church', 'Christian' and even 'God' may take on new meanings. The inner meaning of things said about God at a time when there was a widespread belief in God as a supreme being may still be valid, even if our conception of the God they once referred to has undergone a profound change. As Carl Jung wrote in *Memories, Dreams, Reflections* (1961): 'Not only do I leave the door open for the Christian message, but I consider it of central importance for Western man. It needs, however, to be seen in a new light, in accordance with the changes wrought by the contemporary spirit. Otherwise, it stands apart from the times, and has no effect on man's wholeness.'

3

Anyone for church?

Given the steady fifty-year decline in church attendance, it's not hard to find people who can tell you why they stopped going to church. Nor, these days, is it hard to find younger people who have never been churchgoers and can't imagine taking it up. In Australia, churchgoing was never a mainstream activity, even in its heyday, the way it once was in the US.

In the 1950s, 44 percent of Australians attended church regularly. The figure was 74 percent for Catholics, for whom church attendance was, and theoretically still is, compulsory, but both figures rose dramatically at Christmas and Easter. ('What religion are you?' ran the old joke. 'Oh, I'm C and E,' came the reply. 'Don't you mean C *of* E?' 'No, not Church of England – Christmas and Easter.') Today, about 20 percent of Australians are 'C and E', though the figure is much higher if you add all the 'carols by candlelight' events held somewhere other than in a church. And yet, as reported in the introduction, only 8 percent attend church weekly.

As in most comparable Western societies, churchgoing is simply off the agenda for the majority of contemporary Australians. Even among the new breed of seekers after an experience of spirituality (see chapter 4), churches do not rate highly as places likely to nurture the spiritual life. Nevertheless, between three and four million Australians still go to church at least once a month, in the face of strong social pressure not to. As one of my respondents remarked, 'When we say we go to church, people almost seem embarrassed, as though we'd admitted something they'd rather not know about us.'

So here's a question worth asking . . .

Why do people still go to church?

It's not a simple question. Churchgoing, like most forms of human behaviour, is not something people usually do for one reason: it is an expression of several different needs – spiritual, aesthetic, emotional, social – that seek fulfilment through this particular and highly repetitive action.

It would be easy to assume that people go to church to worship God; that would fit with an orderly view of the world. But the world is not an orderly place and even the motivations for church attendance turn out to be not only complex but sometimes almost inexplicable: 'I don't know, really – I suppose it's mainly habit after all these years. I can't say I particularly like going,' said one of my respondents. We humans do many things we don't always enjoy – such as going to work, for many people – because they add a crucial dimension of meaning to our lives. Churchgoing is like that for some people; the big difference is that it's voluntary.

When people talk about their motivations for attending church, a long list emerges.

Nurturing faith (or a desire for faith)

Regular attendance at church, mosque, synagogue or temple is encouraged by religious leaders for precisely the same reason that regular attendance at meetings of political parties, Masonic lodges, Alcoholics Anonymous, Rotary or other clubs is encouraged: faith in anything – an idea, a cause, a religion – needs to be carefully and regularly nurtured if it is to thrive.

For Christians, church services form an important part of this process of reinforcement by offering regular reminders of the key events in the life of Jesus and the central teachings of the faith through Bible reading, the singing of hymns, the recital of creeds, the exchange of 'the greeting of peace', participation in the communion service, listening to a sermon and, depending on the liturgical tradition, engagement with processions and other rituals associated with festivals and other special events in the life of the church.

We appreciate few things as much as having our world view affirmed. For the duration of a church service, private doubts can be set aside, and even for people who are there in a tentative spirit – possibly looking for reinforcement of their *desire* for faith, rather than faith itself – the internal logic and momentum of the service may carry them along.

A community to belong to

For regular churchgoers, the sense of belonging often seems as important as the religious aspect. To feel accepted, acknowledged and respected within a community of well-meaning and like-minded people is a powerful source of gratification; so powerful, in fact, that it can outweigh other factors that might deter people. Many otherwise liberated women, for example, continue to attend churches with a strong culture of 'male headship', because their sense of belonging to that community – and their friendship with other women in the congregation – is so strong.

> 'I don't approve of the place of women in my [Catholic] church – of course I don't. And I think it will change, given time.

First we'll get married priests, and then we'll get women. I might be dead before it happens, though. In the meantime, I am with a very warm and caring group of women, and we just get on with our lives – the male thing doesn't bother us most of the time. We are all committed Catholics and so we don't really question it – it's just always been like that. I wouldn't stop going to church over that but, as I say, I'm sure it will change. We're all keeping an eye on this new Pope – he might surprise everyone.' —*Marija*

An important ingredient in the rise of the Pentecostal megachurches is their offer of a vibrant, fully functioning community to belong to, though the pressure to conform sometimes becomes too great and the social benefits of belonging may ultimately pale beside a stifling sense of conformity. That's why some megachurches experience a high turnover, especially among young people. They come for the excitement, the strong sense of being accepted and included, and the inspiration of a religious experience, and some of them then leave in a state of confusion or even anger at having been 'taken over' by a highly institutionalised set of expectations about belief, behaviour and belonging.

'Growing up, I was a member of very strong church community. Although it was a pretty strict fundamentalist type of church, now I think back, with the Bible being regarded as literally true and all that, it was very socially supportive. We all knew each other very well, even more than the people who lived in our street, because we saw each other for an hour or two every Sunday and we sort of shared the same values, I guess. So everyone was interested in everyone else, and mainly in a good way. People cared how you'd done in your school exams, or whether you got your driver's licence first go. All your rites of passage happened within the church. You were teased when you appeared in your first pair of long trousers, and that's where your first girlfriend came from. People in the church advised me on what university course to do and where to look for a job.

So when I stopped going to church, it was quite traumatic, like losing a whole circle of friends, as well as an outlook on life. If it had been a different kind of church – more liberal and less judgemental – I think I might have been able to keep going, even though my thinking had changed. Even now, I sometimes hanker after that sense of being part of a caring church community. I do think there's something special about it.'—*Mitch*

In the traditional bucolic picture of village life – but even in the life of a larger town or suburb – local churches played a central role: a place for people to gather not only for church services, but for festivals, weddings, christenings, funerals, fetes, games, 'socials', choral singing etc. Parishioners maintained the church grounds, cleaned the church or served on the parish council as part of their contribution to the life of the village, town or suburb as much as the life of the church.

Today, in a more urbanised and sophisticated society, churches tend to be less integral to the life of their local community, though that sense of the church as a community hub is still strong in some places, and may be on the rise as people look for ways to reconnect with the neighbourhood. Rory Costelloe, the founder and executive director of Melbourne developer Villawood Properties, certainly thinks so: in a 2015 opinion piece written for *VPELA Revue* (the newsletter of the Victorian Planning Environmental Law Association), he refers to the important role that churches played historically in the development of social cohesion in the local community. He believes that the decline of this role has contributed to the increasing problem of alienation – especially of young people – from the neighbourhoods we live in.

Putting Costelloe's conviction into practice, Villawood Properties has integrated a church into an activity hub of a new residential development at Alamanda, in Victoria's Point Cook. The hub comprises shops, restaurants, commercial offices and a supermarket, and the church is located on the first floor, above the supermarket. Costelloe was not concerned about which denomination took up the space, and he recognised that church services were not likely to appeal to everyone. But he believed a church community would have an enriching effect on the broader community: 'We envisaged the church as a community hub to provide youth services, vocational guidance and pastoral care.' (In the same spirit, Costelloe now also includes a Men's Shed and a community garden in his company's developments.)

Among the many reasons why people go to church, the desire to be with other people who share the same convictions is understandably central; social interaction with the fellow faithful is as important an aspect of reinforcement as any sermon could be. Conversely, a feeling of being with a group of incompatible or unwelcoming people, even within the Christian faith, can drive people away in search of a 'better' church to attend.

> 'My husband is a restless soul, I'm afraid. He has this idea of a stable, caring church community that will be like the one he grew up in, but such places are a bit thin on the ground these days. You can't just bowl up to the local church and feel as if you'll automatically fit in. There seems to be a greater variation between churches than there used to be. Anyway, we've tried a fair few, but something always seems to be not quite right for him. They're too judgemental, or they're too liberal, or the music is too modern for his liking. I think he wants to turn the clock back, but you can't do that. I know what he means, though – it would be lovely to find a church where you felt welcome and accepted for who you are, with not too many questions asked. Oh, the other thing is that he wants it to be a thriving place with lots of young people, but no rock bands. See what I mean?

I think we're destined to be nomads when it comes to church attendance.' —*Linda*

Access to pastoral care

There's a strong tradition of ministers of religion also being de facto counsellors, listening to their parishioners' woes, offering a sympathetic shoulder to cry on, or being a supportive presence in times of personal difficulty. In close-knit church communities, much of the work of emotional support is provided by members of the congregation themselves, but the pastor's role remains unique. Rather like an old-style GP, the minister is expected to be available at all hours, especially in the case of serious illness, and she or he will usually be the first port of call, outside the family, when a death occurs. Ministers are often embraced as members, as well as leaders, of the church community, sharing in the joys as well as the trials and tribulations of their parishioners' lives. Though some ministers resist this aspect of their role ('I didn't become a priest to have afternoon tea with old ladies,' an Anglican minister once said to me), most churchgoers would rate the importance of sensitive pastoral engagement more highly than the quality of preaching. In churches with a tradition of great respect for the priesthood, some people depend on their priest for advice and support that goes well beyond the bounds of conventional pastoral care: 'I see more of the priest than my doctor, and I think I trust him more. He was very helpful through the menopause – he listened to me for hours.'

A sense of duty

Regular churchgoing has a self-perpetuating effect: provided no negative factors disrupt the process, the more regularly you attend, the more likely you are to go on attending regularly, and the more likely you are to become dependent on the familiarity, the comfort and the reassurance of the act itself. Before long, the habit of regular attendance may morph into a sense of duty: to miss a service can come to feel like a kind of personal failure, as if you have let the side down. You assume your absence will be noted, but you also feel a kind of personal incompleteness.

In *Summoned by Bells* (1960), the English poet John Betjeman wrote: 'Thus were my London Sundays incomplete / If unaccompanied by Evening Prayer' (a reference to a traditional Anglican evening service).

My late father's habitual church attendance certainly felt to him like inflexible duty: he could not bear to miss a Sunday service, wherever he happened to be. Once, on a school holiday in the Blue Mountains west of Sydney, the family was, as usual, dragooned into going to the local church, but our preparations were stalled by my father's discovery that he had failed to bring a tie (jacket and tie-wearing being de rigueur for churchgoing in the 1950s). A quick search of the family's wardrobe revealed a narrow black satin sash around someone's dressing-gown, and my mother was dispatched to iron it flat enough to pass muster as a tie, though, once donned, it looked as if my father were in mourning. Off we went, arriving late (but arriving late was another lifelong feature of my father's churchgoing habit).

'Keeps me on the straight and narrow'

In *An Unofficial Rose* (1962), Iris Murdoch describes one of her characters, Felix, an ex-army officer, as 'a church-goer and a communicant, maintaining the unreflective unemotional traditional Christianity in which he had been brought up, and which was vaguely connected in his mind with the Brigade and the Queen'. Felix draws moral sustenance from his regular attendance at church, though, typical of Murdoch's characters, he has a history of lapses; in spite of his conviction that he should not go to bed with women he was not married to, 'when he was seriously tempted, he usually succumbed, especially in hot climates'.

Churchgoing feels to many people like a spine-stiffening thing to do and church an inherently virtuous place to be. This is partly because it exposes them to scripture readings and homilies that remind them of their moral responsibilities: 'Keeps you up to the mark' is how one of my respondents put it. But it's also partly because in a relentlessly secular, materialistic and competitive world, churches offer a symbolic refuge; a place where it is assumed that fellow churchgoers will share an attractive moral seriousness.

Peace and quiet

Some churchgoers use the hour of a service for peaceful contemplation of the mysteries of life and death. Others are simply grateful for a break from the demands of family life.

> 'We go to church – not every week, but reasonably often. I think it's a good thing for the whole family, but especially for me. That's one hour a week when I have some peace and quiet – no nagging, everyone just has to sit still and silent. I think that's a good discipline for the kids. And it encourages a sense of gratitude, makes you think about the sick and the disadvantaged, and that's good for the kids, too, as well as for me. I'm not some great meditation person or anything, but I really value that quiet hour. Sometimes I come out and I couldn't tell you what I've been thinking about, but I know it's good for me. It wouldn't happen if we didn't go to church. We go at night, and there's no socialising, as we have to get the kids home. So we're not like fully engaged members of the church community, I realise that. But it's still a precious resource for me, that hour.' —*Julia*

Many of the most numerically successful and fastest-growing churches are quite the opposite of 'still': their services are bustling affairs, full of colour and movement and hardly a moment to draw breath, let alone sit in silence. The new Pentecostal megachurches, for instance, offer a powerful sense of community, a vast array of support services ranging from catering to marketing, special-interest groups, and services that rival any commercial pop music concert for the sophistication, vitality and volume of the music. But when it comes to the encouragement of meditative silence, they are at the opposite end of the spectrum from, say, Quakers. (A friend of mine, a devout Christian, once attended a service at Sydney's Hillsong Church 'to see what all the fuss was about'. He later told me he had suffered an earache for three days as a result of the amplified music.)

For some people, like Julia, church is the *only* place where peace and quiet can be found – and that's not only during a service; the use of open churches as suitable places for quiet meditation can be expected to increase as the need for somewhere to retreat from the busyness and overstimulation of a hyper-wired society becomes ever more pressing.

The aesthetics

From the simplicity of an unadorned chapel to the grandeur of a cathedral complete with stained-glass windows and high altar, the architecture, music, words and other aesthetic features of the churchgoing experience can play a big role in attracting people.

Merely to enter a grand cathedral makes some people feel 'spiritual' (though, for others, such places reek of idolatry and an overemphasis on the aesthetic at the expense of the spiritual). The language of the traditional Anglican or Catholic liturgy, only slightly modified from the way it has been for centuries, is heart-warming and inspiring to those who know it well and are emotionally attached to it. The familiar cadences roll over them reassuringly, the mystery of it being part of its appeal. (By contrast, the language may seem impenetrably weird to those who are either unfamiliar with it or unsympathetic to it.)

In a 2011 article in *The Times*, the Anglican dean of Perth, John Shepherd, argued that whereas the language of theology needs to be intellectually rigorous, the language of liturgy (meaning the language of a formal church service) needs to be poetic, musical, rhythmical and symbolic in order to do the work of inspiration and uplift: 'Like poetry, the words of the liturgy are most powerful when they are only generally, and not perfectly, understood.' He quotes the poet A.E. Housman: 'Poetry is not the thing said, but a way of saying it.'

Music is the crucial aesthetic for many churchgoers – the hymns, the organ, the choir, or the guitars and drums of the gospel-rock band. Indeed, so great is the appeal of sacred music to some people that they sing it, play it and listen to it avidly even when they have lost any faith in the specific ideas being promulgated, because they appreciate its beauty and its power to inspire them. The effects of hymn-singing can be positive enough to keep people coming back for more, year after year, even when the appeal of other aspects of the service may have waned. Given the well-documented therapeutic benefits of group singing, this is hardly surprising: churchgoers are better placed than most people in the community to reap those benefits.

Ross Gittins, the economics editor of *The Sydney Morning Herald*, recounts in his 2015 memoir, *Gittins*, the experience of being brought up in the Salvation Army culture dominated by the music of bands and songsters. Even today, long after abandoning his former faith, he reports that playing recordings of those old hymns can move him to tears.

Engagement with ritual

Many churches – particularly Anglo-Catholic and Roman Catholic – offer a rich presentation of ritual within the liturgy that draws the congregation into a kind of theatre. Some churchgoers become so attached to the liturgical rituals, and to the subtle changes in them that mark different festivals, saints' days and other points in the church year, they can hardly imagine giving them up. Even when faith wavers, or the existence of a traditionally imagined God comes to seem unlikely, the rituals can carry them along.

> 'I don't need to think about the theology too much, but I love those rituals – the processions, the incense, the singing – and I feel as if it's a good thing to be doing. It sort of grounds me in the big stories, the big themes. Maybe they're myths – so what? I like the effect of ritual on the rest of my life. I always leave the church feeling as if something worthwhile has happened, as if I'm better off for having been there, even if the sermon was a bit dreary. Uplifted, I guess.' —*Barry*

That's one reason why many people who have virtually given up churchgoing regularly return for Christmas and Easter festivals.

Interesting sermons

In the contemporary world, a sermon can seem like an anachronistic art form. With Twitter demanding our wisdom be distilled into 140 characters or less, and long emails now typically being only half read ('I scan the first para or two and get the gist'), the idea of sitting through a ten- or twenty-minute talk every week strikes many people as a prospect too daunting to contemplate, especially if their own experience of sermons, starting in childhood, had led them to master the art of switching off. (And, it should be noted, some elderly churchgoers do find the sermon a welcome opportunity for a nap, aided by the soporific sound of the human voice. Ministers of ageing congregations must be tolerant people – rather like the members of string quartets who play, virtually unheard, at noisy social functions.)

But some churchgoers speak with warm appreciation of their thoughtful and articulate preacher; they look forward to the sermon as a unique opportunity to engage with a sustained argument and stimulating ideas. Appreciation of the preaching appears to be quite a rare reason for attending church but, for the fortunate few, sermons are a highlight.

Erotic stimulation

Looking back on their adolescent experience of religion, some people reflect on the possibility that the spiritual and the sexual were very hard to separate: 'I think there was a lot of hormonal stuff bound up with it when I was young – you felt everything so intensely,' said one of my respondents.

It's not only young people who experience the connection – or confusion – between religious practice and erotic stimulation. Throughout history, people have reported ecstatic arousal, sometimes bordering on the erotic, associated with assorted religious practices including music and prayer, both public and private (though, as we shall see in chapter 7, religious ecstasy is hard to distinguish from other forms of ecstatic response). In *Submission* (2015), Michel Houellebecq describes the 'aesthetic, almost carnal delight in the Catholic liturgy' that came through in the writings of the nineteenth-century French novelist, J.K.Huysmans.

For some people, it's a more straightforward question of the charisma of a priest or minister evoking complex emotional responses. Here's a woman in her forties:

> 'I've fallen in love with several priests – I could never tell my husband, or the priests concerned, naturally. But there is

something tantalising about them; their celibacy gives them a special allure, I think – being untouchable. Plus all the gear. And that air of confidence – the occasional young and handsome ones, especially. I can remember feeling pretty aroused in several church services. And I notice a lot of women are quite flirty with priests. I suppose they think they're quite safe. I wouldn't be so sure.' —*Beth*

Use it or lose it

Dwindling congregations ultimately lead to church closures (though there are still many more churches than schools in Australia). Some people who might otherwise drift away from their engagement with a struggling local church – possibly because it has lost its vitality as a direct consequence of falling numbers – stick with it because they believe the presence of a functioning church is beneficial to the community. They might also feel that, if the time ever comes when they should feel the need for advice or support from a minister of religion, it would be a pity not to have access to a local church.

Forced to go

Not everyone attending church wants to be there. Many ex-churchgoers look back with resentment on their childhood or adolescent experiences of being 'force-fed' religion via compulsory attendance at church or school-chapel services.

The 'forced-to-go' category includes people attending on special occasions where parental pressure is still felt: 'We go at Christmas, because we are all at my parents' place and they'd be hurt if we didn't go with them.'

Some adults appear almost to force *themselves* to go, apparently fearing a vague sense of guilt if they stopped: 'I don't really want to go some weeks, but I suppose I just feel I should.'

'To qualify my kids for a church school'

Many parents who have decided they want to send their children to a church school discover that, particularly in the case of Catholic schools, they are expected to have a reference from the local parish priest, and that can't be secured unless the family starts showing up at church reasonably regularly. This has created a new category of churchgoer: 'We need to keep going for long enough to become sufficiently well-known to the priest, so he'll feel comfortable signing the school's application form.'

And the list goes on ...

Some people are looking for specific moral guidance, especially if they are facing a personal crisis; some are hoping for a 'lift' (often from the music or the ambience, but sometimes just from being in that space); some are seeking the classic comforts and consolations of the surrender to faith, including a sense of being in touch with the numinous; some are seeking friendship; some are flagrantly in search of a partner, though churches as meeting places for members of the opposite sex are not as reliable as they once were (except among the bereaved elderly, or in megachurches bursting with adolescent energy).

With all the apparent benefits of church attendance, the obvious next question is:

Why do people *stop* going to church?

Any analysis of why people have stopped going to church needs to take account of the massive bombardment of Western society over the past thirty years by propaganda from two directions – both antithetical to the core messages of religion and spirituality.

The first barrage has come from the world of consumer mass-marketing. Chiming with the emergence of economics as the core of politics and the belief that life can only get better as long as we sustain our economic growth, the blandishments of consumerism have become ever-more seductive. Strategies for the mass-marketing of consumer goods have become increasingly insidious and sophisticated, reinforced by advertising on an unprecedented scale, launched from a burgeoning array of media platforms. The unambiguous message embedded in all this consumerist frenzy is that 'it's all about Me'. If I live in a country that brags about its high standard of living, then surely I am entitled to *feel* rich and *act* rich, courtesy of the magic plastic wand that gives me access to all that beautiful credit. Prosperity is my birthright. I have been conditioned to expect a level of material comfort my parents or grandparents could scarcely have dreamed of, but it all depends on me responding like a dutiful consumer to the injunction to *buy! buy! buy!* and to enjoy the momentary euphoria of retail therapy. And if all this stuff isn't delivering its promise of personal fulfilment (did we ever really think it would?), then we need to *keep buying* for the benefits to be sustained.

The Australian social analyst Richard Eckersley explored the implications of all this in *Well & Good* (2004): 'Despite the cultural propaganda of our times, it is clear that filling up an empty self is a poor substitute for the web of meaning provided by deep and enduring personal, social and spiritual attachments. We are told that a highly individualistic, consumer lifestyle is compatible with strong families, social cohesion and equity, environmental sustainability, and a sense of spiritual connectedness to the universe in which we live.' And then, having reviewed the vast body of research on the subject, Eckersley delivers his verdict: 'It is not.'

The second bombardment has been coming from the merchants of happiness. Marshalling their considerable forces, they have also been telling us exactly what we want to hear: your entitlement isn't confined to material prosperity; you're entitled to happiness as well, and the pursuit of *personal* happiness is a perfectly suitable goal for your life.

Books, blogs, broadcasts, conferences, TED talks, YouTube clips . . . the promotion of the pro-happiness message is every bit as relentless as the marketing of consumer goods. Never mind that our folklore has always said that 'we grow through pain', or that we learn more from failure than success, or that sadness is as authentic and valuable an emotion as happiness and actually has far more to teach us. No, the new message is that happiness is what makes the world go round.

People like Martin Seligman and Roy Baumeister, leaders of the positive psychology movement, must be in despair as they see their serious work hijacked by a cavalcade of pop psychologists trying to seduce us with the proposition that if we're not feeling happy, there's something wrong with us. This denies one of the most precious truths about human existence: we have a full spectrum of emotions available to us, and our emotional maturity – our resilience – depends on being able to recognise and deal with each of them when they visit us. And each emotion can only make sense to us in the context of all the others: we wouldn't even be able to recognise happiness unless we had experienced sadness. (I have developed this theme more fully in my 2013 book, *The Good Life*.)

In any case, as many researchers have found, it is a sense of *meaningfulness*, not happiness, that brings life's deepest satisfactions. Baumeister and other psychologists have been consistently reporting that many of the things that deepen the sense of meaning and purpose in our lives – including things like parenting and work – *don't* necessarily make us feel happy, and most of the things that make us feel happy – including possessions, holidays and a full stomach – don't enrich our sense of life's meaning. Meaningfulness generally comes from giving, Baumeister notes in 'Some key differences between a happy life and a meaningful life' (2013), whereas happiness generally comes from taking. ('Ah,' say some of the slippery apologists for the happiness movement, 'but meaningfulness is what I *mean* by happiness.' So why mislead everyone by using a word that has acquired such a specific modern meaning related to a particular emotional state?)

As mentioned in chapter 2, Seligman's research has led him to conclude that faith in something larger than the self is the one necessary condition for a sense of meaning in life, and the larger that entity, the more meaning people can derive from it. In Western societies, traditional attachments to God, religion, country or even family are becoming both less common and less stable than they once were, so people tend to look within themselves for the meaning of their lives. Yet, as Seligman says, 'self is a very poor site for meaning'. Like many other social analysts, he associates rising levels of depression in the West with increasing individualism.

It is surely no mere coincidence that the rise of the consumerism and happiness industries has been accompanied both by an increase in the incidence of depression and by the dramatic rise in the use of recreational drugs. And why not? The argument is quite simple: If I'm entitled to happiness but I'm not feeling happy, and all my material 'stuff' hasn't done it for me, then a pharmacological strategy might get me to where I want – where I'm *entitled* – to be.

Some versions of Christianity chime with the Me culture, with their emphasis on *my* salvation, *my* access to eternal life, faith as a pathway to *my* happiness, and blessings showered on *me* by a munificent God who is rewarding *me* for *my* faith. But the broader message of Jesus, succinctly expressed in the so-called Sermon on the Mount, is about the need for unfailing kindness and compassion, grace under pressure, and an obligation to care for the poor, the homeless, the sick and the marginalised.

So the core message of Christianity is clearly at odds with the dominant messages of the contemporary Me culture. The rising interest in non-religious spirituality described in the next chapter, and the growth in the practice of yoga and meditation, suggest that the Me culture might be beginning to lose its grip on us – but, as Anne Manne demonstrates in *The Life of I* (2014), we have a long way to go, and the exponential growth in use of social media must be regarded, on balance, as a rich source of yet more fuel for our Me-obsession.

Given all that, you'd expect a steady exodus from the church. In *Turning Point* (1999), I wrote that 'the flowering of a heady consumerism coincided with a sharp decline in the practice of religion and support for its associated moral codes. In the short term, [Baby] Boomers committed themselves to a variety of alternative gratifications, almost as if they were creating substitutes for the religious observance of their parents' generation: sex, food, travel and "personal growth" were all approached with religious fervour and invested with a kind of religious significance.' Their children, not surprisingly, followed suit.

Like the list of reasons for going to church, the following list of reasons for *not* going is neither comprehensive nor presented in order of significance (since each person's motives for leaving the church are the most significant for them).

Boring, irrelevant

The English writer G.K. Chesterton once remarked that there is no such thing as an uninteresting subject, only an uninterested listener. That may be so, but the best preachers, like the best teachers, writers or politicians, have a way of making a subject seem irresistibly interesting by establishing its relevance – especially its emotional relevance – to their audience.

When people say, 'Church was boring', they usually mean: 'It had nothing to do with me.' That's a common complaint among people who were raised in a churchgoing household and attended regularly until a point, usually in adolescence, when they felt sufficiently confident to tell their parents they had had enough.

> ‘I got nothing out of going to church. Nothing! I did it for eighteen years and then I just stopped. There was no crisis of faith, because there was no faith to have a crisis with. I think I was pushed into atheism – well, I'm 99 percent atheist and 1 percent agnostic – by being forced to go to church for all those years. And it was so boring! All those older people . . . I have nothing against older people, but it felt like the church had nothing to offer young people. I felt as if I was simply in the wrong place. I used to occupy myself by checking what all the women were wearing. And I used to watch people praying and think, 'You're not really praying.'
>
> The strange thing is I think I could have been a believer – I mean, there are all those terrific hymns, and the stories are great, and you can pray to Jesus for whatever you want. Some of my friends are still right into it, and I quite envy them, in some ways. But then I think of those interminable church services and I know I could never go through it all again.
>
> It's not as if I wasn't steeped in it – at school, all our sports teams were given saints' names – but I think that was the problem. Too much. Too much religion. Too much compulsion. I guess it worked for some of the girls, but not for me. I sometimes feel like saying to the friends who have stuck with religion: What did you see that I didn't see?’—*Rebecca*

The world is full of storytellers competing for our attention, all trying to demonstrate the relevance of their message to us. No relevance is easier to establish than that of an advertiser's pitch to a potential consumer: 'This is all about *you*! Look what this will do for you! Look how your life will be changed for the better!' The clincher is that the materialist's promise is based on a concrete offer: you pay your money and you get your car/jeans/smartphone/drink . . . or any of the other things that promise to transform your life. In the same way, the 'happiness' pitch has no trouble establishing its relevance. What could seem *more* relevant than your right to personal happiness?

Beside these, the immediate relevance of a more nuanced, reflective and ultimately self-effacing proposition is rather harder to establish. (Which would you rather be: rich and happy, or kind?) Religious faith offers deferred gratification at best, via an enriched sense of the meaning and purpose of your life.

Alien

'Irrelevant' sometimes turns out to be an understatement: many people have abandoned regular churchgoing because they came to feel that it was *so* irrelevant to them, it actually seemed alien: 'I looked around one day – really looked at those people – and said to myself, What are you all doing here? What am *I* doing here?'

For some people, that sense of church and religion being alien seemed to be there from the very beginning, either through the experience of attending church and always feeling uncomfortable or out of place, or through a churchless upbringing that formed a view of religion itself as a strange, even weird, practice that had nothing to do with the life of their family.

'I realised I was neglecting my seven-year-old daughter's religious education,' a colleague said to me recently, 'when we walked past a church and she asked me what it was. I said, "That's a church," and she said, "What's a church?" I'm going to have to do something about that. Ethics classes in primary school can't make up for all the other stuff religion offers you – it's such a big part of our culture.'

Adrian's brush with Sunday school

Adrian McGuigan, the spectator from chapter 1 who follows a strict routine – same seat, same companions, same clothes, same beer intake – to ensure his football team wins (or, as Adrian says when the team loses, 'to give them the best chance of winning') was raised by half-hearted atheists who offered no resistance when their churchgoing neighbours invited nine-year-old Adrian to join their own two boys at Sunday school.

'It'll do him no harm,' Adrian's parents had assured each other. 'Good for him to know all this stuff, so he can make up his own mind later on. Anyway, I don't think Adrian's the type to be taken in by any nonsense.'

When it came to the point, though, Adrian simply wouldn't cross the threshold. Having listened all his young life to his parents making caustic remarks about churches and churchgoers, he had developed a mild phobia about actually entering a church building. The local Sunday school was held in an adjacent hall, not the church itself, but for Adrian it was too close for comfort. It even smelt strange to him.

He went to Sunday school for three weeks, though he firmly refused all invitations to come inside and sit with the other children. Instead, he stood in the doorway and took an intelligent if detached interest in what was going on. A couple of the stories that were told – one about Noah and his ark, and one about Jesus feeding five thousand people with a few loaves of bread and a couple of fish – were familiar from scripture classes at school and struck Adrian as improbable, though some of the songs seemed quite catchy. (In fact, his parents were mildly alarmed when, on one of those Sunday afternoons, they heard Adrian singing a gospel chorus to himself as he bounced a tennis ball against the back wall of the house.)

On the fourth Sunday, the neighbours asked Adrian if he would like to give it one more try and he said no, he didn't think so. His parents were relieved, though they had quite enjoyed the lazy hour they had been able to spend together on those three previous Sunday mornings.

As he grew older, Adrian's sense of churches as a no-go zone increased.

'It wasn't that I thought they were spooky, exactly – more that they just seemed alien. I was really resistant to going to anything in a church, even a concert. In fact, the first time I actually entered a church and sat down was for an uncle's funeral and I remember feeling quite nervous about it. I had a girlfriend at the time who had been raised an Anglican, so she was quite at ease with the whole deal, and it was good having her with me. My parents were there, and I noticed they were pretty edgy, too. Everything seemed strange – the seats were uncomfortable, the lighting was dim, there was this same funny smell I remembered from that Sunday school hall all those years ago, and everyone seemed so quiet and solemn – it was a funeral, of course, but my uncle was over ninety when he died, and he'd had dementia for years, so we weren't exactly shocked at his passing. The clergyman who spoke clearly knew nothing about Uncle Rob, but who did? So he gave us a hammering about the afterlife; he was trying to convince us that the resurrection of Jesus was proof of life after death. I remember thinking that eternal life sounded like a fate worse than death – I mean, forever? I think I'd lose interest, eventually.

'I remember the intense relief when we stepped outside into the sunlight. I felt as if I'd been released from jail. I said to my girlfriend, 'Do you mean you used to go to things like that voluntarily?' and she just laughed. I'd never really thought about what it must be like to go into a church every week.

'These days, I'm more relaxed about it. A few mates have got married in church, though most do the deed under a tree somewhere. When I met Carla, she dragged me along to a Christmas carol service her sister was performing in, which was okay. But I could never see myself signing up. I never felt it had anything to do with me.

'When Carla and I got married, we did it in a church, believe it or not. Carla's like that – her mum wanted a church wedding, so Carla thought: What's the big deal? No point in making a fuss. That's what she's like. She even goes to church sometimes – she says we should be open to it. But I think she's more into yoga, actually.'

'Alien' sometimes means silly as well as strange: many churchgoers have reached a moment when they felt as if the whole situation of being in church no longer made sense to them. 'Loopy', 'over the top', 'weird', 'ludicrous' or even 'funny' are terms sometimes used to describe such a moment.

> 'My parents would sometimes take us all to church. There was this one time, when I was not quite a teenager, and we went to a Christmas service in a very upmarket, stuffy Anglo-Catholic kind of church. They had a procession that went up and down the aisles and someone was carrying a stone baby, to represent the baby Jesus, and people were kind of bowing to it as it went past. Well! My sisters and I just got the giggles – it seemed so ludicrous to us, even as kids. We attracted a lot of disapproving looks and our parents finally hustled us out. They asked us what was so funny, and when we explained how silly it seemed, they could sort of see the funny side of it, too. Anyway, they never took us back.'—*Otto*

'Alien' can also mean something more culturally subtle than that. The experience of migrants, for example, sometimes includes a difficult – or impossible – adjustment to a different attitude to religion or to a different 'vibe' in religious services in the new country. In the case of Frederik, a Scandinavian migrant, the lack of access to a local Lutheran church simply made churchgoing unthinkable.

> 'Where I grew up, the Lutheran church was absolutely integral to the society. It's different these days – the whole society is more secular – but when I was young everyone did religious studies at school and everyone got confirmed. You didn't question it. I think it was more cultural than religious, actually. I was always too much of a realist to believe in the virgin birth or the resurrection, but I have always believed in some form of divine intervention, and I still pray at night – not asking for things, but just repeating prayers I learnt as a child, as a kind of meditation. I would like my family to be able to go to church now – I'd love to be singing hymns,

in fact – but there's no Lutheran church nearby, and everywhere else seems quite alien to me. The children do Anglican scripture at school, because I want them to learn about Christianity, but it's all so hardline, I couldn't possibly go to that church.'—*Frederik*

'I could no longer go along with it'

When a churchgoer reaches the point of feeling uncomfortable with the whole structure of the church and its teachings, it's easy to understand why they might feel it's time to leave. Sometimes the tipping point is over their resistance to a specific piece of doctrine (see 'The all-or-nothing problem', below). Sometimes, the repetitiveness of a service that had once seemed reassuringly familiar may come to feel tedious or uninspiring, particularly if the clergy conducting the service are themselves perceived to be merely going through the motions. Sometimes, a sudden insight changes the way they perceive the tone of the service:

'It gradually occurred to me that the whole thing was making me feel bad about myself. I would hear myself saying, 'We have sinned against you in thought, word and deed,' and I would ask myself, Have I? This week? Maybe I was missing the point. Maybe everyone else's standards were higher than mine.

Sometimes I just wouldn't say it because I really didn't believe it at that moment. Other times I would just go along with it, especially if I thought I might have sinned in some way that week – usually something fairly minor, like not ringing my mother when I said I would or being a bit unreasonable with one of the kids who was exasperating me. I guess it's not a bad thing to focus on whether you're doing the best you can. But 'sinned against you in thought, word and deed'? The whole shebang? It seemed a bit harsh.

In the end, I thought, I'm not that bad. And neither are any of these other people. After that, I just couldn't hack it – I couldn't reconcile all this demeaning worse-than-a-miserable-worm stuff with how I was actually feeling.'—*Renate*

Sometimes, people simply stop believing things they had previously accepted without question.

'I went to church with my family from the time I was old enough to sit still – or maybe they even took me in a pram. It was just part of what the family did. I went along with it until I got involved in a youth group in my teens, and I started to see how judgemental the whole thing was. There was a real lack of tolerance or understanding – or even an attempt to understand – other people's points of view. I came to think it was very unhealthy, very disrespectful. It was alright if you didn't want to think too deeply about it; some of the kids I knew are still there, though I think of them as being a bit weak-minded, to be frank. It was all supposed to be about this religion of love, but I found the hostility to non-believers, or even Christians with slightly different beliefs, quite breathtaking. It certainly wasn't loving.

In fact, I'd say it was the strictness, the punitive nature of it, that finally drove me away. Some of those young people were practically salivating at the prospect of sinners rotting in hell. It was very sanctimonious, very smug – and very triumphalist, too: 'We're the only ones with the key to salvation!' You were expected to accept the whole thing, with no room for questioning or exploring things a bit.

The other thing was the idea of a supreme being, creator, redeemer, whatever. I just found I could no longer go along with it. I remember the feeling of intense relief – liberation, really – when I realised that I simply didn't believe in the supernatural side of it at all.

So there was this lack of love in the way they were interpreting the teachings of Jesus, plus their belief in some God that no one

> could actually explain. It was definitely time to move on. I couldn't play by their rules.'—*Kelvin*

One of history's most famous ex-churchgoers is the Russian novelist Leo Tolstoy. In *How Can We Know?* (1985), A.N. Wilson describes the process of Tolstoy's exit from churchgoing, but not from Christianity: 'After his initial conversion to Christianity, he appeared to accept all the teachings of the Orthodox Church. But when he decided that the rites and ceremonies of the church were ridiculous, it was not long before he had come to the belief that most of the supernatural stories in the Gospels were make-believe ... But the more he discarded the supernatural elements of his faith, the more urgently he advocated the moral excellence of the Sermon on the Mount.' (We'll revisit that famous sermon in chapter 8.) Tolstoy's experience would seem familiar to the many people who have moved away from full-on Christian faith and practice, but who nevertheless retain a deep respect for the values and teachings of Christianity. Though no longer churchgoers, they may still choose to identify as 'Christian'.

'I felt too exposed'

> 'At the church I was attending, I felt as if everyone was looking at me. It was a small congregation and even though they were probably very nice people, I just had this feeling of being the object of too much attention. I eventually went to a Catholic church, even though I'm not a Catholic, and that was better – there were five hundred people in the congregation and I felt as if I could hide. There wasn't the same feeling of pressure.
>
> Another thing that put me off the first church was this heavy campaign to get everyone to give to the church via EFT, instead of putting money in the collection plate. I didn't like the idea

of that at all – they would know exactly how much you were giving and I thought that was a bit too exposing as well. Anyway, I like putting money in the plate – it feels more personal and more like a deliberate act you are performing, as well as being anonymous.'—*Robin*

Too rigid, exclusive . . . or insulting

For some ex-churchgoers, the breakaway has been triggered by unsuccessful attempts to engage in discussion about alternative points of view, by feeling they were being intellectually abused or insulted by things said from the pulpit ('some sermons are just so feeble'), or by the sense that they were not considered worthy of being there.

One of my respondents told a story of his mother's painful departure from the church following the death of her husband and her subsequent wish to marry a divorcee.

'After my father died, my mother met this lovely man who had been divorced long before he met my mother, but the priest said my mother couldn't marry a divorced person in the church. When Mum kept pushing him, he said he had even written to the Pope to get permission, but permission was not granted. There was a great crisis. My mother went ahead and got married, and simply stopped going to church. Then her second husband left her and she eventually met a Catholic man whose wife had died and they got married in the church, no problem. Mum's second marriage was annulled, somehow, in the eyes of the church. Anyway, my mother started going again – not weekly, but occasionally. She never really recovered from that feeling of rejection.'—*Henry*

Henry then told me the story of his own search for a suitable church to attend when he moved from New Zealand to Australia.

‘I was actually trying out a few different churches, looking for one where the family and I might feel comfortable. People were superficially welcoming, but I often got the feeling that this was a sort of club and if you didn’t toe the line, you wouldn’t really be accepted. They felt like closed communities. At one Anglican church, the preacher said from the pulpit that he strongly disapproved of people who just came occasionally and were not prepared to commit themselves to weekly attendance. He wanted nothing less than that commitment – ‘You can’t just pick and choose,’ he said. We felt quite insulted, so we didn’t go back, naturally. We tried another one at Christmas. The music was terrific and the kids were quite intrigued by the crib and everything. And then the same thing happened – we got a tirade from the preacher about how appalling it was for people just to come to church at Christmas, as if it was purely a cultural thing. We didn’t go back there, either.

I ended up getting the kids christened at a Catholic church – the Anglican priest I spoke to wanted to baptise my oldest two in a river by total immersion, but the kids wouldn’t have a bar of it. Anyway, we kind of gave up after that. We don’t go anywhere. The kids get religious instruction at their school, so that will have to do.’—*Henry*

It’s easy to understand how the sense of being an outsider – not knowing the ropes; not cracking the code – can lead to an uncomfortable feeling of exclusion or even alienation that drives people away from church.

In the following two cases, though, it was insiders who were frozen out.

‘I was a youth leader in our church. Mum and Dad were devout Christians and regular churchgoers, and I was totally into it. Apart from being the youth leader, I sang in the church choir and taught a Sunday school class.

After I left school and started at university, my interest in religion and the spiritual life deepened and I began to read widely, including works of theology and Bible commentary that lay outside the narrow scope of the denomination I happened to belong to.

Our youth group met each Sunday afternoon. The meetings usually consisted of a brief talk by one of the members of the group – we all took turns – some discussion, Bible reading and singing, followed by a light meal, and then we all trooped into the evening service in the church.

I got quite fired up by some of the material I had been reading, and so I decided to give a talk on the first chapter of the book of Genesis – the creation story. It was hardly revolutionary, looking back on it. I just presented the idea that this was pure poetry, not to be taken literally, but to be understood as allegory – a way of thinking about mankind's relationship to the earth and to God. I was just as committed as ever – it's just that I had realised how silly it was to take everything literally.

Anyway, a pretty animated discussion followed. Some hardline creationists were outraged by the mere suggestion that Genesis – or any part of the Bible – should be questioned, or read any way other than literally. Some others were more sympathetic, or at least polite.

Soon after I got home from church that night, I received a phone call from the minister of the church, asking me to see him the following morning. That wasn't so unusual, because we sometimes spoke about the program for the youth group. I certainly didn't connect it to my talk. How naive was I!

When I arrived at the church office, I realised this was no ordinary meeting. The minister was grim and unsmiling. He ushered me into his study where he laid out the gist of my talk – obviously relayed to him by one of the tittle-tat creationists – and asked me if that was what I had said. I agreed that it was and began to explain my position, but he held up his hand.

'I want to hear no more of this,' he said. 'You are relieved of your position as youth leader, and I'm sorry to have to say that unless you change your tune, you won't be welcome in this church.'

I was so astonished, I couldn't speak. I sort of stumbled out of his office, caught a bus to university in a state of shock, and never entered that church again, or any other – except for friends' weddings and my father's funeral.

In some ways, the worst thing was that, apart from a couple of my close girlfriends, I never heard from any members of that group again.

My parents were shattered. They kept going to the church, but their relationship with that minister became pretty frosty, and they didn't know what to make of me, either. We never really talked much about it until much later, after Dad died. Mum said she'd heard all about what I had said and she basically agreed with me but Dad didn't. In those days, wives really did obey their husbands, believe it or not – at least in that church they did. So she didn't feel as if she could back me up.'—*Patricia*

Patricia was young and resilient, yet she was temporarily shattered by that experience and bears a long-term grudge against the church. For an older or more vulnerable person, being shown the door can be terminally distressing.

'My mother was an absolutely integral part of the life of her local church. The whole family was. We all had jobs in the church, but Mum was the most involved – she even used to cook meals for a women's refuge run by the church. And then my dad left home. Mum was devastated, needless to say – we all were. As if that wasn't bad enough, the minister of the church came to see Mum soon after the news got out and told her she would no longer be welcome at church. Apparently, the minister couldn't hack the idea of having a woman in his congregation whose marriage had collapsed. Later, Mum suspected that the minister's wife had been behind it – she and a group of women at the church disapproved of Mum after Dad left her. Maybe it was that old thing of married women not liking a divorced woman around their husbands – I don't know. Anyway, Mum left the church and never went back. And that was the day the bottom dropped out of religion for me, too. Since then, I've never seen anything to convince me that religion does more good than harm. The faith-community thing is all very well as long as you're part of it, but when it turns against you, it can be very harsh.'—*Genia*

The treatment of women

For many women who have lived through the women's liberation movement and seen its fruits in a genuine (if unfinished) gender revolution, many parts of the Christian church look increasingly anachronistic. Some churches ordain women to the ministry and encourage female participation in the leadership of the church; the Salvation Army, for instance, has been committed to gender equality from the beginning, and the Anglican, Uniting and Baptist churches are steadily increasing the number of female ministers in Australia. But there are blocks of resistance to these moves, even within some of those churches. The Roman Catholic Church, the large Sydney diocese of the Anglican Church and the Pentecostalists are all heavily male-dominated, their ethos of 'male headship' allegedly based on passages of scripture. The Presbyterian Church in Australia once ordained woman as ministers, but later repealed the church law that allowed them to do so. The Lutheran church does not ordain women in Australia, though it does in many other countries.

As we saw earlier in the chapter, some women who are feminists in other areas of their lives manage to overlook the gender question at church and focus on the comfortable sense of belonging to the lay community. Others, though, have been irritated, bewildered, frustrated and finally exasperated by the intransigence of churches that are so clearly out of step with the changes in the roles and status of women in contemporary society.

> ‘I was very attached to my church for a long time. But when I started having children, I was expected to join mothers’ groups and women’s groups and that wasn’t me at all. I had even been thinking of going into the ministry, but there was no way that would have been open to me. The whole thing became increasingly problematic for me. It was clear the church leaders felt there was nothing to be gained by promoting women to leadership roles; wives were just supposed to be wives, and the leaders’ wives exercised their power, such as it was, by being married to their husbands. That wasn’t the way I saw things.
>
> Every letter we received from the church – mostly about fundraising – was always addressed to my husband. I got totally fed up with it. We just drifted away, basically. I decided that my leadership talents could be better used in education, and these days I rarely go to church. When I do, I’m reminded of just how far away it all is from the reality of most people’s lives.’—*Joanna*

‘We’re too busy, and . . .’

In a society where it was once reported (in 2001 by Sweeney Research) that spouses spend an average of only twelve minutes per day talking to each other, busyness has become a major social issue – and I suspect that if the Sweeney research were repeated today, the face-to-face talking figure might be closer to six minutes than twelve. (‘Twelve minutes!’ exclaimed one of my friends, on learning about Sweeney’s finding. ‘That would count as an eternity in our house, especially if they were twelve consecutive minutes.’)

Everyone's busy, and many people relish their busyness and take pride in it.

'Busyness' is often used as a smokescreen to conceal other factors influencing the way we live. Not surprisingly, busyness has become the favourite excuse for *not* doing things, from exercise, reading, spending time with children and volunteering to walking the dog ... or going to church.

> 'I'm actually a believer, sort of. I mean, I'm certainly not an atheist. I was raised a Catholic, and I want my kids to have that upbringing, too. But the thing is, going to church is a two-and-a half-hour exercise by the time we get them ready, pile into the car, drive there, get settled, go through the service and then repeat the exercise coming home. We were trying to make it at least once a month, now it's more like once every two or three months. It's too hard. Life's a bit out of control – I realise that. I come from a large family, but my parents managed to get us all to church every Sunday. The pace was very different then, and my mother didn't have a paid job, whereas my wife has a career, same as I do. I guess something has to give.
>
> If we have any spare time as a family, we're inclined to have a walk by the water, get some fresh air, buy fish and chips and have a bit of family time together. I'd give church up before I'd give that up. Does that mean we're strong believers? Probably not. We've travelled a fair bit as well, so that gives you a different outlook on it – it would be naive to think our particular tradition is the only correct one. To me, religion is a means to an end, and that end is goodness, I guess. Doing the right thing, being a good person. That's what we want for our kids, and we hope religion will contribute to it. But it's mostly up to us as parents.
>
> In any case, to be truthful, my kids have never really bonded with it. They like the Bible stories, but that's about it. I'll make them go through the six-week preparation for confirmation – I don't

> think that will do them any harm and it's more or less expected if they are going to attend a Catholic secondary school.'—*Richard*

'We're too busy'? What a range of emotions and attitudes may be concealed behind that apparently simple explanation for not going to church! 'No time' to do something almost always means no *inclination* to do it, or a stronger inclination to do something else. (Many ministers of religion may be surprised to find what people really mean when they say they don't have time to go to church.)

Richard's story is a reminder of how nuanced people's motivations can be. The more he talked about his history of churchgoing, the more complex the story became ...

Loss of respect for the integrity of the institution

> 'I knew some of those priests involved in child sex abuse and I must admit that has had a big effect on my perception of the church. I'm more sceptical about the whole thing than I used to be. I sometimes question the validity of an institution that can be so corrupt, especially over a thing like that. I even wonder sometimes whether the church is just a front for evil. I know that sounds terrible, but when you think about what's actually going on, you wonder how anyone in the hierarchy could have thought it was a good idea to cover it up or resist taking action. I would never let my kids go to a Catholic primary school that had a presbytery in the grounds.
>
> I can't see that we'll ever be devout again. I've given it my best shot, but my siblings have all given it away. Even my mother – she's still a woman of faith, but she's been very disillusioned by it all. She knew some of those priests, too. Seeing priests abuse their position of trust – not only with kids, but with women, as well – has really knocked her faith in the church. She clings to her own faith, but she's pretty disgusted with the church as an institution.'—*Richard*

Though Roman Catholic churches, schools and orphanages have received most attention in the media, other denominations – including Anglican, Uniting, Salvation Army and Pentecostal – have also been tarnished by assorted charges of sexual abuse and impropriety stretching over decades.

Child sex-abuse scandals, more than any other single form of institutional corruption, have tarnished the reputation of the church to the extent that many churchgoers have either drifted away in disgust, or now either attend church less regularly or adopt a rather cynical, sceptical attitude to it. As one such person noted: 'There's obviously less respect for the clergy than there used to be. It's no more "Father Bill", it's just "Bill", and I think that's significant.'

(A grim aside: while disgust at the alarming incidence of child sexual abuse by clergy and others in church-based institutions is completely warranted, we need to acknowledge that *most* sexual abuse of children allegedly happens in their own home, often at the hands of a relative or a 'friend' of the family. We also need to acknowledge that much of the institutional abuse of children, especially in some notorious church-run schools, has not been sexual, but emotional and physical in other ways, such as beatings and various forms of humiliation.)

The all-or-nothing problem

One of the most effective ways of discouraging people from attending church is to insist that they meet certain rigid requirements for 'becoming a Christian'.

While the majority of those who identify themselves as Christian in the national census presumably have a broadly sympathetic attitude to Christianity and its values (plus or minus some doctrines), the all-or-nothing approach of some churches leads to a sharp distinction between being 'Christian' – regarded dismissively as a soft 'cultural' term by some hardliners – and being '*a* Christian', implying a full commitment to the doctrines and practices of a particular branch of the church. (Among Roman Catholics, the label is more likely to be 'Catholic' than 'Christian'; as one of my ex-Catholic respondents put it, 'I never thought we were Christians – I thought that was only happy-clappy Protestant types.' And a churchgoing Catholic conceded: 'We're all Christians, but I think there's more prestige attached to being a Catholic.')

It's not hard to imagine the reaction of a seeker after religious truth to the proposition that, when it comes to Christianity, it's all or nothing. Virgin birth, resurrection, ascension, miracles, second coming . . . the lot, New Testament and Old. 'If it's all or nothing,' such a person might say, 'I think I'll opt for nothing.'

If not a church, then perhaps a church school

One of the paradoxes of the current religious scene in Australia is that, as church attendance has declined, enrolments at religious schools have soared. In 1970, only 22 percent of Australian school pupils were enrolled at non-government schools; by 2014, the proportion had risen to 35 percent and that trend appears set to continue. In the case of secondary education, the proportion of pupils enrolled in non-government schools is close to 40 percent.

The overwhelming majority of non-government schools are religious, with schools run by the Roman Catholic and Anglican churches predominating. Even some non-church schools declare that they are based on 'Christian values' and some, like the non-denominational Sydney Grammar School, have 'the promotion of religion' in their founding charter, if not in their current educational strategy.

It might seem reasonable to assume that in a society where religious faith and practice have been in such sharp decline, this would be reflected in parents' increasing preference for a determinedly secular education for their children. In fact, the opposite is the case.

When parents of children at religious schools reflect on why they chose those schools for their children, strong tribal links are often the primary factor, whether the links are with a particular religious denomination or a particular private-school culture. But two other factors consistently emerge, as well: *values* and *discipline*. At first glance, you might think that these would be the very things for which parents would want to take personal responsibility. Yet in a society where parents – especially parents in two-income households – are busier than ever and increasingly challenged by the need to balance the competing demands of work, children, marriage and social life, you can understand why they might want to outsource more and more of their domestic responsibilities, from cleaning to child care.

But there's another dimension to this. Many time-poor parents are devoted to the notion of 'quality time' with their children and don't want to jeopardise that time by letting the need for discipline or heavy talk about values get in the way. If the school offers a curriculum and extracurricular activities that seem to broadly reflect the moral and cultural framework of the family and, in addition, handles sex education, warnings about drugs and advice on managing personal relationships, with a bit of religion thrown in, then this may seem well worth the fees being charged. That is particularly true in cases where parents have managed to convince themselves that private education is generally better than anything on offer in government schools, whether academically, culturally or socially.

To be fair, many parents of children at religious schools would say that they are not outsourcing the teaching of values and discipline, but simply ensuring that the school's approach is consistent with their own. There is often a distinctly tribal dimension to this claim ... and why not? For people raised within a particular religious tradition, the appeal of sending their children to a school within that tradition is understandably strong, even if the parents themselves feel no particular urge to maintain their own engagement with the religion concerned.

As one of my respondents put it: 'My daughter is not remotely interested in going to church at present, but if she ever has kids, she's determined to send them to the local Catholic school. I smile at that – the tribal pull is very strong, isn't it? She just can't imagine sending them to a public school. She's in for a shock when she discovers that the whole family will have to start attending the local church if she wants her kids to get into the school. Otherwise the local priest won't give them a reference.'

The tribal factor so apparent in church communities is equally evident in schools, especially secondary schools. Put the two things together – a school tradition integrated with a religious tradition – and the appeal to parents is easy to imagine. At a time when many local communities and neighbourhoods are fragmenting under the pressure of radical social change, sending your offspring to what you believe is a 'safe' and 'caring' school community run by 'committed' teachers is a growing aspiration among parents who can afford the fees at a religious school.

The effects on an individual of stopping church attendance are not easy to predict. Some ex-churchgoers speak of their sense of relief, or even liberation, at not having to pretend to believe things they can't take seriously any more. 'It was a sham,' said one of my respondents, 'so it was good to move away from it.' Some of the same sense of liberation may come simply from being released from the burden of regular attendance.

But reactions are rarely that simple, and not always so positive. Some people experience residual feelings of guilt; some feel a sense of regret at the loss of that structure in their lives; some miss the comfort and reassurance of the rituals; some miss the community; some miss the music; some miss the opportunity for quiet reflection in a meditative atmosphere; some acknowledge that their fellow worshippers were basically good people and ruefully note that 'good people are hard to find'.

There's lingering hostility to be found, too, particularly among the forced-to-go. They may experience a resentment that lasts for years, as Rebecca has.

'I resented it on so many levels. At the time, I resented the fact that girls couldn't be altar boys, and now I even resent the fact that kids don't have to sit through an entire mass like we did. I resent that fact that when I do go—to please my mum, basically—they've changed the words. I realise that sounds silly, but I can't help it. I guess there's still a lot of anger in me about this, even all these years later. I know I would have been better off without it. But the main source of anger is that it has driven a real wedge between me and my mother. I can't talk to her about it, because I'm too angry and resentful to address it calmly. And she won't talk about it to me, because she knows I gave it away when I left school, and she probably can't quite forgive me for that. I can't even tell her that I wish it was different.

I also think I'm a bit angry that I missed out on really getting it, the way some of my friends did. Anyway, it's a case of take it or leave it, and I've decided to leave it. I get more from my weekly meditation class than I ever got from church. Twenty people sitting in total silence – it's lovely. I think spirituality is a do-it-yourself thing, although I wonder if some older people get the same thing from church. And – am I really saying this? – there's that nagging 1 percent of me that still wonders if something is going on out there.' —*Rebecca*

So much for the individuals who, for various reasons, stopped going to church or never began. What about the effect of declining church membership on a society?

Like many of the other changes that have been redefining the Australian way of life – high divorce rate, low birthrate, shrinking households, widening gap between high- and low-income earners, increasingly mobile population, the IT revolution – this is a change we have brought on ourselves. When it comes to churchgoing, people have voted with their feet.

Yet, as we saw in chapter 2, almost 90 percent of *non*-churchgoers say they like the idea of local churches being present in their neighbourhood, believing they exert a generally benign influence that is as much social and cultural as religious. Activities for young people, support for the frail elderly, visitation of the sick, places for lonely singles to go, school-holiday activities for children, pre-school centres, meditation groups, book clubs . . . local churches are given credit from their local communities for providing such activities as those, quite apart from their conduct of more traditional religious services.

All this creates a conundrum for local churches. While they generally receive a strong tick of approval from their neighbourhood, and while declining church attendance is often associated in people's minds with a general loss of moral clarity and 'shared values' and with the evolution of a less caring, more self-interested society, those attitudes rarely translate into a desire to support the local church by actually going to it.

Even in the case of weddings and funerals, the trend is away from church-based ceremonies; 70 percent of Australian weddings are now conducted by civil celebrants, and an increasing number include a set of – sometimes excruciating – vows composed by the bride and groom (my current favourite: 'I promise to tell you if you become boring'). But there is still a tendency to incorporate some of the time-honoured language of the traditional religious service into the ceremony.

A friend of mine, an Anglican priest, was recently asked to officiate at the marriage of a young couple who were not churchgoers but were among the 30 percent still preferring a church wedding. At a meeting to discuss the order of service, the bride-to-be mentioned that the couple had not yet written their vows.

'Oh, that's all taken care of,' said my friend, something of a traditionalist in such matters.

'Really?' said the bride.

'Oh, yes, we have some standard vows. You can use those.'

'You mean we don't have to write our own?' replied the bride. 'Well, that's one thing we can cross off the list.'

'What a relief,' said the groom.

Can a non-church wedding feel like the real thing?

Dennis Knight could hardly remember how he felt at his first wedding. He was young, his bride was beautiful, both families approved and it took place in the church where his wife had grown up. Now, waiting for his second wedding ceremony to begin, he felt paralysed by nerves. It wasn't nervousness about whether he was making another mistake; Athena felt absolutely right for him, although they both knew the blended family thing would present its challenges. (His seven-year-old daughter Rosie was already jealous of the fact that Athena's daughter, also seven, would be living with him full time, while Rosie herself would continue to see him only every second weekend.)

No, the nervousness, silly as it seemed, was about the choice of venue. Athena was from a Catholic family, and her parents could not bear the thought of their daughter marrying anywhere but in a Catholic church. Dennis, raised a Protestant, was cool with the idea of being married in a Catholic church, though his own parents were appalled at the prospect. But the matter was taken out of their hands when the local priest declared that, as they were both divorcees, he simply couldn't marry them in his church. Under pressure from Athena's parents, the priest had even written to Rome, but the request for special dispensation was turned down. In response, Athena's family had agreed they could marry anywhere but in a Protestant church.

Though Dennis had suggested elopement more than once, and Athena was all for it in theory, she knew her mother would never forgive her, and she didn't want their marriage to start with that cloud hanging over them. Her mother regularly reported that she still had palpitations whenever she thought of her only daughter having been divorced.

So here they were in a nondescript local hall – part of a reception centre that specialised in mounting non-church but church-like weddings.

'We can decorate it to look quite religious,' the manager had said, when she realised how fraught the two families' negotiations had been. 'It will be a whole lot better than a park – the weather won't be an issue and our celebrant wears the most beautiful robe. Your parents will probably think he's a priest. He will even mention God if you want him to.'

Dennis and Athena had met the celebrant, who turned out to be an ex-priest – a fact that disturbed Athena. 'Why ex, do you think?' she kept asking Dennis, who had no satisfactory answer (it was a question they felt they couldn't put directly to the man himself).

When the day came, it was indeed raining, so the park option would have been messy. Dennis had arrived early and then wished he hadn't. Athena's mother was also there early and was refusing to make eye contact with him. His best man was running late and kept sending text messages reporting on the state of the traffic.

Dennis's anxiety grew. His own parents were seated, looking after Rosie and her older brother, Ben, who struck Dennis as suddenly looking very grown-up for a ten-year-old. The guests were straggling in, wedging themselves into the recycled church pews that had been bought from a local Uniting church when it closed. The decorations were mainly floral, but there were also some decidedly un-church-like balloons floating on the ceiling, and Dennis was disturbed to see, hanging on the wall towards the back of the room, a framed print of a sacred heart that he assumed had been insisted on by Athena's mother. (Athena had wisely not mentioned this to Dennis.) He hoped his own mother wouldn't catch sight of it until the knot had been well and truly tied. He thought she might shriek in fright, coming from good Methodist stock.

Organ music was being piped in, sounding to Dennis rather like the background music in a supermarket. Everything felt wrong. Another text arrived from the best man, now a mere three minutes away. The room filled up. The music faded. The celebrant in his promised flowing robe of green silk appeared at Dennis's side. The best man rushed in, panting.

Athena appeared on her father's arm, with her daughter clutching a posy in one hand and Athena's hand in the other. Athena was smiling that broad, beaming smile that had won Dennis's heart the first time he saw it.

The ceremony began smoothly enough. With Athena beside him, Dennis began to relax, though he still felt a niggling anxiety. There seemed so much scope for things to go wrong. A church, he felt – any church – would have been a safer option. This all felt a bit amateurish; a bit inauthentic.

And then Athena's brother came forward to read the 'love' passage from 1 Corinthians 13 that everyone had agreed was mandatory.

'If I speak in the tongues of mortals and of angels, but do not have love, I am a noisy gong or a clanging cymbal . . . Love is patient; love is kind; love is not envious or boastful or arrogant or rude . . .'

The rain was pelting on the roof and beating on the windows – Athena's favourite sound. Dennis glanced across the front few pews. Athena's mother was wiping away a tear, smiling tentatively and clutching her husband's arm. Dennis's mother had an arm around Rosie, while his father gazed benignly at the scene. Ben was sitting erect, taking it all in with an earnest expression on his face.

'. . . bears all things, believes all things, hopes all things, endures all things. Love never ends . . .' The familiar words came to life all over again, as Athena's brother let the rolling cadences take their own good time.

The friends Dennis could see – the Catholics, the Protestants, the atheists, the agnostics, the Buddhists and even Athena's Muslim research assistant – were all smiling or weeping or both, borne up by the very idea of a love like that.

4

SBNR

Over coffee, a young man was talking to me about his post-doctoral research. In the course of the conversation, he said: 'I'm SBNR.' I paused and ran through my mental list of acronyms, but this one eluded me.

'SBNR?'

'Spiritual but not religious. That's what most of my friends are, too. It's what we put in the census.'

The Australian census makes no provision for SBNR as a category, so I imagine he was saying that he and his friends write 'SBNR' beside the 'No religion' box, as a kind of qualification, where others might choose to write 'atheist', 'humanist', 'agnostic' or 'rationalist' – four categories specifically mentioned by the Australian Bureau of Statistics in their commentary on the huge increase in the number of people reporting that they have no religion; as noted in the introduction, the figure has roughly tripled, from 6.7 percent to 22 percent, in the past forty years.

My young friend might equally have written 'SBNR' beside 'Christian', since SBNR is not an exclusively secular category.

Many people who identify as Christian would not choose to call themselves religious. Indeed, the Australian theologian Bruce Kaye declares that he is really CBNR – 'christian but not religious' (and he prefers christian with a small 'c'). Kaye sees christian discipleship as a way of life, a commitment of will, rather than a religion.

Ticking the no-religion box in a census does not imply that you are also an atheist, and there is no census data available on this point; in the 2011 census, only 1.2 percent of those claiming no religion chose to add the description 'atheist'. The Australian National University's Australian 2009 Survey of Social Attitudes reported that 16 percent of the population identify as atheists, though a 2012 WIN-Gallup survey put the figure at just 10 percent.

To give that some international context, in the US, 3.1 percent of the population are self-declared atheists, according to a 2015 survey by Pew Research. In the UK, a 2015 YouGov poll conducted for *The Times* came up with the figure of 19 percent. In Sweden, a country where religion is generally regarded with benign indifference (a mere 10 percent of Swedes say religion is important in daily life), a Eurobarometer Poll in 2012 reported that 13 percent of the population are atheists, though a further 30 percent identify themselves as agnostics.

All these figures are open to furious debate and interpretation, partly because of different survey methodologies, including different question wordings, and partly because the attitudes of many people – especially young people – towards such matters as God, faith, religion and spirituality fluctuate constantly. Both fence-sitting and fence-jumping are easy to do in any society that sets little store by a person's religious beliefs and vigorously opposes any discrimination on religious grounds.

To further complicate the picture, many theists and agnostics distance themselves from organised religion, as a quite separate question from their belief or non-belief in a god. In Australia, those who occupy the gap between the 15 percent who attend church at least once a month and the 61 percent who identify as Christian may include a great many SBNRs.

On a US-based SBNR website, it is claimed that an estimated 100 million people worldwide identify as SBNR, though I suspect not all SBNRs would appreciate this attempt to formalise their status (and not all people who claim to have a spiritual life outside religion would even be aware of the SBNR acronym or its meaning). The SBNR website proclaims that 'Love is the answer; you are the question', which looks very much like the kind of slogan you might see on a church noticeboard. The website also suggests that while all religions contain some wisdom, 'no one religion contains all wisdom', which sounds like an echo of the Baha'i position. (The institutionalisation of the formal SBNR movement itself into a quasi-religion can't be far away: today a website with an executive director, tomorrow a 'spiritual leader' and, before long, local – or possibly online – congregations and an explicit set of beliefs and practices.)

According to a 2010 survey, 72 percent of Americans aged eighteen to twenty-nine identify as SBNR. 'If the trends continue,' said the head of the survey company, LifeWay Research, 'the Millennial generation will see churches closing as quickly as GM dealerships.'

The label might be new; the concept is not. SBNRs are located in a rich tradition of thinkers, mystics, doubters, agnostics and passionate theists who have resisted formal connections with institutional religion while never losing interest in the spiritual. Before he was executed by the Nazis towards the end of World War II, the German theologian Dietrich Bonhoeffer predicted the emergence of 'religionless Christianity'. In despair, he observed that many professing Christians were acting in ways incompatible with their beliefs, and when there appeared to be no 'religious' resistance to the war, Bonhoeffer came to believe that 'we are proceeding towards a time of no religion at all: men as they are now simply cannot be religious any more'. Bonhoeffer was writing from the bleakness of a prison cell (he had been charged with complicity in the plot to assassinate Hitler) and the concept of religionless Christianity was, for him, the only realistic response to a war so horrific that, to his mind, it proved that the religious impulse once thought to have been inherent in human nature did not exist after all. He also saw religionless Christianity as a way of describing how Christians could continue to express their faith in a determinedly secular society, outside the crumbling structure of traditional religious institutions and denominations, as least in Europe.

The French social activist, philosopher and mystic Simone Weil, Jewish by birth and upbringing, turned towards Roman Catholicism in later life after a series of mystical experiences. But she stopped short of declaring herself a Christian, partly because, like Bonhoeffer, she despised the institutional church. Her language was more colourful than his: in *Gravity and Grace* (1952), she called the Roman church 'the Great Beast of atheism and materialism, adoring nothing but itself'. She also felt that aligning herself with the church in a formal way would alienate her non-Christian friends with whom she felt a strong solidarity.

Christian faith does not always require an institutional context, and the spiritual life may exist quite independently of any particular religious affiliation. But when SBNRs speak of the spiritual dimension of their lives, or of their hunger for spiritual nourishment, what do they – or any of us – mean by that word 'spiritual'?

Those who argue that the mind–body distinction is itself a false dichotomy – since everything that happens in 'the mind' is located in the brain and central nervous system – are unlikely to be comfortable with the addition of yet another element like 'spirit' or 'soul', in any but the most metaphorical or poetic terms. But for those who think of human identity as having three aspects or layers – body, mind and spirit – the idea of spirituality is easy to define: it's not physical (as in the body); it's not cognitive or intellectual (as in the mind); it's what's left – neither material nor mental, but something beyond those realms.

For people who conceptualise soul in this way, spirituality is 'what goes on in the soul'. Albert Schweitzer, the renowned fourfold doctor – philosophy, theology, music and medicine – most famous for his work as a 'jungle doctor' in Africa, acknowledged that no one can give a definition of the soul but nevertheless claimed that 'we know what it feels like'. In *My Life and Thought* (1933), he described the soul as 'the sense of something higher than ourselves'; something that stirs thoughts and aspirations towards 'goodness, truth and beauty'.

Elizabeth Alexander, the Frederick Iseman Professor of Poetry at Yale, is in no doubt about the meaning of 'soul'. In an article written for the *New Yorker* (2015), she described her experience in the minutes and hours following the death of her husband, Ficre, from a heart attack:

> When I held him in the basement, he was himself, Ficre.
>
> When I held him in the hospital as they worked and cut off his clothes, he was himself.
>
> When they cleaned his body and brought his body to say goodbye, he had left his body, though it still belonged to us.
>
> His body was colder than it had been, though not ice-cold or stiff and hard. His spirit had clearly left as it had not left when we found him on the basement floor and I knew that he could hear us.
>
> Now I know for sure that the soul is an evanescent thing and the body is its temporary container, because I saw it. I saw the body with the soul in it, I saw the body with the soul leaving, and I saw the body with the soul gone.

In that account, Elizabeth Alexander was not necessarily saying that Ficre's soul survived, or *went* anywhere, though she does write of her late husband: 'Where is he? I often wonder.' Her description is consistent with the much simpler idea – supported by some neuroscientists – that a vestige of the life force remains briefly with the body after death.

Since we don't even really know what *consciousness* is – let alone soul – it's not surprising that we resort to metaphors when we try to discuss the nature of such concepts. In *The Mind's I* (1981), Douglas Hofstadter writes: 'There seems to be no alternative to accepting some sort of incomprehensible quality in existence' and presents the idea of the soul as an aspect of self-consciousness – knowing that this is 'me' and no one else. In a joint reflection, Hofstadter and Daniel Dennett suggest that 'soul' is the name we give to 'that opaque yet characteristic *style* of each individual'. But they wonder whether this unique core or essence of each individual might actually consist of nothing more than a particular set of moral principles or personality traits, or whether it is 'something we can speak of in physical terms – in brain language'. As Hofstadter remarks: 'We all fluctuate delicately between a subjective and objective view of the world, and this quandary is central to human nature.'

Regardless of how people might define them, words like 'soul' or 'spiritual' are almost always used in association with our responses to positive experiences – from human love ('soul mates') to the beauty of a sunset; from hearing a Bach chorale to seeing a film that moves us to tears of sadness or joy; from a moment of silence and stillness – an emptying – to an overwhelming sense of being part of 'something bigger than me'.

A spiritual experience is usually described as being mystical, transcendental, sublime or revelatory in some way. It is often associated with a feeling of great calm, peace or tranquillity, a shedding of stress and anxiety. Such experiences appear to yield something more than heightened awareness of the self; they are typically associated with an intense awareness of the human story and our place in it.

Enlightenment. Inspiration. Hyper-clarity. Consolation. Vision. Bliss. Ineffability. Luminescence. Transcendence. Cosmic awareness. Oneness. Connectedness. Suffused with loving-kindness. An expanded sense of what's real and what's possible. Loss of fear – especially fear of death. These expressions are commonly used by people trying to describe a specific spiritual experience, though the term 'spirituality' will sometimes amount to no more than a claim that 'I acknowledge the importance of the non-material aspects of life' or that 'I felt totally alive' or that 'I was fully present in the moment in a way I had never experienced before'. For some people, the spiritual is merely a heightened sense of the emotional – *feeling* things with great intensity rather than thinking about them in a rational way; for others, it refers to the accumulated values, attitudes and beliefs we use as a basis for the sense of our life's meaning and purpose. Most commonly, 'spiritual' is used to convey something beyond the intellectual, beyond the emotional, beyond the cultural: a heightened sense of consciousness that illuminates or enriches our human potential; a glimpse of something we might call sublime, or even 'divine' (without needing to attach that idea to a Divinity-with-a-capital-D).

In *What Days Are For* (2014), the Australian writer Robert Dessaix remarks, with evident disapproval, that the word 'spiritual' seems to have 'broken free of any sort of semantic tethering at all'. Compared with his own intense interest in the radical spirituality of Christian Science in his youth, he is dismissive of 'bushwalking or a bit of homeopathy' being described in such lofty terms. He recalls a time in his life when he 'ardently pursued eternity – or timelessness, to be more precise: timelessness and spacelessness, the art of seeing through the glass of time and space still darkly but with hope and wonder'. He mocks a radio personality who claimed to have felt 'spiritual' when he looked at the stars; Dessaix assumes he meant 'awe-struck and small'. Yet 'awe-struck and small' would strike many people as a precursor, at least, to some acknowledgement of a spiritual dimension to their lives that could incorporate 'hope and wonder'. In any case, there's not much doubt that the very word 'spiritual' is undergoing a shift in usage, partly under the influence of all those SBNRs who want to wear it as a badge of authenticity.

David Lodge's 2012 novel *A Man of Parts,* based on the life of H.G. Wells, includes a fictionalised encounter between Wells and Beatrice Webb, a prominent member of London's 'Bloomsbury group' of intellectuals and writers. Lodge writes of Webb: 'Though like most intelligent people of her generation she had shed her Christian faith early in adult life, she retained its dualistic opposition of flesh and spirit ...' and, later, he has Webb saying to Wells: 'I believe men and women will only evolve upwards by subordinating their physical desires and appetites to the spiritual and intellectual side of human nature. That is the faith that sustains me.' (It was not, however, the faith that sustained Wells: he is portrayed in the book as a man in the very grip of his physical desires and appetites.)

Most of us use words like 'spirituality' and 'soul' quite confidently – even if purely metaphorically – as if no explanation is required. On ABC Classic FM in April 2015, after the presenter Christopher Lawrence had played a piece of music he described as being 'good for the soul', he interviewed Professor Anne Boyd, the Australian composer and music educator, about her receipt of the Sir Bernard Heinze Memorial Award for her lifelong service to music. In the course of the interview, Boyd referred to the influence of the Australian composer Peter Sculthorpe on her life and work. She said that the spirit of Sculthorpe (who died in 2014) was so vividly with her as she wrote her third string quartet, it was as if he were its co-author. She was clearly not speaking of his presence as someone might describe seeing a ghost; she was acknowledging the power of memory, the richness of Sculthorpe's professional and personal legacy, and his lasting influence on her. Her listeners would have understood that she was referring to that lingering non-physical connection as 'spiritual', in the same way as both she and Sculthorpe had often referred to the influence of indigenous spirituality on their music.

In many towns and suburbs you can find a relatively new category of retail outlet, its ethos somewhere between a massage therapist's studio and an astrologer's tent, that claims to offer access to an enhanced spirituality via everything from crystals, incense, herbal medicine, psychic guidance or chakra-balancing to naturopathy, homeopathy or colon hydrotherapy (don't ask). They might also put you in touch with a 'narrative consultant' to help you sort out the story of your own life, a counsellor to promote your spiritual growth and wellbeing, classes to help you 'hear the Earth' or gain access to 'the temple of your daily life', possibly through participation in 'spiritual dancing'. In the marketing of wellbeing, 'spiritual' is taking on some of the cachet of 'organic' in food retailing.

Some of this sounds like a close relative of spiritualism – the system of beliefs based on communication with the spirits of the dead, that was a more significant Western phenomenon in the late nineteenth and early twentieth centuries than it is today (though spiritualists will tell you theirs is the most ancient form of spirituality). One of my respondents described her mother's encounters with spiritualism, theosophy and the occult, blended with Christian spirituality.

> 'My mother used to go to a medium, séances ... all that, yet she was a Christian with a strong sense of Christian spirituality expressed through charity. Those two things are not supposed to mix, but they did in her. So I grew up thinking that all this 'spirit world' stuff was neither batty nor evil. My daughter would say

she's spiritual, but not in that rather old-fashioned, nineteenth-century way. For her it's vaguely pantheistic, mixed with the need for kindness – sort of sixties-hippie, with some Buddhism thrown in. She believes that by doing good, you'll become good, so it's a very practical form of spirituality, based on her faith in the idea that being a good person is both desirable and possible. And it was like that for my mother, too. We would often come home from school and find a homeless person in the house tucking into a meal she had prepared. Spirituality was meaningless for her unless it was expressed in goodness and kindness. At the same time, she really believed that when she died, she would see her father again, and she died with a smile on her face. So that brand of spirituality is a kind of secret resource some people have. I wish I had it myself.' —*Megan*

Spirituality as a secret resource? That's a thought echoed in many of the conversations I've had with people – both professionally as a researcher and personally as a friend or colleague. Though institutional religion has become unattractive and even repugnant to many people, spirituality remains an appealing concept, based on the assumption that whatever a spiritual life might offer, it would be beneficial. When people reveal a kind of 'faith envy' (as many people do), they are as likely to be hankering after faith in the inherent goodness of humans, or 'some power beyond ourselves', or some interpretation of life's meaning that offers more than biology, as they are to be yearning for conventional religious faith.

Patricia, whose story of being expelled from her church for giving a talk on the metaphorical poetry of Genesis was recounted in chapter 3, puts it like this:

'For me, spirituality is all about connectedness – union – trying to get in touch with the meaning of life for a community. What is 'our moment' about? What does it all mean? I want

> my involvement in the community to be informed by my spirituality, and vice versa. I think we nurture our spiritual life through silence, contemplation, meditation, reflection, but in the end it's calling on the essential goodness in our collective consciousness.' —*Patricia*

The Australian social analyst Richard Eckersley strongly supports the idea of a link between spirituality and connectedness. In *Well & Good* (2004), he defines spiritual meaning as 'a sense of having a place in the universe', and regards spirituality as 'the broadest and deepest form of connectedness ... the only form of meaning that transcends our personal circumstances, social situation and the material world, and so can sustain us through the trouble and strife of mortal existence'. He warns against attaching too much meaning to things that are transient and fragile, such as 'our looks, careers, sex lives, romantic relationships, personal development, health and fitness, even our children (when we burden them with our own expectations and dreams)'. Eckersley's views are part of a strong tradition, also echoed by Albert Schweitzer, who believed that the communal nature of humanity was central to its spirituality.

In a 2015 radio interview with Natasha Mitchell on ABC Radio National's *Life Matters*, a nudist claimed that nudism has a spiritual dimension and, again, the link with connectedness emerged: his view was that when nudists get together, the sense of individual differences are quickly submerged beneath their sense of common humanity. Far from drawing attention to their physical characteristics, nudity makes their bodies seem less distinctive than when they are 'dressed up' and bodily differences become less significant than the sense of oneness: 'We are all the same.'

Though some people prefer to avoid the word 'spirituality' because it is too reminiscent of religion, the irony is that people are increasingly using the word to *distance* themselves from religion: 'I'm spiritual but *not* religious.'

Magic moments

Suddenly I realize
That if I stepped out of my body I would break
Into blossom.

Those are the last three lines of 'A Blessing', written in 1963 by the US poet James Wright. The poem describes an interlude when the poet and a friend stop just off the highway near Rochester, Minnesota, and come upon two Indian ponies who emerge from willows to welcome to their pasture these visitors, to whom 'they bow shyly as wet swans'. One of them walks over and nuzzles the poet's hand. Moved to caress her long ear, he finds it 'as delicate as the skin over a girl's wrist'. And then . . . those final three lines.

Break into blossom? Step out of my body? We acknowledge those as purely poetic images, yet many people experience moments like that – moments so pure, so ethereal, that they are alerted to something that seems to transcend the here and now. Such moments often seem magical, or mystical, or deeply insightful (or, yes, spiritual), and they generally stay with the person as a reference point. Here are five examples drawn from my recent personal interviews.

'I love nature. That's why I love bushwalking so much – it's always made me feel a part of nature. But, until recently, I had never connected it with spirituality. Then, one day, when I was out walking, I had this sudden sense of myself as energy particles. I saw my skin as mere casing – a thin layer between me and the universe. I had a sense of unity, as if I was not a separate being at all, as if the boundaries of my body could dissolve. That experience was very real to me, and it has changed me.

I had an echo of that experience when I was looking over a rainforest in North Queensland from a viewing tower high above the forest canopy. I felt as if the forest was singing to me, or as if a light had turned on inside me. I didn't want to come down. It was quite magical, really.

Ever since that moment when I was walking, I have felt differently about yoga – the breathing and the stillness; it's like preparing the ground for spiritual growth. A lot of people get into yoga thinking of it as a form of exercise or relaxation, but they soon realise there's more to it than that – and the 'more' is the spiritual dimension. They learn about the eight-limbed path that is the essence of yoga, and that's about everything from morality and personal discipline to our compassion and sense of union with the divine. Body postures and breathing techniques are part of it, too, but they serve a deeper purpose than mere relaxation.'—*Karen*

Karen had a conventional Protestant upbringing, going to church with her parents, attending youth fellowship, but gave it away in her late teens. Her more recent awakening spirituality is, for her, completely unrelated to the religion of her earlier life. Whereas that had seemed perfunctory, dogmatic and judgemental, this seems liberating, authentic and generous. Her disposition towards other people now feels more compassionate than when she was a churchgoer, and she herself detects some irony in this.

Here's another example of a person who abandoned conventional Christian faith but then came back to a strong sense of (non-religious) spirituality via an unusual pathway.

'I remember the moment when I abandoned the religion I had grown up with. I had attended a first-year anthropology lecture at university and listened to our lecturer describing primitive religious beliefs and the vast array of religious experience. I walked out of that lecture theatre and said, 'It can't be true', and that was it. My parents were very disappointed.

By the time I was twenty-one, I found myself trying to make sense of the whole thing from a different perspective. I was interested in the broader question of mysticism and I wondered how – or if – that could fit into Christianity. While the rational scientific view was that religion is just 'made up', I was intrigued by the fact that every human society has had its stories of divine influence.

After I graduated, I went to live with an indigenous tribe in a Malayan forest. Having secured the permission of the tribe, I walked into the forest with a guide and was adopted into a family. I lived the life of the village and the headman of that village was the senior shaman for the area. I sat with him as people sang and chanted themselves into a trance. They believed the soul left the body at these times. They believed in astral travel – that the heavens had seven layers and each had a special melody. The spirit guides were healers. The shaman's task was to bring back the part of the soul that had been lost through illness.

Because I lived with them I became fully immersed in this way of thinking. Those people were not idiots, and they had many stories of miraculous healing to tell. I saw some of it with my own eyes. Later, I came to think of it as part of the evolution of consciousness.

When I came back home, the culture shock was extraordinary! I knew what I had experienced, but I knew it would be almost impossible to explain to anyone back home in a convincing way. They would think I was mad.

I gave up on the academic life. Although I'm a rationalistic person, I'm open to all possibilities. There has been a constant movement in my understanding of all this. We tend to think everyone is basically the same, but the shamans showed me a different way of experiencing the world, based on this idea of the evolution of consciousness. The idea that consciousness evolves reminds me that the so-called Christian values were there long before Christianity. I see Christianity as part of that evolutionary story. I try to live up to Christian precepts and Christian ethics. I notice that, among the young people I work with, it's not cool to be Christian – yet they are all interested in a spiritual life. I think the real question is: how can we live well? The answer to that is going to come from your spiritual understanding.'—*Graeme*

Graeme never abandoned the ethical underpinning of Christianity, but he no longer attends church.

Michaela was also raised in a Protestant family, but her exit from formal religion was more abrupt and came at a younger age than either Karen's or Graeme's. Her subsequent re-engagement with the idea of spirituality came via an unnerving encounter with the occult.

'I was raised in a nominally Christian household but at the age of twelve I gave it all away. I declared myself an atheist, to the great distress of my parents. Then, when I was sixteen, I went with some friends to a séance and that gave me a real shock. Don't laugh – I really felt that ouija board move! The whole experience had a profound effect on me. I felt I couldn't deny the reality of the spirit world. It was quite scary, actually, and I realised it could be dangerous to play with this stuff. So I didn't go on with it, but I certainly stopped describing myself as an atheist.

A year or so later, I went to a Catholic mass with a friend from school who was quite devout. I can't remember why I went – I was pretty tentative about going. But I was overwhelmed by it. I had a real sense of the sacred in the silence. A kind of vision. I felt the presence of God in a really personal way. It was a holy presence, like a good version of what I'd felt in that séance. It felt like I was encountering the spirit of forgiveness – there was no sense of anything judgemental at all.

I attached myself to a Protestant church and settled into the life of a very committed Christian. Then I almost lost it all again over a strange experience at work. I was in the running for a big promotion. Everyone thought I would get the job. All my Christian friends knew I would get the job. I prayed about it. I felt utterly convinced that this was God's will for me. But I missed out. When that happened, I was devastated. Shattered. I felt as if God had turned his back on me.

In despair, I went on a religious retreat – so I suppose I was still clinging to my faith. I felt angry with God, let down, as if God had cheated on me. The people running the retreat gave me some material to read about God having to find 'the well in the heart'. That really spoke to me. I saw that God's love was above and beyond all. I was overwhelmed by tears. I'm not describing this very well – but I felt as if I rediscovered myself through meditation and thinking differently about the very idea of God.

I now think of my spiritual life as a journey. I think of faith as a process of constant discovery. Specific propositional beliefs are less important to me now, and I know there's no such thing as an absolute interpretation of scripture – though I still hold to some of the doctrines of the church.

By the way, I left that company and ended up with a far more suitable job in a completely different line of work. And it all started with that ouija board! Or maybe it was the Catholic mass. Or maybe it was the retreat. But I've never lost the sense that there is a spirit world, and our spiritual life connects us with that.❞—*Michaela*

Michaela's ouija-board experience might strike you as an unusual pathway into Christian faith (though, as we saw in chapter 3, Megan's mother managed to combine the occult with her Christianity). The insights and consequences of a magic moment are unpredictable; they are by no means certain to point us towards religion, let alone God, but, unfailingly, they seem to convince us that there's more to life than the obvious, the rational, the material. One of my respondents put it like this: 'There's probably an entire spiritual world, like a parallel universe, that we only occasionally get a glimpse of.' Even one of my emphatically non-churchgoing friends recently said, 'I live with a sense of mystery and perhaps even a vague sense of the numinous. I wouldn't be surprised to find there was something going on under my nose. Anything is possible.'

Otto certainly thinks 'anything is possible'. He was the boy in chapter 3 who left a Christmas church service with his siblings in a fit of uncontrollable giggles. Here's what happened to him later in life:

> 'I once went on a ten-day Buddhist retreat. On the fourth day, I had this incredible feeling of going up into my head. I had not moved for a whole hour. I had to ignore the pain – just observe the pain, they told me. It was like going into a void, into the gap between your thoughts, as if my head really was in the clouds. I had a real sense of positive energy. Like a sweet spot – my brother talks about feeling like that sometimes when he's rowing.
>
> I also had a smidgen of this same feeling after yoga once – a peace that makes you feel connected to everything, so that there is all compassion and no judgement. When you look at people in the street, their troubles are your troubles – even whether they get across the street safely or whatever – because you feel part of everything. How can there be judgement if there is no separation between us? It is the difference between compassion and pity, but more than that: it's to do with the interconnectivity of all things. Quantum science scratches away at it too. You can only see or feel it when you're in a state of equilibrium.
>
> The thing about seeing this – even ever so slightly – is that you can't un-see it. It's an experience that can affect people

profoundly. You can't go back. Eastern religions often talk about universal truth – truth being like the sun, and us all going about our daily routines by candlelight. If you happen to catch a glimpse of the sun through a crack in the blind, or even get a full window's worth of sunlight, you couldn't un-see that. You would spend the rest of time telling people about it, seeking it, helping others to see it, trying not to appear mad.

Spirituality? There's so much to it ... concentration, non-attachment, non-seeking, forgiveness of self, compassion and empathy for others, persistence, patience. You need all these things for equilibrium and a state of grace; to become somehow subtler in life, attending to the nuances, listening to your subtle body ... which doesn't mean sitting quietly in a corner like a hermit, by the way. You have to be fully engaged. You have to realise you are part of the life of those around you. It's really that sense of oneness. You can get it watching a sunset or hitting a ball, or meditating. Or even listening attentively to someone else's story.'—*Otto*

A recurring theme in these stories is that more open, generous, compassionate attitudes seemed to emerge as a natural consequence of some spiritual experience. Even Michaela, who returned to the church after her several 'magic moments', has adopted a more relaxed, more liberal attitude towards the specific beliefs traditionally associated with her faith – and towards the beliefs held by others. In my conversation with her, she spoke lovingly and tolerantly of people she disagreed with, and expressed horror at a story she'd heard about a person who had been encouraged to leave his church because of his unwillingness to assent to every last scrap of doctrine.

The link between spirituality and compassion shouldn't surprise us. In *Wisdom* (2010), Stephen Hall reports on the growing body of research into the sources of compassion in the human heart (metaphor alert!). Having spent time in a neuroscience laboratory in Madison, Wisconsin, where the effects of meditation are being studied, Hall writes that 'the first neural traces of compassion have begun to appear in our twenty-first-century measuring machines. In the neural geography of wisdom, we have even managed to locate a few places in the brain associated with loving-kindness'. If meditation is indeed one of the well-worn pathways to the inner life, and meditation has the capacity to stimulate compassion (remember the research on loving-kindness meditation reported in chapter 1), then it's no wonder compassion is so widely regarded as one of the most visible manifestations of spiritual maturity.

A magic moment of a very different kind, more frightening than inspiring, occurred when one of my respondents was a boy of no more than ten.

> 'I had an experience – I suppose now I'd call it an epiphany – when I suddenly realised that everything was just a veil, that something lay beyond the form of everything I could see and so-called 'reality' was just a working hypothesis. Obviously, I didn't think of it in those terms back then. It certainly wasn't a religious experience, but it left me wondering why everyone wasn't talking about this. Nothing else seemed important. But when I tried to discuss it, people just thought I was crazy, so I put the whole thing on hold. It was many years before I was able to face up to it again and realise that it was an authentic experience and was telling me something about the way the mind works. Eventually that led to my interest in mental training and mindfulness.
>
> As I grew older, I came to realise that so much of what troubles us is just like a veil or an illusion. I would feel as if I had a real mountain to climb and then, when I'd climbed it, I'd realise there never was a mountain there. One teacher who was urging me to let go of my anxieties said to me, 'There's nowhere to fall.' And that really rang true – it reminded me of a beggar I once

knew who was living on the street. I kept pressing him to explain why he wasn't trying to better himself and he simply said, 'I've got nothing to lose – I'm in the perfect position' ❞—*Duncan*

One of the common threads in these various stories is that, after an experience of some kind of spiritual insight, specific beliefs – to say nothing of concrete labels like 'theist' or 'atheist' – come to seem less important, as if spiritual enlightenment involves moving beyond dogmatic beliefs. That's an idea we'll return to in chapter 8.

'Religion is history'

In explaining why they are SBNR, people sometimes draw a distinction between formalised, institutionalised religion that is rooted in the past, and spirituality that seems more immediate, spontaneous, free-floating and potentially more *personal*, because it grows out of here-and-now experience. To people who see it like that, religion is an historical phenomenon, based on doctrines, rituals and institutional structures that evolved over centuries, whereas spirituality, as a concept, seems both present and timeless. The distinction is sometimes expressed in terms of religion being static, 'set in stone', whereas spirituality seems more dynamic, being about personal growth and development.

This distinction may be both unfair and spurious, since many people report spiritual experiences and insights in the context of their formal religious practice that are as personal, present, growth-producing and timeless as the spiritual insights of any freelance mystic. (Indeed, most of the world's great mystics – including Buddha – have, in one way or another, become 'religious' in the sense of formalising and even prescribing ways for people to practise the art of living simultaneously in the spiritual and physical realms.)

While many SBNRs might think of a church as one of the last places they'd go if they were looking for ways to enrich the spiritual dimension of their life, many churchgoers themselves would claim that that is exactly what they are doing, and that they are actually better positioned than most to tap into ancient spiritual wisdom. However, the shrinking of Christian congregations in many Western societies does suggest that people with a spiritual yearning are likely to look somewhere other than the local church for ways to satisfy it. It may be worth repeating the Jung quote from chapter 2: 'Not only do I leave the door open for the Christian message, but I consider it of central importance for Western man. It needs, however, to be seen in a new light, in accordance with the changes wrought by the contemporary spirit. Otherwise, it stands apart from the times, and has no effect on man's wholeness.'

If Jung was right, then adaptation is the alternative to ultimate irrelevance for the Christian church in the West. As one of my respondents said, 'Why does the church find it so hard to persuade us that its message is important and that this is a good way to be in the world? On the face of it, it makes sense, but people – including me – seem generally unconvinced by it.' The English poet Philip Larkin captured that rather wistful perception of declining relevance in his 1955 poem, 'Church Going', especially in the lines describing his almost compulsive visits to country churches on the brink of falling into disuse. He wonders why he even bothers to stop and look:

> Yet stop I did: in fact I often do,
> And always end much at a loss like this,
> Wondering what to look for; wondering, too,
> When churches fall completely out of use.

The 'religion is history' idea helps to explain why, to people unfamiliar with the forms and rituals of the church, a church service – as well as the church building itself – can seem like a museum piece. The recital of a creed, for example, can strike outsiders, or even ex-churchgoers, as strange to the point of bizarre. 'Why do they say those things if they don't really believe them?' is a question frequently asked by people who find it hard to accept that many contemporary Christians would seriously believe, for example, in the literal resurrection of Jesus or the virgin birth or, indeed, that God is 'the maker of heaven and earth'. The justification sometimes offered – that such creeds have historical and institutional significance as statements of 'the faith of our forefathers' or 'what *the church* believes' – rather proves their point.

> 'I believe that divinity is universal and timeless. Religion tries to capture it and limit it, and that's when the spiritual side gets threatened by the organisational side. Imagine anyone fighting a war over the nuances of a spiritual life! But they do it all the time over religious differences. Doctrine written so long ago in such different times can't be treated as gospel now (sorry about the pun). It doesn't make sense. I know of a couple where one partner is Muslim and refuses to get a home loan because of the part of the Qur'an that forbids taking money from others. Refusing to eat pork in this day and age seems equally strange to me, though I try to respect people's traditional beliefs.
>
> I think love has a lot to do with it – people who are in touch with their spiritual side are more likely to be compassionate, and that applies to some religious people, too. Look at all the good work religious charities do.
>
> The esoterics say we are moving from a masculine age into a feminine age, the masculine age being structured religion and the feminine being spirituality. Interesting idea, isn't it?' —*Otto*

The primary concern of those who declare that they are SBNR is their resistance to the idea of spirituality being institutionalised. Even though they might find inspiration in the architecture or music of the traditional church, they find the whole idea of a vast and complex organisation – rife with factional politics and power plays – at odds with the essence of spirituality.

Even when SBNRs acknowledge that churches are *supposed to be* about fostering the spiritual life, they typically offer two reasons for avoiding them.

The first is that churches run on dogma – formal doctrine – and SBNRs typically regard prescribed beliefs as anathema to the whole idea of a spiritual life. In fact, their reservations go even deeper than that: they blame strictly defined religious beliefs for most of the tension and enmity between people who are supposed to be worshipping the same God. Sectarian tensions between Catholics and Protestants, for example, might have eased in Australia in the past fifty years, but plenty of people are old enough to remember when that divide seemed unbridgeable, though never to the extent of Ireland's 'Troubles'. (Bitter conflicts between Sunni and Shiah Muslims in the Middle East exemplify the same point.)

Such divisions aren't always on a grand scale; plenty of disillusioned ex-churchgoers can tell tales of congregations splitting over doctrinal or ecclesiastical – or even architectural – questions, leading either to the formation of breakaway churches or a mass exodus of dissenters. (In the US, for instance, the huge Baptist denomination comprises more than fifty sub-groups, each with its own subtly distinctive theological or doctrinal character.)

The other big source of SBNRs' resistance to institutional religion, sometimes amounting to repugnance, is that the church, like so many other institutions over the centuries, has been tarnished by various forms of corruption. If, as is widely acknowledged, power tends to corrupt, and institutions typically involve the concentration of power in the hands of an elite hierarchy, then it follows that *any* institution is vulnerable to corruption, or at least to shady practices designed to protect its power.

Clearly, the church has been no exception to that rule. Various forms of child abuse; the subjugation of women; the concentration of great wealth in buildings surrounded by poverty; the torture and execution of so-called heretics; the suppression of scientific knowledge; endless scandals involving financial embezzlement, sexual impropriety, the abuse of power ... the list goes on. The church may be no *more* susceptible to dubious, self-serving practices than many other institutions – political parties, the media, commercial organisations, schools, local government, trade unions etc. Considering its foundations in the teachings of Jesus, the remarkable thing is that the church seems no *less* susceptible, either.

The resort to religion in a crisis

'There are no atheists on an aircraft in a bad storm.'

So said a rather cynical colleague, himself an atheist (except, presumably, on an aircraft in a bad storm). His claim might not be literally true, but it points to a revealing fact about us: we are less sure of our rationality and more disposed to surrender to superstition, or to the language and practice of religion, when the going gets tough.

'Something like a serious car accident will drive people back to religion – at least for a while,' said one of my respondents. And there's a good reason why airports and hospitals provide chapels for the use of nervous flyers, anxious relatives or people gripped by the fear of losing a loved one. The people who use them are by no means all theists, and some are likely to be SBNRs.

> 'I've come and gone a bit as far as church is concerned, but I do find that life's traumas bring you back to your core religion and faith. If I analyse my own life, it's been the grief, the upheavals, the crises that have always brought me back, and then I've thought, 'How did I lose my spiritual fitness? Why did I ever stop praying?' But I can tell you the answer: when things are going well, and your life is busy, you get caught up in the good things; it's only through

pain that you rediscover God. My children are good Christians, but they're not good Catholics – won't have a bar of it. But their life experience will probably change that. My daughter says when she gets married it will be in a church and she'll send her kids to a Catholic school. The big moments in life – getting married, becoming a parent and all the tragedy and misfortune everyone suffers – these are the things that bring you back.' —*John*

When the Australian test cricketer Phillip Hughes was killed in a freak accident, felled by a fast ball, his teammates, not previously noted for their religious sensibilities, took to gazing skywards at significant moments in matches following Hughes's death (such as reaching the same number of runs he had scored before he was killed), as if they thought Hughes's spirit might be 'up there somewhere'. Even if none of them really believed that, their gestures were clearly reminiscent of primitive religion. They were also an example of how religious rituals, practices and language offer us a structure for articulating and dealing with our most intense emotions, especially those involving shock and grief.

News bulletins announcing the safe recovery of a young autistic boy, lost for four days in the bush near Victoria's Lake Eildon, referred to 'prayers answered'. While it may well be the case that the boy's family and friends, and others, had been praying for his safe return, the concept of 'answered prayer' is something of a conceptual and theological minefield, as we shall see in chapter 7. Nevertheless, at a moment of such euphoria and gratitude, the language of religion is almost instinctively harnessed by the media.

The 2015 terrorist attacks in Paris led to a succession of foreign leaders offering their 'thoughts and prayers' in support of the French people. In less horrific circumstances, we may speak of our admiration, our respect or our support for others; when death and destruction are involved, the language of religion invariably surfaces.

Governments are usually quick to offer a state funeral when a notable public figure dies, the assumption being that the ceremony will take place in a church or cathedral, and that's usually what happens, whether or not the deceased had any discernible religious faith or church affiliation. (There are exceptions for declared atheists: memorial events were held for former Australian prime minister Gough Whitlam in Sydney's Town Hall, and for media and casino mogul Kerry Packer in the concert hall of the Sydney Opera House.)

In Australia, Anzac Day has become the closest thing we have to a national day (Australia Day being a rather controversial runner-up), and it is characterised by a curious mixture of religion and revelry. The morning is given over to dawn services and other ceremonies of remembrance for those killed in battle and, more broadly, to honour those who have served in the armed forces; the afternoon morphs into an extended party, fuelled by alcohol and two-up at pubs, clubs and backyard barbecues. At services around the country, people solemnly stand and sing such hymns as 'God of Our Fathers, Known of Old' and 'Abide with Me', glad of the familiar cadences to inspire thoughts of sacrifice. Clergy are usually on hand to offer prayers, and people who neither sing hymns (apart from Christmas carols) nor pray from one Anzac Day to the next are evidently moved and uplifted by the experience. As churchgoing has steadily declined, attendance at outdoor Anzac Day services has steadily grown. Is this because these services have such a specific focus? Because they offer a simpler and more readily accessible ritual than church-based liturgies? Because they are less intimidating as a result of being held outdoors? Because 'it's only once a year'? Because of a desire to maintain some semblance of religious faith and practice? Because young people, in particular, are intrigued by the whole idea of sacrifice in defence of our way of life, or curious about what it's like to take part in such a ritual? No doubt the answer is 'all of the above'.

Sitting at the bedside of a gravely ill loved one, many people who would not regard themselves as religious find themselves unable to resist the urge to utter some kind of prayer – if not for recovery, then for release – and derive comfort from doing so. When someone is killed in battle, in a natural disaster or in other traumatic circumstances, the survivors instinctively turn to a minister of religion for the words that will bring peace. If no ordained person is present, someone may try to recite the Lord's Prayer ('Our Father in heaven . . .'), or the 23rd Psalm ('The Lord is my shepherd, I shall not want . . .'), dredging up a distant memory in response to the feeling that 'religious words' are needed to bring the appropriate dignity and solemnity to the occasion.

Stories of people who were converted to Christianity in extreme or troubling circumstances are legion. Among the most famous is the remarkable tale of John Newton, the composer of one of the Christian world's favourite hymns, 'Amazing Grace'. Newton was a slave trader who continued to ply his trade even after his dramatic conversion to Christianity during a storm at sea. He eventually renounced slavery, became a minister of religion and joined William Wilberforce in the fight for its abolition.

None of this proves anything beyond the fact that in a culture partly shaped by religious faith and practice, there are momentous occasions when even some committed atheists may feel fleetingly drawn to participation in a religious activity, when agnostics may veer closer to faith, and when SBNRs may struggle to come up with words that will match the language of religion.

The meaningless death of Fran Turner

Laurie and Fran Turner were in the habit of taking an evening stroll after dinner. Fran was working two days a week in the local school library, Laurie had recently retired from teaching, and these walks had become a precious time for them both. They talked about their grown-up sons' lives, their own travel plans, and, occasionally, they veered towards the topic that had been the only serious source of tension between them in forty years of marriage: religion.

Fran had been a churchgoer all her life and she and Laurie had met in a church youth group. But Laurie had never been committed to Christianity and stopped going to church soon after the birth of their first child: 'I'll stay home and look after the baby,' Laurie had suggested. 'It will give you a break – an hour of peace and a chance to catch up with your mates.' He never went back after that and admitted to Fran years later that he had only ever gone to that youth group because he knew she went there and he was keen to meet her.

On their last evening walk together, a passing motorcyclist lost control of his bike and struck Fran from the rear. She was dead before the ambulance arrived.

Paralysed by shock – and guilty about the fact that he had been walking on the inside of the footpath – Laurie relied entirely on his sons to make all the arrangements for the funeral. After consulting some of Fran's friends, they approached the minister of her church, Peter Munro, to conduct the service. Though he was new to the church, he knew Fran well enough to deliver a eulogy that offered some consolation and comfort to Laurie and his sons, and to Fran's friends.

A month after the funeral, Peter Munro was walking through the local park on his way back to his church office after having bought a sandwich for lunch – a daily ritual. He spotted Laurie sitting alone on a park bench, staring into space. Laurie flicked a glance in his direction, so Peter walked over, sat down, unwrapped his sandwich and offered Laurie half of it. Without speaking or making any further eye contact, Laurie accepted the offer and bit hungrily, almost angrily, into the bread.

'Are you eating properly, Laurie?' Peter enquired.

'Mm.' Laurie continued to chew his sandwich.

Peter also began to eat, and they sat in silence.

'I'm always around if you need someone to talk to, Laurie. Or just someone to sit with you.'

After an almost imperceptible nod from Laurie but no further sound, Peter lingered for a few more moments, stood, smiled at Laurie, and went back to work.

A week later, on his way to the sandwich shop, Peter noticed that Laurie was sitting on the same bench. He bought a sandwich for each of them, walked back and sat down beside Laurie, offering him the sandwich and a bottle of water.

'Egg and lettuce. Is that okay? I'm not very imaginative, I'm afraid.'

'It's fine. Thanks,' said Laurie, again devouring the food with a gusto that seemed more aggressive than enthusiastic.

They sat in silence for a while and then Laurie spoke: 'I'm not looking for religious comfort, thanks. I don't believe half what Fran believed, you know.'

'I'm not offering religious comfort, Laurie. I'm just buying you a sandwich and sitting here. By the way, neither do I.'

Laurie shot him a look. 'Neither do you what?'

'Believe half of what Fran believed.'

'Really?'

'Try me. As a matter of fact, I don't think what you happen to believe or not believe about the doctrines of the church matters all that much. There are far more interesting and important things to think about than that.'

'Such as?'

'How to think of God in a way that has nothing to do with Fran's death.'

Laurie stiffened at the sound of the words 'Fran's death', but he was intrigued by Peter's directness.

'How do you mean?'

'Well, I couldn't have faith in a god that could be responsible for terrible accidents. Could you? All this talk about the so-called "problem of pain" and why God allows dreadful things to happen to people – it's all cock-eyed. It's all based on a very strange view of what God is.'

Laurie paused and seemed to withdraw. Eventually, he said, 'Can we talk about this another time?'

5

Reasonable faith

Like most people, I occasionally board an aircraft to travel long distances. I regularly drive my car across bridges. I post letters in a well-maintained postbox I have used many times previously. I confidently click 'send' on emails and text messages, even though I know emails occasionally go astray. I deposit my money in a bank. I pay good money to see a film I know little about, at an art-house cinema where I have had mixed results in the past. I eat meals in restaurants where I never see the kitchen or the chef. I jump into a taxi driven by someone I don't know. I let a gastroenterologist put a camera down my throat. I make appointments for face-to-face meetings with people I have never met before.

What a trusting person I must be! What faith I must have in engineers, pilots, the postal service, the internet, banks, filmmakers, chefs, doctors and taxi-drivers.

But what if I boarded a small charter aircraft to fly through a severe storm to a destination famous for its turbulent weather – a place with a string of aircraft crashes to its credit – because I was desperate to get there in a hurry? What if I dropped a letter into an antique postbox, beautifully restored and located inside a museum, because I thought it looked cute? What if, desperate for a cab, I jumped into a battered car with a roughly painted sign on the door and a red-eyed driver at the wheel? What if I ordered a meal in an otherwise deserted cafe on a hot day in a foreign country, where the buzzing of flies and the surliness of the staff seemed less than reassuring, but my hunger got the better of me? What if I agreed to meet someone I didn't know in a dark alley on a wet night, because they had promised to give me access to a get-rich-quick scheme?

Suddenly, I seem more stupid than trusting. Now it looks as if I am prepared to place my faith in people or enterprises unworthy of it. Such faith seems, from every point of view, unreasonable. It might turn out that it was worth the risk – the plane landed safely, the food didn't kill me and neither did the man in the alley – but, on balance, you'd probably say my faith was misplaced, or even 'blind'.

No faith need be blind. However fleetingly or unconsciously, we calculate the risks before we board a plane or cross a bridge or enter a restaurant, and if our prior experience reassures us, and the reputation of the people in charge is sound, we do those things without a moment's anxiety. History is on our side, and so is rationality.

When it comes to religion, blindness is often touted as a virtue. 'Take the leap of faith,' we're urged, 'because that's the only way to receive the full benefit. Surrender yourself. Don't ask too many questions. Take it all on trust. Only *after* you've believed can you make sense of your faith. And if you're being asked to do or say things that make you feel uncomfortable, or you're expected to believe things that seem highly unlikely to be true, just go along with it.'

Some churchgoers regularly recite a creed beginning with the words, 'We believe in one God, the Father almighty, maker of heaven and earth ...', while insisting that they don't actually believe it themselves, but are happy to say it as a way of identifying with the church – *We believe* rather than *I believe* – like an act of solidarity or affirmation, rather than a description of me and my faith. Some recite it as if it were an allegorical poem. Others prefer to keep their mouths shut at such moments.

Rethinking agnosticism

I was once asked in a television interview whether my 2013 book *The Good Life* had been written out of a religious motivation. I assured the interviewer that it had not. When pressed about my own position, I said that I supposed I was a 'Christian agnostic', meaning that I was neither a believer nor an unbeliever when it came to the existence of a supernatural God, but that my view of the world was sympathetic to Christianity and its values, making me 'Christian' rather than '*a* Christian' (depending what hoops you might ask me to jump through in order to qualify for that tag). For several months after that interview, I was approached by people wanting to declare – sometimes shyly, sometimes almost secretively, and sometimes with evident pleasure and relief – that they thought 'Christian agnostic' was a label they, too, would like to adopt.

Throughout history, agnostics have had a hard time at the hands of ardent believers, whether at the theistic or atheistic extremes of the spectrum of belief. The agnostic says, 'I don't know; I can't be sure,' and means it; the hardline theist and atheist both say: 'How pathetic – make up your mind!' The true agnostic may even think that the existence of a supernatural God is neither a central nor crucial (nor even particularly interesting) question when it comes to finding a sense of meaning in our lives: 'Why try to settle a question that can never be settled?' Passionate theists and atheists, by contrast, regard the question as absolutely central: they *need* to settle it, at least in their own minds.

In *The God Delusion* (2006), the British biologist and renowned anti-theist Richard Dawkins admits to having had his harsh attitudes towards agnosticism coloured by the experience of having a schoolteacher, a so-called 'muscular Christian', railing against agnostics as 'namby-pamby, mushy pap, weak tea, pallid fence-sitters'.

Bible-believing Christians have some basis for such immoderate attacks. In the third chapter of Revelation (the strangest book in the Bible, and one that very nearly failed to make the final cut when the composition of the New Testament was being decided) there's an outburst against those who are neither hot nor cold: God says, 'I will spit you out of my mouth,' no less. Dawkins's schoolteacher probably found his inspiration right there.

Yet even Dawkins acknowledges that since it is just as impossible to *disprove* the existence of God as to prove it, he couldn't in all honesty call himself an atheist. In a 2012 interview with Rowan Williams, the former Anglican Archbishop of Canterbury, Dawkins said, 'On a scale of seven, where one means I know he exists and seven means I know he doesn't exist, I call myself a six.' (Rather intriguingly, Dawkins used the traditional male pronoun to refer to God, suggesting the kind of god he might have had in mind.) While that sounds more reasonable than the sledging he gives agnostics – let alone theists – in *The God Delusion*, it is entirely appropriate for him, as a scientist, to identify himself as an atheistically inclined agnostic. Even so, it was a bit rich for Dawkins to have weighed in with such force against religion in any form, when most of his attacks were aimed at a rather extreme form of fundamentalism. 'The God he attacks is not the God I have faith in,' was a common response of non-fundamentalist Christians to *The God Delusion*, and many reviews of the book, including some by atheists, criticised Dawkins's unscientific approach as the opposite of open enquiry, being based on virulent anti-theism from the start.

Towards the other end of the spectrum, many people who might describe themselves, on balance, as believers will nevertheless acknowledge that their faith is tinged with doubt. Indeed, faith without doubt is a moribund, calcifying faith that you could hardly call faith at all; faith is by its very nature fluid and evolving. How could it be otherwise? Doubt is the very engine of faith, the oxygen that keeps the flickering candle of faith alight. There is no need of faith when we are certain of something; it's when we can't be sure that we are free to explore, to imagine, and to wonder.

Even if we choose to invest our faith in something unprovable, that's not necessarily a once-and-for-all choice or even a boots-and-all choice. For most of us, faith in anything is an unfolding process, not dependent on a moment of black-and-white acceptance or rejection. As John Shepherd, the former Anglican dean of Perth, put it in an email to members of his Heretics Anonymous discussion group: 'Can faith be reasonable without having embraced the challenges that doubt creates? If we have no doubts, does this mean we have stopped thinking? And if we have stopped thinking, does this mean we have stopped imagining? And if we have stopped imagining, are we stifling the growth of faith?'

We may have faith, but the doubts arise. We may abandon our faith, and the doubts tease us and draw us back into faith's orbit. We may persist in a pattern of religious practice, even while wrestling with doubts that threaten to undermine the whole edifice of faith, for an edifice it is: one we ourselves construct, often painfully, with the work often interrupted by periods of neglect or episodes of partial demolition.

> 'Christianity doesn't have a monopoly on goodness and compassion, and I've never felt it had the whole story, either. I'm actually pretty impressed with Buddhism, but that just doesn't happen to be the tradition I'm most comfortable with. I love a story I heard about the Dalai Lama – someone asked

him if he would still be a Buddhist if he had been born in Italy and he said, 'Of course not – I'd be a Roman Catholic, eating pizza.' So Christianity is the one that feels most natural for me. But it's all a work in progress, isn't it? I do believe there's something greater than any one of us – not supernatural, but a kind of bank of collective goodwill we can tap into, and contribute to, as well. If you pressed me, I suppose I'd call that God, but I'm not sure I'd give it a capital G and I certainly wouldn't give it a gender. And I'm not a hundred percent sure it makes sense. But that's okay – it's a kind of working hypothesis.'—*Bernice*

Faith is about weighing the balance of probabilities, and then deciding to go – or even to lean – in one direction or the other. Agnosticism doesn't preclude the possibility of faith, but it precludes the possibility of *blind* faith. Agnosticism allows a person to experience *reasonable* faith – the kind of faith that allows many Christians to keep an open mind about institutionally based belief systems, even those that bear the great weight of tradition, while trying to come to terms with a satisfactory idea of God, no matter how unformed and tentative. That's the world the Christian agnostic lives in.

Some level of agnosticism is essential to growth. It's the natural state for anyone who is open to the possibility of change to any aspect of their belief system. Agnosticism is not a pathetic no-man's-land; it is the place where many atheists and theists probably dwell, even when they give out other, more confident-sounding addresses. And yet, for believers to admit to their doubts can be a liberating experience.

Faith is a creative act; a leap; a tentative, hopeful encounter with the numinous; a reaching-out for certainties that keep eluding us. We don't place our faith in visible, tangible certainties, but in ideas, prospects, promises, probabilities – things we can imagine to be true or that seem to fit the available evidence. When it comes to the imagination, nothing is certain; nothing is finished.

Belief and unbelief mingle in all of us. Sometimes we feel ourselves swinging to one extreme or the other – *I really know this to be true; I really know this to be untrue* – but most of us can't stay too long in a doubt-free zone. These are big questions, these questions of faith; why wouldn't we doubt our own convictions? Why wouldn't doubt become our travelling companion, even if it is sometimes subdued or ignored when we are temporarily dazzled by little flashes of certainty?

It is doubt that saves us from arrogance; doubt that maintains our humility; doubt that actually bolsters faith by forcing us to examine it, test it, possibly reshape or refocus it and, in the process, make it more resilient.

It is doubt that allows many people to maintain their religious practice through their darkest periods of unbelief.

> 'At the bleakest time of my life, when I was struggling with a divorce and felt as if my religion had become empty and meaningless, I kept going to church. Don't ask me why. I actually said to the minister, 'I don't know why I come any more – I don't think I believe anything I used to believe, but I still love the music.' He said, 'Why not keep coming for the music, then? That's enough for now.' And it was. The music and the silence. It was very sustaining, I suppose in a vaguely spiritual way. And then, gradually, I came to feel I still had a skerrick of faith, but that feeling comes and goes, too. I no longer attend church regularly, but I'm glad to go sometimes, sort of on my own terms, and it mostly turns out well. At least I'm not pretending to believe things I don't believe.' —*Mitch*

Show me the believer – in anything – who doesn't harbour doubts about their belief, and I'll show you a person who has withdrawn from the process of intellectual, emotional or spiritual growth and cut themselves off from the possibility of deeper understanding of life's mysteries. To echo the theme of John Shepherd's email, no faith is worthy of the name if it can't meet the challenges of doubt. Whether we're talking about religion, philosophy, science or personal relationships, certainties are hard to come by; at best, they are a transitional state.

Changing fashions in philosophy would make your head spin. Where have all the logical positivists gone? Is postmodernism dead already? And uncertainty is fundamental to the process of scientific discovery. In his 1962 classic *The Structure of Scientific Revolutions*, the American physicist-philosopher Thomas Kuhn argued that scientific theories are both subjective and constantly evolving constructions and that the integrity of any theory lies in its falsifiability – in other words, its openness to the possibility of repudiation in the light of new evidence or fresh insights. Those insights might come from a more creative interpretation of existing data whose significance was not previously understood. That applies as much to theology as to any other discipline whose theories are constantly being tested through experience.

Here's some encouraging news: uncertainty is good for us! It keeps us mentally young, maintains brain plasticity and stimulates our cognitive and emotional development. The more routinised our lives, the less 'alive' we are. It's when unexpected events or challenging ideas crash into our world and disrupt our comfortable routines that we are at our best. Although we resist change, the truth is that we thrive on it. A month or so before the 2014 Scottish referendum on independence, a wise Scot in a crowded meeting at Kingskettle said, 'Let's have a Scotland where the energy of uncertainty is still there after September – whichever way we vote.'

Most people who survive the trauma of life-changing events – serious illness, retrenchment, separation, divorce, bereavement – will say that these were the great testers of their faith (including their faith in themselves) and the great developers of their resilience. Travel to unfamiliar places changes us, and most of us would say the changes are for the better: broadening the mind; increasing our tolerance of other people's values; appreciating a different way of life. Moving house, changing jobs or falling in love can be both destabilising and energising experiences (though doing them all at once might overwhelm you). Developing an ability to absorb change and entertain new ideas is part of the process of becoming whole.

The idea that agnostics are by nature lukewarm is deeply unfair to them. Agnostics tend to be centrists. Like social democrats on the political spectrum, they have resisted the seductive comfort of extreme and inflexible positions. But this by no means implies that the agnostic is indecisive by nature or unable to commit to action. Agnostics may have as much passion for social justice as any theist or atheist; agnostics may be as concerned as anyone else for the plight of the poor or disadvantaged. Living with uncertainty about the existence or nature of a supreme being does not disqualify agnostics from responding to charitable impulses traditionally associated with religious faith any more than it disqualifies them from participation in religious practices that nurture their interest in the spiritual life or respond to their occasional yearnings for faith.

Whether they incline towards the theistic or atheistic end of the spectrum of faith, their position is that of the sceptic. In fact, the very term 'agnostic' was coined in the late 1880s by the English biologist Thomas Huxley, initially as a joke. According to a 1996 lecture by the self-described 'agnostic Buddhist' Stephen Batchelor, Huxley belonged to a small philosophical circle in London in which he felt increasingly out of place, partly because everyone else in the group readily labelled themselves as Christian,

Rationalist, and so on, whereas Huxley felt no such term applied to him. He decided to call himself an agnostic so that he, too, could 'have a tail like all the other foxes'.

For Huxley, agnosticism involved taking one's reason as far as it would go, and not accepting that anything is true unless it can be demonstrated – which stands as a fair description of agnosticism, whether in the Christian, Buddhist, humanist or any other tradition. When it comes to belief in a supernatural, transcendent God, agnostics typically see themselves as more reasonable than both theists and atheists, because they refuse to commit themselves to either position in the absence of sufficient evidence for doing so.

There are many shades of agnosticism, just as there are many shades of theism. Lazy agnostics may simply throw up their hands and say, 'It's all too hard – I can't decide', and lose interest (just as lazy theists may settle on the way they thought about God in childhood and close their mind to any other possibilities). Some agnostics wrestle constantly with the question of God's existence as if it is the central question of their lives. Others may reserve judgement about the existence and nature of God, but choose to live as if some type of god exists (possibly attracted by another version of 'Pascal's Wager' – the idea proposed by the French philosopher and mathematician Blaise Pascal that it is better to live as if there is an afterlife, because nothing is lost if there isn't, and everything is gained if there is). Closely related to them are the people who count themselves as believers but live with serious reservations about the value and integrity of those beliefs.

Agnosticism is, by its nature, a searching after truth: just don't ask agnostics whether they have arrived at their destination yet. And don't be surprised if you start to encounter some members of the growing band of 'subtle agnostics', who seem to have switched their attention from the traditional God question (*Does God exist?*) to the exploration of new ways of bringing divinity – godliness – into their lives, without needing *a* Divinity or *a* God to call on.

Does this make them theists? Or atheists? In fact, as we shall see in the next chapter, this more subtle form of agnosticism raises big questions about the usefulness of all such labels.

Three tests of reasonableness

If you were considering placing your faith in anything – whether a god, a religion, a teacher, a leader, an ideology, a philosophy, an economic system or an alternative to conventional medical practice – there are a few questions you might like to ask yourself first. The following three work for me (though not, I realise, for everyone):

Does it make sense?

To sacrifice Reason in the name of Faith is too dangerous a trade-off. Your faith is a precious commodity, not to be squandered: it's the mast you nail your colours to; the key to your identity. If you were going to invest your faith in something, shouldn't you be sure it is compatible with reason? Shouldn't you be sure, for a start, that it doesn't contradict what you know to be true about yourself and the world?

If someone tries to tell you that adopting their faith demands that you meet certain prescriptive criteria that don't seem sensible or reasonable, run a mile. Prescriptions about belief are one of the ways institutions – religious and otherwise – get their hooks into you. And if you abandon your reason in order to become 'acceptable' to a particular institution, you will have surrendered too much; if there is to be room for growth, there must be room for doubt. Changing your mind in response to new evidence – or being prepared to rethink old evidence – is a sign of strength, not weakness.

> 'Growing up on a farm and coming from a strict Methodist family, we had lots of rules about Sunday. First thing, the girls had

to go out to the henhouse and let the rooster out, and the boys had to move the bull to a separate paddock from the cows. There was to be no hanky-panky on Sundays, even for animals. I kid you not – that's what we had to do. There was no swearing on Sundays, no playing cards and no telling jokes. Later on, I realised you could be a perfectly good Christian without all these rules, but it was the rules that drove me away from it when I was young. I just thought one day, This doesn't make sense! What kind of God would want anyone to act like this? It didn't turn me off God, but it certainly turned me off religion.'—*Patrick*

Another respondent, also from a rural background, had a very different reason for deciding, at a young age, that religion didn't make sense to her.

'I remember the moment quite vividly – the moment when I gave up on religion. I couldn't have been more than eight or nine at the time. I had begun to realise that our animals went to the abattoir, and I had asked the minister of our church whether animals went to heaven. He solemnly assured me that as animals have no soul, they couldn't go to heaven. Well, I knew animals had a soul – I could see the way they looked at me, and the way they became distressed. I had a pet dog at the time, and I saw the way she responded to things – I just knew she had a soul. So that was it. I couldn't make sense of that at the time, and I still can't. I have some reverence for Christianity, but I knew it wasn't for me.'—*Josie*

If you were inclined to join a political party but were told you first had to sign a charter of political conviction, you'd want to study that charter pretty carefully. If there were items on it you couldn't subscribe to, then why join? Your faith in that party's broad political aims might be more likely to remain intact if you didn't complicate it with specific commitments that posed a problem for you. And if you were told that, in order to be a member of the party, you would have to use certain words and phrases that seemed alien or meaningless to you, why would you do it? It wouldn't make sense.

If you were about to sign up for a course of alternative treatment for a condition that had failed to respond to orthodox medicine, wouldn't you first want to see some evidence of its efficacy? Unless you had cheerfully fallen under the spell of a guru or were banking on the placebo effect – *If I believe it will work, it will work* – surely it would be unacceptably risky to throw yourself on the mercy of an unproven therapy.

Evidence matters. When you're contemplating a faith commitment of any kind, ask yourself: Where's the evidence for this? And there's another closely related question worth asking: Do I want to be like the people who have already placed their faith in this? Is this a club I want to join? Can I imagine myself being part of this tribe, while still being true to the person I know myself to be?

Our faith must feel as if it is authentically ours or it will be a vain faith, a conformist faith, a faith for show rather than something positive, productive or transformative. If you find yourself attracted to the idea of faith in God but you can't stomach the notion of a creator-god 'out there somewhere', then find an alternative way of thinking about God. Millions of people experience faith, including Christian faith, in ways that don't entail belief in a supreme being or a supernatural entity of any kind (see chapter 6, 'When we say "God" . . .').

Why place your faith in something that seems a bit weird, a bit pointless, a bit suspect, or a bit too irrational for your liking?

Does it point to a better world?

The best reason for investing your faith in something – whether a god, a philosophy, a religion, your own ability, the justice system, science, the joys of meditation or the essential goodness of humanity – would be that it offers a pathway to the good life. And since 'goodness' is a moral concept that can't be separated from our obligations towards each other, 'the good life' means finding ways of making the world a better place for all of us.

In other words, save your faith for *goodness* – good causes, good people, good intentions, good work. Avoid the deadly trap of regarding faith as a pathway to personal happiness.The idea that you are entitled to happiness, or that the pursuit of personal happiness is a suitable goal for your life, is seriously misguided. If we know anything, we know that's a fruitless, pointless quest – doomed to disappoint – because it overlooks the fact that, as we saw in chapter 3, our deepest satisfactions come from a sense of *meaning* in our lives, not from experiencing any particular emotional state like happiness or contentment. (Remember Roy Baumeister's 2013 conclusion that happiness is mostly about taking, meaningfulness mostly about giving.)

Ideally, any belief system, movement, cause, institution or process worthy of your faith should offer a sense of meaning and purpose that transcends self-interest. It should have a clear moral purpose, meaning that it will both encourage and equip you to be of value to those around you – in the family, in the neighbourhood, in the workplace, in society at large. Morality is always, and only, about the way we relate to other people, the way we respond to their needs and our determination to treat them the way we ourselves would like to be treated. Everyone who's ever thought about goodness, from Socrates or Jesus to the most contemporary humanist, will tell you that.

Given the current fashion for yoga, meditation and mindfulness as spiritual exercises designed to achieve peace of mind, it's worth remembering that these practices are ultimately worthless unless they are geared to our destiny as social beings with a responsibility to the communities we belong to. If we construe the 'spiritual' as something essentially private – something we do for ourselves – we will have missed the point: the value of a spiritual life is to equip us for the business of living courageously and lovingly in the material world.

In *The Good Society* (1991), Robert Bellah and his co-authors point out that many of the institutions that influence our lives most powerfully – whether political, economic or educational – tend to encourage competition rather than cooperation, and 'empty out meaning from our lives when they structure our existence as a race for money, power, prestige or the consumer goods that symbolize them'. They argue that religious communities, by contrast, foster a sense of membership, recognition and meaningfulness in people's lives: 'They help us grapple with the ultimate problem of meaning ... of whether we have a place in the universe at all and any abiding purpose to pursue here.' This is true for many people, but it is a rose-tinted analysis; Bellah and his colleagues could well have added that while religious communities foster all those things for their members, they sometimes promote tribalism in ways that foment prejudice, and even hatred, against outsiders.

The psychotherapist Thomas Moore warns in *Care of the Soul* (1992) that spiritual convictions don't always lead to a better world: 'It's easy to go crazy in the life of the spirit, warring against those who disagree, proselytizing for our own personal attachments ... taking narcissistic satisfactions in our beliefs rather than finding meaning and pleasure in spirituality that is available to everyone.'

> 'One of the things that disturbed me as I moved through my teens was people's certainty that their brand of religion was correct and everyone else's was wrong. I don't just mean that they were critical of Hindus or Muslims – they were critical of other Christian denominations that didn't accord with their own dogma. I've known a lot of Catholics who looked down their noses at Protestants – as if they just thought we were a sort of pale

imitation or something. (So what about the Reformation? I used to think.) And, in return, we were pretty down on Catholics, too. We accused them of idolatry and we disapproved of the fact that they were drinkers and smokers and gamblers – no one in my church was surprised when a priest turned out to be part of some horse-racing scandal that made the news at the time.

It's so weird – most people follow their parents' religion, so it's not as if they made this big decision to be a Catholic or Protestant, let alone a Christian or Muslim! So I see religion as promoting a lot of division in the world. It polarises people and encourages them to ridicule each other, or at least to judge and devalue other people's views. Some of the differences become really bitter and last for years, or even centuries. How is that good? One of the things I hated most about our church, before I left it, was that we were supposed to go around 'witnessing' – telling other people about our faith and trying to win them over. I couldn't do that. I wouldn't do it. I felt it would be intrusive and terribly presumptuous. It's one of the things I admire about Buddhism – they have this rule: don't try to influence anyone. They respect that people have to find their own pathway and work out their own vision of a better world.'—*Jenny*

What is your personal vision of a better world? As a social researcher, but also as a citizen, my sense is that most of us dream of a world where poverty is reduced or eliminated, where sickness is cured and suffering relieved, where equality of opportunity (especially educational opportunity) is adopted as a serious goal and the problems of isolation, loneliness and social fragmentation are addressed; where the rich accept their obligation to help the poor, the strong to help the weak and the advantaged to help the disadvantaged. It would be a world animated more by loving-kindness than materialism, a world of peace and shared prosperity.

If we dream of that kind of world, it makes sense to align ourselves with faiths, ideologies and organisations that are working to make it happen, to seek out those who will enlarge our vision, not shrink it. It makes sense to support the peacemakers, and those with a deep commitment to kindness, respect for all and a compassionate view of the human condition – frailties, foibles, foolishness and all. We should look for the signs of hope, the signs of love; they will point us to the best places to invest our faith in.

Does it matter?

When confronted by any faith-based proposition you're tempted to embrace, ask yourself this: What difference would it make to the way I live my life if it were true?

> 'Ever since I was a kid, I've been interested in religion and spirituality. In fact, I was in love with the whole idea when I was young – I just couldn't get enough of it. But I knew the answers weren't in all the dogma and doctrines of the church. I always wanted it to be more esoteric or mystical or transformative or something. Of course, I didn't think in those terms when I was younger, but I do remember thinking that I couldn't see what difference it made if Jesus was resurrected or not. That didn't seem to be the point – surely it was more about what Jesus taught and how he lived rather than what happened after he died. And I was never impressed with miracles, either, except that they gave me the idea there might be more going on than meets the eye. But I think I knew they were more like fables than history. Later, when I became interested in Buddhist meditation and other practices, I found the same thing – some people were really turned on by the idea of levitation, but I could never see the point; why get worked up about something that really doesn't matter? Meditation is only valuable if it helps us live more lovingly. And so is religion.' —*Duncan*

Faith, at its best, makes a positive difference to the kind of people we are and the way we act in the world. Faith that enriches and enlarges us deserves to be incorporated into our world view. By contrast, the kind of faith that obliges us to believe in the impossible – or the highly improbable – is likely to diminish and cripple us by distorting our sense of reality.

Why cling to beliefs that feel like excess baggage or, worse, distract you from the things you think really matter? To live a good life – a loving life, a meaningful life, an engaged life – requires us to travel lightly, unencumbered by dogma. We need to be morally and spiritually fit, flexible and ready for anything. For many people, faith in a god of some kind – a supreme being, a life force, an idea greater than themselves – acts as a powerful motivator to live a good life. For others, religious faith is neither here nor there; the motivation to act well comes out of their sense of responsibility as citizens committed to the common good.

What counts as professional misconduct for clergy?

On the night the Reverend Dr Philip Druggett left his wife, Marie, for a recently separated woman in his congregation, his children were away at a school camp. He had chosen the moment carefully, leaving Marie to explain to their ten-year-old daughter and seven-year-old son that Daddy still loved them and would be coming to visit them as often as he could but would be living somewhere else from now on.

His clothes were packed in a suitcase already loaded into the boot of his car, his model train set – carefully boxed – was on the back seat, and twelve cartons of books were stacked in the carport, ready to be collected by a removalist the following morning.

As he prepared to leave, Druggett placed his hand on his white-faced wife's arm and said, with the utmost sincerity, 'I will always love you, you know. It's just that God has chosen a different direction for me.'

That was the moment when Marie's misery turned to blazing anger. She seized the nearest object – a metal-backed hairbrush – and clouted him across the face, bruising his cheek and splitting his lip. Bright blood began to drip onto his collar. When Marie raised the brush to administer a second blow, Druggett made for the door and left without another word being spoken by either of them.

As the sound of his car receded, Marie went calmly to the laundry, took a half-full bottle of household kerosene from the shelf, picked up a box of matches and walked to the carport. She doused as many cartons of books as she could before the bottle was empty, and set them alight. The effect was more symbolic than damaging, though the top layer of books in three of the cartons had smouldered satisfyingly.

She went inside and sent a text message to the woman for whom Druggett had left her – a former university friend of both of them: 'The rat is on his way. You'll make a good pair.'

Then she ran a hot bath.

Bella Browning was settled comfortably in Wild Thyme, her favourite cafe, with Penny, her favourite person. Bella and Penny, now in their late fifties, had been friends since primary school and had shared everything, somewhat to the chagrin of their husbands (Penny's now ex-husband), who knew that no topic was off-limits when these two got together.

For many years, the two women had attended the church where Philip Druggett had been the minister, before he moved on and was replaced by Peter Munro. Religion turned sour for Penny when her marriage collapsed; her husband continued attending the same church, and Penny couldn't face the prospect of seeing him there. ('He said we should be civilised – I'm not that civilised.')

'Well,' said Penny, 'I have some gossip. I was going to text you, but I wanted to see the look on your face when I told you.'

'So tell me.'

'SPP has bitten the dust.'

Philip Druggett had always insisted on being known as Senior Pastor Phil, though the junior pastor had long gone. Bella and Penny had taken to calling him 'SPP', even to his face. They both despised him – partly for his arrogance and his male chauvinism, but also for the dreary predictability of his sanctimonious sermons. By the time he announced his transfer to another parish, Penny had already left the church and Bella had begun wondering whether she might use the change of minister as her cue to pull back.

Bella raised a sceptical eyebrow. 'What happened? Are you going to tell me another all-too-predictable story of human frailty? What's old SPP done? Made off with the cash? Anyway, how did you hear about it, you infidel?'

'Nothing as simple as embezzlement. He's made off with the wife of a parishioner at his new church. The woman's neighbour works in our office, that's how I heard.'

Penny studied Bella's face, looking for signs of shock and dismay.

'Silly, silly man,' Bella said. 'And, by the way, silly, silly woman. I assume she wasn't drugged at the time. Did this of her own free will, did she? Oh well, perhaps they've been swept up in the great passion of the century, and we're supposed to give them our blessing and forgive them everything because they have surrendered to a force greater than themselves – not.'

'I thought you'd be more . . . shocked.'

'No. I can't say I'm shocked. A bit irritated. No doubt it's wrought havoc on two families – although if I was his wife, I'd be relieved to see the back of him.'

'Quite.'

'You know, Pen, this reminds me of something Peter Munro said.'

'Peter Munro? Oh, your new minister.'

'I think you'd like him. A total contrast with SPP, I can tell you. Anyway, when Peter hears of clergy who have morally lapsed one way or another, he says he feels sad and angry, but not nearly as upset as when he comes across clergy who are deliberately keeping their congregations in the dark, refusing to keep them abreast of contemporary scholarship. He thinks that's an even greater shortcoming, and I know what he means. People from all walks of life make a muck of their love lives, but if an accountant falsifies your accounts or a surgeon's scalpel slips, that's a very particular kind of breach. Professional misconduct, I suppose. Do you get what I'm saying?'

'So your lovely Reverend Peter thinks ministers who continue to preach as if we're all still in the Dark Ages are guilty of professional misconduct, is that it?'

'Absolutely. And that's a more serious lapse than a bit of hanky-panky because it's a betrayal of the very thing a minister is supposed to have been trained to do. Professionally, I mean. Theologically. What's the use of continuing to present myths and metaphors as if they are literally true? It's unconscionable!'

'Myths and metaphors? You are steamed up. I've never heard you talk like this before.'

'No, because I hadn't really faced up to it before. I just sat through all those awful sermons, year after year – and not just SPP's – thinking everyone else was swallowing it as if it made sense, so why couldn't I? I never spoke up, naturally. No one ever does.'

'Well, you won't get any argument from me. Anyway, we'll see what happens to the old SPP. If he ends up in court, it won't be for heresy. It'll be another boring family court case, wrangling over a property settlement and the custody of the kids, and I suppose he'll go on mouthing all the same platitudes he always has. No doubt he'll be praying for the wellbeing of the wife he's abandoned.'

They drained their coffee and looked at each other as thoughts of their own past sexual exploits, openly discussed at the time but now never mentioned, bubbled silently to the surface.

'Well, that fell a bit flatter than I was expecting,' Penny said.

After an exchange of family news, they kissed and parted, neither in a hurry to leave. Bella's husband was cooking the dinner, and Penny had no one to go home to. At moments like this, she was painfully aware of how the church worked like a kind of enfoldment: Ray, her ex-husband, was in; she was out. Bella alone had stuck by her. She had been deserted by all those church people she had thought were her friends and she wasn't sure whether the greater sin in their eyes was leaving Ray or leaving the church.

Faith envy

In previous chapters, we have encountered several people who have expressed a kind of 'faith envy'. Some of these have been agnostics with an unfulfilled yearning for faith; some have been wistful atheists recalling a time when they counted themselves as believers; some have been churchgoers who, for a variety of reasons, have drifted away; some have been people who've never had a brush with religion but occasionally encounter a person of faith and marvel at their buoyancy.

We are at a point in our social evolution where there are far more ex- and occasional churchgoers than regular churchgoers, which means there are millions of people in our midst who have had some contact with the church, and some experience of religious faith and practice, but no longer engage with it.

As chapter 3 suggested, most of those people are unlikely to resume church attendance. Yet many of them retain a tiny thread of connection to the idea that faith *can be* a good thing. While most of them continue to believe that the presence of a church in a neighbourhood is likely to do more good than harm, the increasingly popular view is that the church as an institution does more harm than good.

Here are some snippets from recent conversations with people who, even if only half seriously, have expressed faith envy:

> 'I saw the look on my mother's face when she died – she was utterly confident she was going to see her father again, and it's hard to argue that that was anything but a good way for her to die. I kind of envy her that.'
>
> 'I wish I believed in God – I wouldn't have to be so responsible. I don't think I really mean that, by the way. But it's so easy for Christians – they can leave everything to God. With Buddhism, there's nowhere to hide.'
>
> 'What if they are right and I am wrong? If their faith gives them a reason for living and makes them a better person, then I'm all for it. It's just that I don't have it.'

> 'I miss church. I really do. There's nowhere else you can go where people talk about the spiritual life, and I think we all have a need for that.'

> 'I admit I'm frustrated by my own lack of faith. I'm quite angry with God for not existing, as a matter of fact. I'm sure life would be better if I had something to believe in – to rely on.'

> 'I definitely call myself an atheist. Well, maybe an agnostic. But I don't believe. On the other hand, I sometimes think wouldn't it be good if I could? In some ways, it would make everything easier. One of my friends is quite devout – sometimes I want to attack her for being so weak-minded, and sometimes I wish I was devout, too.'

> 'I don't go to church, but it's kind of reassuring to know that people still do.'

What does all this mean? It suggests that in this post-churchgoing (if not post-Christian) era, there is a significant residue of people who still hanker after the consolations of religion, the confidence enjoyed by believers and the peace of mind they associate with women and men of faith – or, at least, the *best* examples of women and men of faith. (SPP would not qualify.)

Some of them will find comfortable lodgings in the SBNR movement, a yoga class, a meditation or 'mindfulness' group outside the structure of organised religion. They, like many people inside the church, may begin to explore new pathways to a more reasonable and sustainable faith than the kind they previously experienced.

Next question: What kind of god might it be reasonable for them to believe in?

6

When we say 'God' . . .

The 2009 Australian Survey of Social Attitudes conducted by the Australian National University found that 67 percent of Australian adults believed either in God (47 percent) or in something they preferred to call a 'higher power' (a further 20 percent). A less nuanced Nielsen/Fairfax poll in the same year reported simply that 68 percent believed in God. (To put this in a historical context: in a 1949 Gallup poll, 95 percent of Australians declared their belief in God.) The figures for Australia almost exactly match those for New Zealand and the European Union.

The question is, what do people mean when they say 'God'?

There's no shortage of attempts to explain God, some of them highly poetic. God is love. God is light. God is life. God is Being. God is Now. God is the soul of the universe. Listening to people struggling for words, it soon becomes clear that God, like faith, is a product of the imagination. This is why we have so much trouble getting to grips with the idea and why so many people slide away from the word 'god' itself in favour of some equally ill-defined alternative: 'something out there', a 'higher power', a 'life force', a 'cosmic imperative'. There isn't a thing or a person called God we can to point to, touch or even describe in a way that will produce general agreement. I imagine my god; you imagine yours; they imagine theirs. Are those gods the same? Who knows? Rather enigmatically, the US Catholic mystic Thomas Merton suggested that 'God approaches our minds by receding from them', which was presumably his way of saying that even trying to conceive of God is an inappropriately rational process.

To say that God is a product of the imagination is not to denigrate the idea, nor to suggest that God doesn't exist. Even if God does not exist as an objective external being or entity, the subjective experience of God and the widespread evidence of faith in God indicate that we mean *something* when we say 'God'. And when did we ever reserve the idea of reality for objects we can directly see, hear, feel, taste or touch? As a species, we're pretty accomplished at dealing with imaginary things – ideas – as if they are real. There is no entity called Democracy-with-a-capital-D, for instance, any more than there is an entity called Justice-with-a-capital-J, but we believe in them both and talk as freely and confidently about democracy and justice as we do about other intangible ideas like beauty and truth.

Take the case of *the mind*. We use that term without blinking – *it's all in the mind*; *he's losing his mind*; *mind over matter* – and we imagine that's where thinking takes place, but we know it isn't that simple. There is actually no tangible thing called *the mind*, and no place where it could exist. 'Mind' is simply a useful metaphor; a way of referring to the operation of a brain and central nervous system and all the other organs and processes of the body that influence how we think, feel and act. The eminent British neurosurgeon Henry Marsh has never doubted the material nature of thought and feeling. 'You cannot see people whose very personality and moral being has been altered for the worse by damage to the frontal lobes and maintain belief in some kind of mind or human soul separate from the brain,' he writes in 'Better not look down ...' (*The Psychologist*, 2015). Marsh nevertheless acknowledges that the brain is infinitely mysterious and that scientists 'cannot even begin to explain how consciousness and subjective feelings arise from the electro-chemical activity of nerve cells'. For most of us, 'mind' works nicely as a shorthand way of summarising all that highly complex (and often well-hidden) activity. To take a simple example, our moods, which we sometimes think of as 'states of mind', are notoriously tied to things like digestion and hormonal activity.

Another of our favourite metaphors is *the heart*. We talk easily of the heart in a non-physical way, as though it is the wellspring of our emotions, the place where we feel love most intensely, the place where we are most deeply hurt, the source of our generosity and charity towards each other. *Have a heart*, we say, or, *She's all heart*. We know this has nothing to do with the pump that keeps our blood supply moving. It's a poetic concept, a metaphor, that works for us as a way of representing one aspect of human experience.

We do the same thing with *the soul*. We don't look for the physical properties of a soul; we don't think of it as inhabiting the brain or the liver or the lungs. And yet, as we saw in chapter 4, we routinely use 'soul' as a metaphor for deep inner feelings, or as an imaginary space where spiritual experiences take place just as we imagine thinking takes place in the mind. 'Good for the soul' is a phrase that makes perfect sense to most of us.

I'm a social psychologist and researcher, not a theologian, so I'm not equipped for a full-scale exploration of a topic like 'our knowledge of God'. In any case, there are countless books on that subject, dating from antiquity all the way up to yesterday. (So many books! So much speculation!) All I can do is try to make sense of what people mean when I hear them say 'God'.

In my experience, people attach five primary levels of meaning to that ubiquitous and ambiguous word. There's a lot of overlap between the five levels, but most people tend to focus on one more than the others.

> Level 1: *Something out there* too mysterious to define – possibly a life force, a 'presence' of some kind, bearing no similarity to human existence; immortal, invisible, unknowable, ineffable.
>
> Level 2: *A supreme being* with the properties of creator, ruler and judge – to be worshipped and obeyed; omniscient, omnipotent and omnipresent.
>
> Level 3: *A heavenly father* – the supernatural version of a human father – characterised by unconditional parental love and care, though capable of stern discipline ('tough love'); accessible through prayer.
>
> Level 4: *An imaginary friend* we can talk to, bounce ideas off and share experiences with – an enchanting blend of the human and the divine.
>
> Level 5: *A spirit within and among us* whose 'divine' qualities emanate *from* us, rather than coming *to* us from an external being or power.

In this chapter, we will explore some of the many shades of meaning attached to those five categories. We will also consider whether, at level 5, it is possible to reimagine god, minus the heavily freighted capital G, in ways that make sense of the idea that we could stop believing in *a* God without losing faith in the presence and influence of godliness in our lives – just as I have previously suggested we don't need to believe in *a* Truth or *a* Beauty in order to acknowledge the presence and influence of truth and beauty in our lives.

★

God is quite possibly the brightest idea humans have ever had. In one hit, it responds to our need for an explanation of why we are here; our need for something to account for our sense of the numinous; our need for a sense of life's meaning; and our need for attachment to something greater than ourselves. This one grand idea proposes that there is a powerful but ultimately indefinable God; some kind of guiding spirit abroad in the world, a mystery beyond all mysteries, a life force that has brought us into being and sustains us – possibly even beyond our physical death. If we're operating at levels 3 and 4, we may also imagine that this God takes an interest in us personally: 'His eye is on the sparrow, and I know he watches me,' says the old gospel song.

> 'I used to know this old guy, Barry – he was a friend of my parents – who talked as if Jesus was right there alongside him, as a kind of confidant and carer. I remember Dad coming home one day after visiting him, shaking his head as he described how Barry had pointed to a damp patch on the ceiling of his living room – not just damp, but dripping – and said to Dad, 'He knows,' as if he was simply going to leave it with the Lord and the drip would miraculously disappear, or some kind soul would spontaneously show up – sent by God, presumably – and fix it for him. Dad even wondered if he should offer to help out. I don't know whether he ever did or not, but if he did, no doubt Barry would have given the credit to God, not Dad.' —*Carrie*

You can see why primitive people might have assumed there was a supernatural agency behind illness and death, success and failure in hunting or agriculture, the vagaries of the weather, or misadventures ranging from a lightning strike to a tree that fell on someone. And you can see why, once these matters were better understood, the species was reluctant to abandon the idea of a higher being that could be blamed, thanked, praised, obeyed, adored, deified . . . or defied.

Once the idea of God lodged in our consciousness we were – and are – reluctant to let it go. (Even atheists are obliged to imagine the thing they are asserting does not exist. Only agnostics can decline to define it.)

There is an almost infinite variety of ways of interpreting the word 'god'. Is a Muslim's Allah (*He neither begets nor is born, nor is there to Him any equivalent*) the same as (some) Hindus' concept of a formless and attribute-less Absolute that is an integral part of the universe and everything in it? Is a Jew's Yahweh (*I the Lord your God am a jealous God, punishing children for the iniquity of parents, to the third and fourth generation of those who reject me, but showing steadfast love to the thousandth generation of those who love me and keep my commandments*) the same as a Christian's God (*God is spirit; God is love*)?

What about the meaning of 'Allah' when it is occasionally used by Baha'is, Maltese and Indonesian Christians or Mizrahi Jews, or by Arab Christians who used it before the advent of Islam? Is a Roman Catholic's God the same as a Protestant's? Is a fundamentalist's God the same as a liberal's? And is *this* liberal's God the same as *that* liberal's?

Two people may agree that they are both talking about, let's say, the God of level 3, yet disagree passionately about how that God should be described, interpreted or responded to – or what might follow from faith in a God like that. As we saw in chapter 3, even a congregation of apparently like-minded believers may represent many different conceptions of God, just as those conceptions may evolve, for a single person, through a lifetime of devout theism.

How could it be otherwise? God is an idea we can only try to imagine, each in our own way. Men are naturally inclined to imagine a male God and so, in Christianity's male supremacist culture inherited from Judaism, God was masculinised. Many women go along with that, especially if they believe Jesus of Nazareth was the embodiment of God, or accept the idea of male headship in the church as some kind of reflection of the masculinity of God. Other women (and some men, jumping on the feminist bandwagon) will insist that *their* God is female, as many ancient gods of other religions have been. Those who conceive of God only as spirit would regard any discussion of the gender of God as absurd: for them, God is as genderless as gravity, as charity, as clouds . . . and the appropriate pronoun is therefore neither 'he' nor 'she', but 'it'.

'There's something out there'

God turns up – either explicitly or as a source of inspiration – in the art, music, poetry and literature of every age. The fact that you or I might not personally be able to imagine this or that kind of God is irrelevant; it's clear that many people *can* conceive of 'something out there' (level 1), even if they don't choose to call it 'God'. In the ANU survey quoted at the beginning of the chapter, the 20 percent of respondents who claimed to believe in an unspecified 'higher power' wanted to distinguish that from the idea of a personal God, but were presumably thinking of something supernatural.

At levels 2 and 3, many people have been able to imagine a supernatural intelligence that purposefully created the universe and maintains a close interest in it, dispensing justice, rewarding good behaviour and even, from time to time, sending messages to the human world via prophets, signs, visions and other revelations. 'Him upstairs,' people say in a joking way, parodying the ancient, primitive idea of a divine entity parked in the sky, ultimately responsible for the whole show.

The concept of a higher power is sometimes colloquially captured in the term 'the universe', as in 'I'll put it out to the universe'. This is roughly the same idea that is sometimes expressed in religious terms as 'I'll leave it in God's hands'. In fact, 'the universe' has become a popular alternative to 'God' in the lexicon of many atheists and agnostics, as though 'something out there' – nothing as specific as God, but *something* – will look after me, or at least has things under control. The same kind of thinking leads to the fatalistic proposition that 'the universe meant this to happen' and the popular idea that 'everything happens for a reason' (which is why we try so hard to make sense of whatever happens to us).

If you believed that the natural world was formed according to some vast eternal purpose – some cosmic design or plan – it would not be a great stretch to imagine there must have been a creator behind it, since words like 'design' and 'plan' cry out for designers and planners. Then it's a short step to praying for rain – 'the controller of the universe ought to be able to control the weather' – and the belief that the creator could intervene when necessary to warn or even to punish us; for example, through plagues, famines, floods or fires. (In recent Australian history, some apparently intelligent people have interpreted the extended bushfire season as evidence of God's wrath.) Every time we use words like 'creatures' or 'creation' to refer to the natural world, we encourage those ancient cultural impulses towards the idea that we are part of a universe under the control of a creative intelligence.

Creative intelligence? Many theists are as deeply uncomfortable with such talk as any atheist. They would regard people who take the biblical creation story literally – even if they want to stretch the 'seven days' into the aeons of cosmic time – as embarrassingly naive. The fundamental difficulty with the idea of a creator-god – already identified at the beginning of chapter 1 – is that if 'eternity' and 'infinity' mean what they say, there can have been no beginning of existence in the same way as there can be no end, so the question of a creator simply doesn't arise.

Yet many people who reject the idea of a creator-god still cling to a quasi-theistic belief in 'something out there' – an indefinable 'spiritual presence' that watches over the world rather like a benign grandparent who's seen it all and doesn't worry too much about the transient vagaries and absurdities of its offspring. This view sometimes includes the idea that, if pushed too far, this 'presence' or 'higher power' *could* intervene.

'There are more things in heaven and earth, Horatio, than are dreamed of in your philosophy,' said Shakespeare's Hamlet. Some of us are inclined to go along with that, without feeling the need to discover what those 'more things' might be. Life is puzzling, we may say, and that doesn't mean there has to be a solution to the puzzle. But many theists believe those unsolved mysteries point to an all-knowing God for whom there are no mysteries. (The rationalist-atheist, on the other hand, may anticipate that all mysteries will ultimately yield to the instruments of science.)

A modern Hamlet could equally say: 'There are more things in the human psyche, Horatio, than are dreamed of in your philosophy.' Sigmund Freud and his disciples would have cheered at that; Freud once remarked that the conscious mind is like the tip of an iceberg, meaning that most of what is going on inside us is inaccessible to us, even if we were to surrender ourselves, for years on end, to the ministrations of psychoanalysis. More recently, in *Strangers to Ourselves* (2002), Timothy Wilson wrote that the conscious mind is more like a snowball on the tip of that iceberg, since so much of who we are remains hidden to us.

If we are, indeed, strangers even to ourselves, ignorant of most of what's going on 'in here', then we shouldn't be surprised when we find it impossible to imagine what the mysterious but influential 'something out there' might be like. A disembodied mind of inconceivable power and energy? Some Natural Law that is the source of all other natural laws, like the fruitlessly dreamed-of Theory of Everything or the philosophically discredited Uncaused First Cause? A unifying life force as active in the operation of the cosmos as in the affairs of mere mortals? An Infinity of

Existence that unites all existence? In *A God for This World* (2000), the Australian theologian Scott Cowdell writes of God as the soul of the world that is inseparably 'in, with and under' all the struggles of human life, and the novelist Amanda Lohrey has one of the characters in *The Short History of Richard Kline* (2015) refer to 'a cosmic consciousness, a form of intelligence that pervades everything . . . you swim in the ocean of that consciousness like a fish in the sea'.

Is your head spinning? The fourteenth-century English mystic and hermit Robert Rolle thought he had it sorted: 'He truly knows God perfectly that finds Him incomprehensible and unable to be known.' Yet even old Robert, opting unequivocally for level 1, was prepared to say 'Him'.

It is precisely this kind of puzzle that leads many people to abandon any quest for an understanding of God and simply to lose interest in the whole idea. Others, like Rolle, may cling to a concept of God they say is so far beyond human understanding, there's no point in trying to articulate it, let alone argue about it. Such people may find the very idea of 'reasonable' faith repugnant, because it seems to diminish the grandeur of their idea of God.

> 'Don't ask me to tell you who or what God is. I just don't think about it. If you pushed me, I'd say there's got to be something out there. This can't all be an accident. I certainly don't go along with the idea of a God as anything like a person, or even a God that cares about me and my kids. But when I think about the way the world works, or even the way the universe hangs together, it does seem pretty unlikely it was just due to chance. On the other hand, I don't really think about these things most of the time, to be honest. I just get on with it, unless one of my kids asks me an awkward question. If someone said to me, 'No, there's no God – it's all a big mistake,' I don't think it would make much difference to

my life. I'd still think there's some power, or some . . . I don't know. Something greater than ourselves. I've read Richard Dawkins and I see what he's driving at, but I still think there's more going on than meets the eye. It's not about biology – it's about theology, I guess, or psychology. People say religion is just a human construct to satisfy the human need for something to believe in. Well, okay, but where did that need come from? I think you can't ignore the spiritual dimension. There's got to be something, or someone, out there.'—*Ricky*

A brief history of the death and revival of God

In 1882, the German philosopher Friedrich Nietzsche famously declared that 'God is dead'. Nietzsche was a bit like the Marshall 'the medium is the message' McLuhan of his day: a broad and intuitive thinker given to grand generalisations that sometimes seemed to go too far. (You can almost imagine Nietzsche saying, as the Canadian McLuhan supposedly did: 'By the time I've said something, I've already changed my mind.') Much of what Nietzsche wrote was in the form of rather cryptic notes published after his death, and philosophers are still deeply divided on the question of how seriously he should be taken.

Nevertheless, his pronouncement of the death of God was widely interpreted as predicting the eventual death of religion, too; if there were no God, what could be the point of religion? (This was a naive assessment since, as we have seen in chapter 2, there's more to religion than God.)

In 2012, another cheeky philosopher, Alain de Botton, wrote a book called *Religion for Atheists* suggesting ways that atheists might gain access to some of the benefits of religious faith and practice without actually believing anything, but that was never a serious response to Nietzsche. In any case, there already is a kind of religion for atheists: Buddhism. Though Buddhism is conventionally described as one of the world's four great religions, many Buddhists resist 'religion', preferring to call it a philosophy, or a mental discipline, without a deity. They are not alone in that; many people follow traditional religious practices without believing in a deity. The concept of 'cultural Jew' makes perfect sense in the Jewish context, and there is a growing band of 'cultural Christians', too – people who observe the Christian festivals, sign up, broadly speaking, to Christian values, admire Jesus of Nazareth as a prophet, teacher and exemplar, send their children to Christian schools, but profess no faith in a supernatural God. They may well describe their Christianity as a philosophy rather than a religion.

Nietzsche's claim that God is dead was based on two observations about life in nineteenth-century Europe. First, in Nietzsche's increasingly secular, post-Enlightenment world, the idea of transcendence (an 'out there' God, beyond and independent of the universe) was losing its grip on the culture.

Nietzsche's second observation was that, in a society adjusting to the idea that morality is subjective and relative, the traditional idea of God as the ultimate source of objective and absolute morality was indeed dying, if not dead.

Following the pronouncement of the death of *that* God, Christian believers either shrugged and went right on believing in *their* God, or began looking for new ways to think about the very nature of God. In the wake of Nietzsche, many twentieth-century Christian theologians tried to recast our thoughts about God in ways that would avoid the whole idea of a god that could conceivably be dead or alive. For example, the German theologian Rudolf Bultmann urged Christians to recognise the supernatural aspects of Christianity as mythology and to focus on the life and death of Jesus Christ, not the resurrection. He believed that the endless quest for historical proof of the miraculous events reported in the New Testament was really an inward quest for faith. For him, the resurrection was not a bodily thing, but a metaphor for the rise of Christian faith in the wake of the crucifixion. Needless to say, Christians who not only believe that the resurrection literally happened but use it as the main justification for their faith have been appalled by Bultmann's argument, but he turned a decisive corner in the development of Christian thought and, for many people, there was no turning back.

Writing at the same time, the German American theologian Paul Tillich – widely hailed as one of the great thinkers of the twentieth century – proposed that we should conceive of God as 'the Ground of our being' while not itself a being. This allowed Tillich to sidestep traditional arguments for or against the existence of God as a supreme-being-in-itself and yet to regard God as the ultimate source of meaning and purpose in our lives. In *The Shaking of the Foundations* (1948) he wrote that we are estranged from others and ourselves because we are estranged from this unifying Ground that gives us a sense of the origin and aim of our life. As a result, he believed, 'We are separated from the mystery, the depth and the greatness of our existence.' Currently fashionable talk of being 'grounded' points to a similar idea: that our lives need a foundation of meaning and purpose, not only to make sense of our own existence but also to equip us to live rich lives, fully engaged with society and responsive to others' needs.

The 1960s was a revolutionary time in Christian theology, as in many other aspects of Western culture, from music and art to politics and education (the Beatles, the waves of student protests in Paris and around the world, the anti-Vietnam War demonstrations, the Prague Spring, the anti-nuclear-weapons campaigns, 'flower power', psychedelic drugs, hippies, New Age gurus etc.). In 1963, an English Anglican bishop, John Robinson, shocked many Christians – though not many theologians – with his book

Honest to God, in which he echoed some of Tillich's arguments, especially those in favour of rescuing God from a kind of 'supranaturalism' and reinterpreting the idea of transcendence to take it away from the childish notion of an 'old man in the sky' presiding over a triple-decker universe. Robinson encouraged Christians to be more honest about what they *actually* believed, and how they *actually* experienced faith, rather than simply mouthing the pieties of antiquity. He was responding, eighty years later, to the same kind of situation that had led Nietzsche to pronounce God dead, but Robinson's project was radically different from Nietzsche's: he wanted to revive Christian faith by sweeping away some of its rigid and simplistic approaches to the idea of God.

In 1965, the English theologian Leslie Weatherhead published *The Christian Agnostic*, proposing that agnosticism about many of the traditional doctrines of the Christian church (virgin birth, resurrection, Jesus as the Son of God, the Bible as the inerrant word of God etc.) was not incompatible with a deep and meaningful Christian faith, and that too many so-called believers had placed their faith in the kind of God that simply could not exist. He wrote: 'No honest mind can exclude doubt, or ignore criticism, or shut its ears against reason. And if we could do these things we should be left, not with faith, but with a head-in-the-sand superstition.'

Over four decades, the now-retired American Episcopalian bishop John Shelby Spong published a series of worldwide bestsellers, including *Rescuing the Bible from Fundamentalism* (1991), pointing out the dangers – in his view, the absurdities – of trying to cling to literal interpretations of scripture as a basis for understanding God. According to Spong, new religious insights always emerge out of the old traditions as they begin to die.

The UK philosopher, theologian and Anglican priest Don Cupitt has gone further: his 'sea of faith' movement (the name borrowed from a line in Matthew Arnold's poem 'Dover Beach') sees God as no more than a projection of the human desire for faith – 'an imaginary focus for the religious life'; a potent symbol or metaphor that has no objective reality beyond the practice of religion. Although he has done nothing but try to wrestle with the possible meanings of 'God', Cupitt's critics label him an atheist – or at least a non-Christian – as many have labelled Bultmann, Tillich, Robinson, Weatherhead and Spong.

The mass readership of such authors – and the *New York Times* bestseller *Zealot: The life and times of Jesus of Nazareth* (2013) by Reza Aslan – says something about the appetite for a new interpretation of religion in a Western world no longer as willing as it once was to embrace supernatural notions of God nor to engage with institutional religion in the traditional way. *One* kind of god may be dead, but the yearning for *some* kind of god lives on.

> 'When I finally left the church I was attending, I started spending more time with friends who were quite militant atheists. Everything they said made sense, and I started talking the talk – I was sounding quite militant myself. It was true that once I stepped away from it, I could see there was a lot of crazy stuff about the beliefs I used to have . . . and yet, something was missing. Partly, I missed the habit of churchgoing – the structure, the rituals, even the formality of it. Once that went, there was nothing in my life to replace it. And even those beliefs – I started to feel as if they did have some value as metaphors, or myths, even when I could no longer think of them as being literally true. Strangely enough, it was only after I had left the church that I started thinking more seriously about what I really believed. That has gone on for twenty years. I still read books about religion and spirituality, and I still go to church at Christmas and Easter – I love all the music – though I don't dare tell my atheist friends I do. I think what I've come to realise is that it's not simply an intellectual exercise, like they

> think it is. Life is a bit empty without faith in something greater than ourselves – the challenge is to work out what that might be. Love? Goodness? Is that what God is? I suppose the idea of God hasn't left me, and I might yet be able to find some way of making sense of it.'—*Mitch*

When theologians' definitions of God become more and more removed from the traditional notion of a supreme being, the line between believers and non-believers becomes more and more blurred. And who will be the one to decide where – or if – that line should now be drawn? In *The Unheard Cry for Meaning* (1978), Viktor Frankl suggested that the concept of God need not be 'theistic' at all. His own operational definition, formulated when he was a teenager and returned to in old age, was an entirely interior one: 'God is the partner of your most intimate soliloquies' (a neat combination of level 4's Imaginary Friend and level 5's Spirit Within Us).

For theologians like Cupitt, it does rather appear as though all vestiges of the traditional idea of God have gone, to be replaced by an essentially psychological concept that allows Cupitt to cling to the word 'god' as a name given to the human need for there to be one.

As the US psychologist Abraham Maslow wrote in *Religions, Values and Peak-Experiences* (1964):

> Even the word 'god' is being defined by many theologians today in such a way as to exclude the conception of a person with a form, a voice, a beard etc. If God gets to be redefined as 'Being itself,' or 'the integrating principle in the universe,' or as 'the whole of everything,' or as 'the meaningfulness of the cosmos,' or in some other non-personal way, then what will atheists be fighting against? They may very well agree with 'integrating principles' or 'the principle of harmony'.

The Western retreat from the God of traditional, institutional religion has coincided with a revival of pantheism, the most ancient religion of all. Pantheism imagines God as somehow embedded in nature; the creator integral to the creation or, less mystically, the planet Earth itself; a living being that sustains us and must, in turn, be respectfully (even worshipfully) tended by us. The latest scientific manifestation of this idea is the 'Gaia hypothesis' co-developed by scientists James Lovelock and Lynn Margulis, borrowing the name from a Greek goddess. In popular books such as *The Revenge of Gaia* (2006), Lovelock presents the idea that earth is a self-regulating system at risk of disruption by human activity. The motivation of true pantheists goes one step further than the scientists: they think the natural world *is* God and it is therefore appropriate to revere it.

Who created whom?

The biblical story of creation (Genesis chapter 1) is quite explicit about God creating Man 'in his image' (note the masculine gender, inevitable in a masculinist culture). Though atheists and agnostics – and most Western Christians – might dismiss that as neither literal fact nor even metaphor but simply wild poetic licence, the concept of Man-in-God's-image has had remarkably enduring cultural power. It has encouraged a human-centric view of the universe: we are the creatures closest to God; we resemble God in some mystical sense; we are therefore uniquely positioned to have a relationship with God.

Not surprisingly, believers in that idea welcome it as a sign that humans alone reflect something of the character of their creator. (The sceptics' counter-argument is obvious: even as a metaphorical narrative, it makes no sense to talk of a creator and one of its creatures as though they could have some qualities in common, just as it would make no sense to assume that a baker has the same qualities as bread, or a watchmaker as a watch.)

From the perspective of people at level 5, the idea of a god creating humans is both inconceivable and pointless: it's an idea that simply doesn't work in the language of spirituality. For them, as for atheists and many agnostics, the correct interpretation of the creation story is simply that 'Man created God in his image', given that the early books of the Bible, including Genesis, reflected the culture of their time and were written by unknown authors grasping for a human metaphor to tell their story.

The psychoanalyst Carl Jung, himself a Christian firmly located at level 5, saw it rather differently. In *Psychology and Religion* (1938), he wrote: 'We do not create "God", we choose him.' Jung's point seems to have been that God is always present in the human psyche – as the unconscious mind is always present – and we can choose either to engage with this aspect of our psyche or ignore it. (This was part of Jung's general view that we choose who we will become.) He described most of his clients as 'lost sheep': people who had lost their faith and, with it, a crucial source of the meaning of their life. So convinced was Jung of the idea that God is an aspect of the human psyche that he spoke of our potential *knowledge of* God rather than mere *belief in* God, and felt that conventional religious symbols were often inadequate in pointing to this deep inner reality.

The contemporary German Canadian mystic Eckhart Tolle agrees with Jung, but expresses the point slightly differently in *The Power of Now* (2004): 'I don't call it finding God, because how can you find that which was never lost, the very life you are?' In fact, Tolle prefers to avoid the word 'God' altogether, partly because he believes it has been consistently misused over millennia, and partly because it implies an entity independent of us. 'God is Being,' he says, 'not a being.'

By contrast, Don Cupitt believes that creating God in our image is precisely what we do, in the sense that we conceive of a god that can satisfy our yearning for there to *be* a god, and we choose to believe only in the kind of god we can imagine – just as the author of Genesis did, all those thousands of years ago.

> 'I still remember the moment when it suddenly dawned on me that we had created God in our image. I was sitting in church, believe it or not, and I realised all my doubts and confusions were about that one idea – that God had created us in his image. I mean, it's obviously a poetic thing – a lovely thing in its way – but it would do your head in if you tried to think about it in a literal way. I mean, where would you start? I don't think it's even a matter of faith; I think I have more faith in the goodness of people now than I ever had before. It was a real liberation to walk away from that. It was like the second stage in my proper conversion. The first was when I was about twelve years old and I looked up into the sky one day and said to myself, 'No way, there couldn't be a god up there. If there is a god, it's not that kind of god.' We live and learn, I guess. I've still got some way to go, but at least I feel as if I'm heading in the right direction – inwards rather than upwards!' —*Dean*

People who are content to stick with level 1, conceiving of God only as a mysterious 'higher power' or 'something out there', will typically claim that they never imagined the 'something' as having human qualities. Indeed, they may well object that when people try to ascribe to God such human qualities as loving, avenging or judging, the essential mystery of that 'something' is diminished: 'If God is just a bigger, grander version of us, I'm not particularly awestruck by that.'

Those operating at level 5 conceive of God as the source of all that is most noble and wonderful in *human* nature: love, compassion, kindness, grace, tolerance, sensitivity, fairness, forgiveness, courage and creativity. They see these things, metaphorically, as evidence of a 'divine spark' within us, as did the eighteenth-century English poet Alexander Pope in his famous line: 'To err is human; to forgive, divine.'

Most people would simply call such admirable qualities by their names and leave it at that. But many theists, including some at level 5, claim that because humans are rather unattractive creatures in their natural state – easily distracted by self-interest, gripped by assorted passions, blinded by ambition or greed, capable of aggressive and even violent behaviour towards each other – such 'unnatural' motivations as compassion or forgiveness must come from a higher plane of consciousness or reflect a higher sense of purpose than is normal for humans.

Talk of a 'higher purpose' naturally appeals to believers in a supreme being, because it seems to imply something transcendental. 'Yes,' they will say, 'those noble qualities on your list come to us from somewhere beyond us, and I happen to know where they come from – God.'

In response, the atheists, doubters and sceptics may say: 'Why can't we just accept that the impulse to behave well – even gloriously, jaw-droppingly well – comes from within us? If it did come from God, that would surely mean God was within us.' (Which was precisely Jung's point.)

Christianity's big idea: 'God incarnate'

Many mainstream Christians believe that Jesus of Nazareth was, quite literally, God in bodily human form ('God incarnate'). In the words of the Australian theologian Bruce Kaye, 'God revealed himself in a particular person at a particular time and place.' That's why such Christians resist any attempt to bracket their God with other gods that might be the focus of other faiths but were never incarnate.

By no means all Christians believe that Jesus *was* God, but those who do are naturally quite comfortable talking about God in human (and specifically masculine) terms, ascribing to God such human characteristics as mind, will, choice, emotion, and the capacity for judgement, revenge, punishments or rewards. Belief in the incarnation of God via the divinity of Jesus has created some obvious complications for the Christian concept of God. It's easier for the Jews: when Old Testament writers referred to 'the Lord', this unambiguously meant 'God'. In the New Testament – and among contemporary Christians – 'the Lord' is generally taken to mean 'Jesus', but is interchangeable with the traditional father-figure God as well (indeed, John's Gospel has Jesus saying 'I and the Father are one'). Then there's the Holy Spirit, yet another manifestation of God, introduced in the second chapter of a New Testament book called The Acts of the Apostles and referred to by conservative Christians as 'the *person* of the Holy Spirit'. So it's easy to see why Christians had to come up with the idea of a Trinity – Father, Son and Holy Spirit – as their concept of the 'godhead' became more complicated.

But it didn't happen quickly. In *A Short History of Myth* (2005), Karen Armstrong points out that the doctrine of the Holy Trinity was devised by Greek theologians of the fourth century as a deliberate piece of myth-making – a non-rational way of expressing an idea about God: 'As Gregory, Bishop of Nyssa (335–395), had explained, Father, Son and Spirit were not objective, ontological facts but simply "terms that we use" to express the way in which the "unnameable and unspeakable" divine nature adapts itself to the limitations of our human minds.' Then, in the manner of these things, the idea took hold and became a doctrine of the church; a 'fact' about the Christian God that has provoked endless theological debate.

The Swedish philosopher and mystic Emanuel Swedenborg (1763) saw the trinity simply as a metaphorical way of describing three aspects of one God, as opposed to the complexity of 'God in three persons'. For Swedenborg, the Father was the mind (the thought), the Son was the body (the action) and the Spirit was the influence (the effect on others). In that sense, we are all walking, talking trinities, capable of expressing the three aspects of our 'divine' nature: a mind possessed by the spirit of loving-kindness, a body that acts compassionately and the benign influence that flows from that to the world around us.

What if God *is* Love?

There is an entirely different way of thinking about 'God incarnate' that doesn't involve belief in Jesus as God. This is the idea that God exists *only* in the lives, and through the interactions, of ordinary mortals – the classic level 5 view.

Support for this way of thinking comes from some New Testament references to the nature of God. While theological debate rages over the intention of these statements, with some theologians staunchly resisting the idea that they should be regarded as *definitions* of God, they have profoundly influenced the views of those Christians (including Christian agnostics) whose understanding of godliness does not depend on there being *a* God.

The first reference is in John's Gospel (John 4:24): 'God is spirit, and those that worship him must worship in spirit and truth.' The idea that God is spirit makes perfect sense to those who have rejected the idea of a supreme being, an 'out there' creator-god or a punitive judge. For them, the idea of *spirit* brings God closer to their experience and resonates with their idea of a spiritual life. It also removes many of the difficulties people have in trying to imagine God: *God is spirit* presents no difficulty for people who are accustomed to talking about all kinds of spirit in everyday life – school spirit, the spirit of adventure, the Christmas spirit, the spirit of enterprise, the spirit of optimism, or the zeitgeist (the spirit of the age). In none of those cases do we ever think of the spirit as existing independently of the people who are experiencing it. The Christmas spirit, for example, is within and among us, and nowhere else.

Imagining God as *spirit* removes many of the intellectual difficulties people have traditionally had with the idea of God as a being with the capacity to intervene in human affairs. For example, the eternal question of why God would 'allow' certain things to happen in the world (war, disease, pain, suffering, poverty, inequality) simply evaporates for people who no longer cling to the idea of a God with a 'mind' or 'will' like ours.

Next question: what *kind* of spirit might God be? In response, some Christians point enthusiastically to one of their favourite New Testament verses: 'Whoever does not love does not know God. For God is love' (1 John 4:7). That proposition – *God is love* – resonates strongly with people across the entire spectrum of Christian faith because it seems to capture the essence of the teachings of Jesus himself, which were about compassion, tolerance and the need to behave charitably, especially towards those who are most different from us. So 'God is love' wraps those teachings into one neat idea: the best way to think of God is to think of Love (let's give it a capital L in this context).

Taken together, these two verses explain why the spirit of loving-kindness is often regarded as the defining characteristic of the Christian life – which is not to suggest that Christians have it on their own, since many non-Christian lives are similarly motivated. It is only to acknowledge that, at least in theory, this is what lies at the heart of Christian faith and values. God conceived as 'the spirit of loving-kindness' is a far cry from any talk of cosmic minds or 'something out there', since it's very clearly 'in here', for a start. It's also the polar opposite of a wrathful, edgy, jealous, vengeful or prescriptive ruler of the universe – which is presumably why some

Christians have trouble reconciling the Old and New Testament versions of God.

> ‘When I think about God these days, all I can think of is that verse that says ‘God is love’. It was painted on the wall of the church I grew up in, so I guess it's forever printed on my mind. But I like it – it says all you really need to say. And if that's what God is, then it's pretty obvious what ‘putting your faith in God’ means. It means you're putting your faith in the power of love. I just wish that was more obvious among the Christians I know. A lot of them aren't really that loving when it comes to people with different opinions from theirs. Some of them obviously can't wait for the infidels to be punished.’—*Cathy*

Godliness – holiness – wholeness

The idea of a spirit of loving-kindness – charity, compassion – being present in and among us is not particularly hard for most of us to grasp. We know such a spirit exists because we experience it as both givers and receivers, we note its effects on human interactions and, conversely, we observe the disastrous effects on people when it is withheld from them.

And it's easy to see the difference between that *motivational* form of love and *emotion-based* forms – romantic love, parental and familial love, love of friends, love of food, love of pets, love of autumn, love of the bush or the ocean, love of a good book, love of the latest IT gadget. By contrast, expressions of ‘godly love’ – like compassion for the disadvantaged or oppressed, kindness to strangers in distress, or a willingness to listen attentively and patiently to someone's story – aren't necessarily accompanied by positive emotions at all. They are better thought of as the product of a particular psychological/spiritual predisposition, a frame of mind, a permanent state of readiness and willingness to act kindly. It's the sort of love that exists independently of liking someone; the kind of love that makes sense of the saintly concept of 'loving the unlovely'.

For people at level 5 who embrace the idea that this kind of love is what God *is*, the proposition that 'God is dead' is unthinkable because it would imply the death of loving-kindness.

> 'The thing that always keeps me coming back to the idea of Christianity is that it's supposed to be a religion of love. It often isn't, but the fact that it's meant to be a source of love in the world – charity, compassion, tolerance – is still very appealing to me. And you do come across it in some people – people who are unobtrusively devoted to making the world a better place by acting in a loving way towards everyone. They are often very humble people. I admire them. I envy them, actually. I'm sure they are not all Christians, but some are. And maybe religion, when it's working properly, does foster that in people. I've seen the opposite as well – religious people who are angry or prejudiced or cruel or arrogant – but the thing is, you feel they are letting down their religion. That's real hypocrisy, to say you belong to a religion of love and then act in such an unloving way.' —*Dean*

Those who have found spiritual meaning and satisfaction at level 5 are inclined to regard all other possible meanings of God as elaborate and redundant constructs, though some of them may occasionally wonder about the 'something out there' – not as a source of godliness, but as a separate question, belonging more to the realm of physics than faith.

The 'God is love' proposition certainly shifts the basis of the argument; no one is going to argue that the spirit of loving-kindness doesn't exist, but only whether that selfless, transformative kind of love comes from within us, or from somewhere beyond us. Even those who think it is within us are divided into the same old camps: atheists, who think 'godliness' is simply an esoteric name for an aspect of human nature that might just as well be called 'goodness' or 'loving-kindness'; theists, who think those qualities are evidence of God at work in us; and agnostics, who aren't prepared to take either side in that debate because they can't see how it would make any practical difference either way.

When conservative theists argue that a loving, compassionate, altruistic disposition is but a pale shadow of an infinitely grander, divine version of those qualities, they are treading a well-worn path of philosophical argument stretching back at least to Plato (pupil of Socrates, teacher of Aristotle, founder of the Athenian Academy). Plato believed that every quality in human life was merely a particular, specific, human expression of a perfect, spiritual 'form' of the quality that existed only in the realm of the gods. For example, he argued that we could never directly perceive Truth, Beauty or Justice in their pure form; we could only ever encounter their rather feeble 'particulars' in human life – a poor substitute for the real thing, but the best we mere mortals could manage.

That's why traditional theists believe there must be more to godliness than anything we normally mean when we speak of love, kindness, charity, grace or compassion in everyday life. How else, they will say, would we find the motivation to behave well towards someone we don't know, someone we may never see again, or someone who has treated us badly? Why would we place our own safety at risk to go to the aid of someone who isn't a 'loved one'? Why would we resist the dictates of our own ego in order to contribute to the common good?

The non-theistic answer to such questions would be to say that we are all bound together by our common humanity and that, as social beings who rely on communities to sustain us, we are culturally conditioned – and may even be genetically programmed – to be cooperative and to subordinate our own needs, at least sometimes, to the needs of the wider community.

A spiritual extension of the idea of unity or connectedness is captured in a greeting widely used in yoga classrooms all over the world: *Namaste.* There are many ways of interpreting that ancient Sanskrit word, still in everyday use in India. The simplest and most common seems to be: *The divine in me acknowledges the divine in you,* implying that the quality of divinity is simply an aspect of human nature that we all share – a point made explicit by Karen Armstrong in *A Short History of Myth.* This is not to suggest there is an external Divinity that is the source of the divinity within us; simply that there is a 'divine' aspect of our nature that can be acknowledged and nurtured.

There are more elaborate interpretations of *Namaste.* One yoga expert tells me that the full meaning is: *I honour the place in you of love, of light, of truth, of peace, and if you are in that place in you, and I am in that place in me, then there is only one of us.* The underlying proposition here is not supernatural, but simply that the 'divine' aspect of our common nature is the basis for a spiritual affinity and sense of connection between us.

Viewed in these terms, godliness is much the same concept as 'holiness', which is, in turn, just a religious word for 'wholeness'. In fact, the line of demarcation between godliness and wholeness seems impossible to draw; they are two ways of expressing faith in the 'spiritual' idea that compassionate love is the greatest thing in the world.

> 'The thing I ask myself, ever since I gave that whole man-in-the-sky thing the flick, is this: what difference would it make to my life if I thought that Christian love came from some supernatural source? Answer: zilch. In fact, I despise some of the religious zealots who devalue other people's essential goodness, as if they can't really be loving and kind unless they buy into one particular idea of God. Those days are gone for me.' —*Cathy*

You might have noticed that this discussion of possible meanings of God has barely touched on the question of formal religious doctrine or dogma. Faith is like that: it transcends specific, prescriptive beliefs, and many people have spoken of their liberation from dogma as a prerequisite to faith – especially faith in the idea that God is the spirit of loving-kindness, no more and no less. Whether we choose to place our faith in any god at all is rarely a matter of which boxes we're prepared to tick. Faith is a product of the imagination (you might even choose to call it the 'divine imagination'); dogma is the product of an institution.

'Why don't you ever talk about God?'

Another lunchtime in the park. Another sandwich shared by Peter Munro and Laurie Turner (the man from chapter 4 whose wife died when she was hit by a motorcycle). Out of the blue, Laurie said, 'I used to be a churchgoer, you know, but only for Fran's sake. I never got anything out of it. Couldn't make head nor tail of it, to be frank. Sounded like a foreign language.'

'I know what you mean,' said Peter.

Laurie turned his head to look at Peter. 'Are you joking?'

'Not at all. I stopped going to church myself, for very similar reasons, when I was about sixteen.'

'So how come you started again?'

Peter had been asked this question many times, most persistently by the selection panel that had finally admitted him to a theological college in Canada.

To Laurie, he simply said, 'I felt something was missing.'

'Yeah. I can relate to that alright. But it's not church that's missing in my case.'

There was a long pause, and then Laurie said, 'Why don't you ever talk about God?'

'Because I'm a clergyman, you mean?'

'Sort of. I guess. After the funeral and everything.' Laurie nearly choked on the word.

'If you had lunch with your dentist,' said Peter, 'would you expect him to talk about teeth?'

'Not quite the same.'

'Oh?'

'You once said you couldn't believe in a god that would be responsible for Fran's death.'

'Of course not. Could you?'

'I don't want to, that's for sure. I just find it a bit unexpected that you don't ever seem to mention God.'

'Laurie, I try to live as if everything I do is "talking about God". It's not very complicated. I believe God is in all the good stuff – the kindness, the courage, the compassion, the charity we show to strangers, the respect we have for each other, our readiness to forgive. Does that make any sense to you?'

Laurie, puzzled and a bit embarrassed, said nothing.

'Sitting with a poor bastard whose wife was killed in an accident is "talking about God", as far as I'm concerned. Plus learning how to keep your mouth shut when words would only get in the way. Communication isn't only about words – you know that as well as I do.'

'I assume you also think there's a god somewhere that inspires you to do these things?'

'I do, but it mightn't be the kind of god you're thinking about. Maybe that's a subject for next time.'

They stood up to go their separate ways.

Before they parted, Laurie said, 'I don't always know what you're talking about, but I rather like talking to you.'

Footnote: We do *say* 'God' rather a lot

Omigod! Or *OMG* in a text or, in the fashionably drawn-out spoken version, *Oh . . . my . . . god!*

God only knows!

Thank God!

For God's sake . . .

God help us!

These IVF doctors are 'playing God'.

My husband thinks he's God – we get along fine as long as I worship him.

God forbid!

That's not to suggest that every time we say the word 'God', even as an expletive or exclamation, we are declaring our belief in the existence of a God. On the contrary, the evidence suggests that the less we believe in a traditional, supernatural, institutionalised God, the more we resort to the use of 'God' in our language.

There's a long history of religion being a rich source of expletives (once known as blasphemy, or 'taking God's name in vain'), not as an acknowledgement of God's existence, but as a way of thumbing your nose at religion: *Strewth* (God's truth); *bloody* (by Our Lady – a reference to Mary, the mother of Jesus); *Jeepers Creepers* (Jesus Christ); and all the slippery variations like *gosh, golly, jeez*.

> 'I've wrestled for years with the meaning of God – swinging backwards and forwards between thinking yes, there is, and no, there isn't – yes, there must be, and no, there can't be. I read, I study, I think. Sometimes I even pray. Last Christmas I had pretty much come to the conclusion that there is no need for a supernatural interpretation of God. I'd been reading a book about godless Christianity and I was quite persuaded by it, even though I still think it's a pretty weird idea, and I'm back to not being sure. Anyway, I found myself at a family gathering – the usual Christmas thing – and I ran into a cousin who's always ribbed me about my faith, even though it's been pretty wobbly most of the time. He himself has always been a rabid atheist – the kind of guy who can't keep his atheism to himself; wants to persuade everyone to give religion away, thinks the world would be a better place without it, no room for God at all. He's a real fan of Dawkins, naturally. Inevitably, he asked me about the state of my 'tortured soul' – that's how he put it, in his rather sneering way – and I said I'd pretty much come to the conclusion that there was no God in the supernatural sense. Guess what he said, with a perfectly straight face? 'Thank God for that.'' —*Jesse*

As with God, so with Jesus: the less we put our faith in the idea of Jesus as God in human form, or as a performer of miraculous deeds, or as the saviour of the world, the more easily we slip his name into colloquial speech:

> *Jesus Christ!*
> *Christ almighty!*
> *Jesus Christ on a bike!*
> *Jesus H. Christ!*
> *Jesus wept* (an actual verse of scripture, that one).

All this reckless talk of God suggests, at the very least, that we grant the word a legitimate place in our vocabulary and therefore in our culture. Whatever other functions language may serve – communication, self-expression, tribal codes designed to exclude outsiders – it remains our most obvious repository of culture. The frequent utterance of 'God' in everyday life also suggests that we have at least a vague notion of what the word might refer to. Existence in language obviously does not imply existence in the world: I can *say* 'three-headed green monster with purple spots' without there having to be one; I can imagine time travel without its being possible.

But God? We might be so comfortable with the word because we know, however unconsciously, that *some* kind of god is integral to our life, however much we may try to deny or conceal it. Many of those most hostile to the idea of a religious deity have deities, and indeed religions, of their own. If we are sufficiently devoted to the accumulation of wealth or power, the achievement of status or fame, or even the pursuit of personal happiness, these things will become our gods. Martin Luther, the man who triggered the Protestant Reformation in the sixteenth century, explained it like this: 'Whatever your heart clings to and confides in, that is really your God.'

Sex, democracy, freedom, scientism, travel, food, education, careers, even spirituality . . . all those things have godlike status for some people. Beside any of them, the spirit of loving-kindness, with or without a religious framework, stacks up quite well as something to revere, especially for anyone who has understood what it means to say that we are social beings whose communities need us as much as we need them.

7

Proving the existence of *which* God?

'God' is one of the most ambiguous words we ever use. Because it refers to something we can only try to imagine, it is always going to be difficult for people to agree on what they mean when they say it.

When someone sets out to prove the existence of God on the basis of either logic or personal experience, their quest is doomed from the start. The reason you've never heard of the definitive proof of God's existence is that there isn't one. Centuries of scholarship and argument have led us nowhere, because there is no reasonable way to prove – or disprove – such a thing. This is a matter of faith, not logic.

Plato thought otherwise: whereas the atheists of ancient Greece believed science had disproved the existence of God (or 'the gods', since the Greeks worshipped many gods), Plato insisted that the *only* pathway to certainty was through science, and he is generally acknowledged as the first philosopher to attempt a proof of the existence of God through formal argument.

For the believer, such intellectual gymnastics are both uninteresting and pointless because they deny the very nature of faith.

You don't commit yourself to believing in something provable: that would be a waste of faith.

But the quest goes on. Some people look to the natural world for their proof: as we saw in chapter 6, a severe weather or seismic event is sometimes interpreted, even today, as 'God's judgement', and the devastating effects of epidemics like AIDS and Ebola virus tempt many religious people to look for a supernatural explanation.

On the other hand, sceptics have long argued that the presence of pain and suffering caused by disease and other natural disasters is evidence that there is *no* creator-god in control of the natural world, since no god would permit, let alone cause, such suffering among its creatures (though, if you were seriously entertaining the idea of 'the mind' of such a paternalistic god, you could just as easily argue that a wise god would build suffering into the system, using adversity as a way of teaching us some important lessons about what it means to be human).

People have always used 'bargains with God' as a test of God's existence in general and God's interest in their personal survival in particular. A person carried away in the surf by a strong rip may pray for survival in return for a commitment to becoming a better person. As we saw in chapter 4, many terrified passengers in aircraft buffeted by severe turbulence have prayed to a God they might previously have barely acknowledged and, again, the deal most often proposed is 'If you get me out of this, I'll become a Christian/live a blameless life/give up the grog/terminate my sexual affair/go to church . . .' or similar offers. It is not known how many of these bargains are kept by the survivors. I would guess very few. Nor is there much evidence to suggest that survivors give God the credit for their survival. Once you're safely on the ground, it's the skill of the pilot you'll most likely praise.

Similarly, people who would claim no religious faith may pray for seriously ill friends or relatives as a last resort: 'There's nothing left to do except pray.'

Theists may say that, in such extreme situations, people turn to God because they have a deep-seated consciousness of the existence of God, and this was the moment to convert that into active faith. Sceptics would merely note that some cries for divine help go unheeded, and some apparently 'miraculous' rescues – like people dug from the rubble several days after being buried by an earthquake – occur in the absence of any appeals for divine intervention. The weakest of all the attempts to prove the existence of God are those based on events that can be equally explained by coincidence or by naturally occurring phenomena, such as medical remissions.

Seeing with the 'eye of faith'

All such logical argument is, in the end, irrelevant to women and men of faith. Once you believe *anything*, you see things differently. The 'eye of faith' is like any other predisposition or preconception – social, cultural, professional or political. As we saw in chapter 1, our own convictions provide a filter through which we view the world. If you're a social democrat, the ills of rampant free-market conservatism seem obvious to you. If you're an economic conservative, you may see 'welfare' as a burden on the system. If you're an ardent supporter of a particular sporting team, you'll interpret everything you hear about its players (even nasty stuff about drug use or loutish off-field behaviour) in the most charitable terms possible; the same information about the members of other teams will reinforce your existing negative attitudes towards them. (In love, war, commerce and sport, few people harbour charitable feelings towards their rivals.) If you believe in astrology, you'll see the 'proof' of it in everyone whose behaviour conforms to the pattern you associate with their star sign.

> 'I know it's ridiculous. I know there couldn't be anything in it. Yet there is something in it. It can't all be coincidence. After I've got

> to know someone a bit, I can usually pick their star sign. Sometimes I check, and I'm nearly always right. It's just so obvious that there are these different personality types, and their characteristics are very apparent once you start looking for them. I notice it especially at work – there's this one man in our office who is such an Aries, it's, like, laughable. People talk about control freaks, or paranoia, or obsessive compulsives – all that stuff – but astrology cuts straight to the chase. The star sign says it all. I'm a Virgo and you can see that in my extreme tidiness, my cautious approach to relationships, my tendency to perfectionism. I've always been like that, but it became clearer to me, and I understood why, when I started studying astrology. I've heard all the arguments against it, but the evidence is right there in my own experience. Totally. If you study it, you'll come to the same conclusion.'—*Renée*

The UK economist E.F. Schumacher, author of the bestselling *Small is Beautiful*, wrote in *A Guide for the Perplexed* (1977) that 'higher grades of significance and Levels of Being cannot be recognised without faith and the help of the higher abilities of the inner man'. That's an intellectual's way of saying that faith – in *something* – is the precursor to making sense of life's deeper mysteries. It is also another way of saying that, once we're equipped with the eye of faith, we will tend to see what we're looking for.

Our ability to see things we want to see is legendary, as is our tendency to notice things that were always there but have suddenly become relevant to us: as soon as you've booked your trip to Cuba, stories about Cuba will start popping up everywhere. When you come across information about something that's on your mind – like the prospect of terminating a relationship, the possibility of undergoing cosmetic surgery, the idea of moving house or training for a new career – your selective perception may turn a passing remark by a friend or a news item in the media into 'a message' designed specifically for you. And that process affects the seeker after religious truth as much as anyone else. Our beliefs, predispositions and expectations all strongly influence what we see and hear.

Visions and visitations

Sometimes we see things even when they could not possibly be there – like recently bereaved people who 'see' the figure of the deceased person suddenly in the room with them. In *Hallucinations* (2012), the neurologist Oliver Sacks relates the story of a fourteen-year-old girl visiting her grandparents' house six months after her grandfather had died. She was in the kitchen, her grandmother was at the sink, her mother was engaged in some domestic chore and the girl was still finishing her dinner at the kitchen table, facing the door to the back porch. As she sat there, the girl told Sacks, 'my grandfather walked in and I was so happy to see him that I got up to meet him. I said, "Grampa," and as I moved towards him, he suddenly wasn't there.' The grandmother was so visibly upset by the incident, the girl thought she might have been angry with her. When she told her mother that she really had seen her grandfather, her mother replied, 'You saw him because you wanted to.' The girl claimed she had not been consciously thinking of him and was at a loss to understand how she could have seen him so clearly.

To experience hallucinations that seem utterly real is not to prove anything supernatural, but only to remind us what a complex and unpredictable organ the brain is. As Sacks has demonstrated, the experience of hallucinatory voices, visions and illusions of 'presence' can seem as vivid as if they were real – and they are real in the sense that they are the result of altered brain states. But all such experiences, whether occurring spontaneously or under the influence of drugs, are irrelevant to any notion of spirituality, let alone the existence of a supreme being.

The impact of visions or voices – *I really thought she was talking to me but when I looked, there was no one there* – may be inspiring, frightening or reassuring. Throughout history, people suffering from hallucinations have been regarded as special – either especially blest or especially evil. Knowing what we now know about the operation of the brain and central nervous system, we simply acknowledge that such phenomena originate within us and are not the 'visitations' they seem to be.

> ‘I had an extraordinary experience that I suppose would once have been called a vision. I had been involved with a woman called Inga for many years – we lived together in Europe for a while and even after we split up we remained close friends. She told me she was ill, but it didn't sound serious and then, very unexpectedly, I heard that she had died. I was desperately sad, not only because I knew I would never see her again, but because I had not been able to see her before she died or even be with her when she died. Her sister told me she had died alone, which made it all seem worse.
>
> Soon after that, when I was still grieving deeply, I was driving my car and Inga was suddenly beside me, in the passenger's seat, telling me she was okay, it was all okay, that I shouldn't be distressed on her account. We had this beautiful, warm conversation – it seemed perfectly normal, really – and it simply didn't occur to me that this was strange, let alone impossible. I was just so happy to see her and be with her again. Then I was distracted by the traffic for a moment and when I looked back, she had gone. I felt sad that she was no longer there; it was like waking up from a beautiful dream, I guess. But from then on, I felt better about everything.
>
> I can see how strange it must seem that I didn't question what was happening, but I didn't. It was as real to me as it is sitting here talking to you.’—*Daniel*

Sometimes such experiences are spontaneous and puzzling. Sometimes they are reactions to traumatic events, like projections of grief or loss. Sometimes they are experienced by isolated individuals; sometimes by small groups or even crowds. The so-called post-resurrection appearances of Jesus are of that kind: disciples who were in grief and shock over his death by crucifixion were textbook cases of the kind of people most likely to 'see' the risen Christ. (It is notable that evangelical Protestants, who set great store by these alleged post-resurrection appearances, are more sceptical about Roman Catholic claims regarding appearances of the Virgin Mary – for example, in the famous 1916 case of Mary's alleged appearance to three young shepherd girls in a meadow outside the Portuguese hamlet of Fátima.)

The power of prayer

When I was a child, I was told that God always answers prayer, it's just that the answer is sometimes 'no'. (Try telling that to drought-stricken farmers praying for rain.)

If you are convinced that God answers prayer, you will be able to see the supporting evidence all around you through the eye of faith. Because our perceptions are so heavily influenced by our predispositions and expectations, that same evidence will strike a non-believer (or a believer in a different kind of god) as nothing more than welcome coincidence or the result of a vivid imagination.

There's no doubt that reflective, meditative prayer as opposed to a shopping list of requests to the Almighty (known in religious parlance as 'intercessions') can be an effective means of stilling your mind, getting things into a better perspective or seeing the world in a different light. The very experience of praying can clarify your thoughts – or banish unwanted ones – and equip you for a more constructive approach to problems that might previously have seemed intractable. Meditative prayer of this kind is also associated with the 'emptying' of the mind, a discipline widely recommended by mystics of all faith traditions. So the therapeutic benefits to the one doing the praying are potentially very significant – as are the reported benefits of secular meditation. Remember the story of Frederik, in chapter 3, who no longer attends church and is no longer as certain as he once was about the meaning of 'God', but who still prays regularly at bedtime – not asking for things, he says, but just repeating prayers he learnt as a child, as a kind of meditation. He reports that this has a reliably calming effect, and he enjoys saying the familiar words even though they mean less to him now than they once did.

Some studies suggest there may also be positive effects of prayer on the health or wellbeing of the one being prayed for; others do not. This is one of those classic cases where, in the face of contradictory and inconclusive data, we would be wise to suspend judgement. The most famous example – a 2001 study of the alleged positive effects of prayer on female fertility, sponsored by Columbia University and published in the prestigious *Journal of Reproductive Medicine* – turned out to be a monumental fraud.

In the case of anecdotal evidence for the power of prayer, it is always hard to isolate the effects of prayer from a larger pattern of loving and supportive behaviour towards the one being prayed for. And it would be almost impossible to identify which factors were most influential in determining the outcome when, for example, parents pray for the return of wayward children, separated lovers pray to be reunited, or people pray for the safety of loved ones in risky situations.

But this is not a closed question. Who knows what impact activity in the brain of one person, or a large number of people, might have on the brain state or wellbeing of another? So-called paranormal or extrasensory activity, from telepathy to clairvoyance, usually turns out to be no more than intuition or coincidence (or a deliberate trick), though there's growing scientific interest in the phenomenon of telepathy. Who's to say that inter-brain transmission – stimuli sent from one brain to another via electrical impulses – might not occur through channels we don't yet understand? If 'prayer effects' could be demonstrated, it would make more sense, surely, to assume that they were the result of a non-obvious mode of interpersonal influence rather than being the result of supernatural intervention by an omnipotent God whose attention had been drawn to specific cases of hardship or distress.

Since two of our deepest desires are to be taken seriously and to be loved, the news that someone is praying for us can be a deeply affecting and comforting symbol of their concern, and a sign that we are valued by them. An Australian Salvation Army officer who works as a first-response person at the scene of accidents and natural disasters commented in a media interview that he always offers to pray for people affected by the event and has 'never been knocked back'. And why would he be? There's every chance that knowing people are praying for you is itself therapeutic. (If we don't *know* that such prayers are being offered, those social-emotional benefits are not available to us, so if you wanted to study the effects of prayer in a formal research project, the first requirement would be to recruit two matched samples of people in similar need, none of whom would know whether they were in the 'prayed-for' or 'not-prayed-for' group.)

Prayers for peace during times of war might appear to be answered in the long run – since wars always end eventually – but most such prayers imply an appeal for victory, and have been offered with equal fervour by believers on both sides of many conflicts . . . so is the answer 'yes' to one side and 'no' to the other?

The fact that people sincerely believe they are praying to an external god does not mean that such a god exists. When the evidence is so patchy and unconvincing, it seems that prayer is no proof of anything except the undeniably positive effects of quiet contemplation and concentrated meditation.

So is it pointless for religious parents to teach their children to say their prayers at bedtime, as Frederik did? Is saying grace at mealtimes a meaningless ritual? Not at all. Such disciplines help to focus the mind on the need for gratitude and to nurture our loving disposition. When regarded as a form of meditation, bedtime prayers, for children and adults alike, encourage reflection on the events of the day and on the blessing of having family, friends, neighbours and others who care for us. Where such rituals still happen, their intention is honourable and their outcomes more likely to be positive than neutral.

The therapeutic effects and, indeed, the point of prayer are more dubious when the act of praying is thought of as 'wrestling with God' – seeking favours and demanding God's intervention in human affairs and in the operations of the natural world, like death and drought. (Even here, there may be some therapeutic benefit from 'having your say' or 'getting things off your chest' via prayer, especially if you actually believed that you had God's ear.)

> 'One of the things that turned me off church was the emphasis on prayer as a means of asking God for things. I hated the tone of it. There was this one time when the minister was praying for the safe return of a boy who'd been kidnapped – it was all over the news – and everyone was saying loud 'Amens'. When I got home that night, I turned on the TV, and the boy's body had finally been found, abandoned in the bush somewhere. He had been dead for a week. I thought, 'What was the point of praying for him when he was already dead?' and then I thought, 'The whole thing of praying for outcomes like that is really weird.' Like, as if God would be waiting to see if enough people were concerned about this boy to pray for him, and then maybe God would intervene in some miraculous way? I don't think so. I also used to find

prayer meetings an acute embarrassment – everybody trying to outdo each other in public piety. That's how it seemed to me, anyway, especially as there's a verse in the Bible about Jesus saying we should pray in secret – a point that most churchgoers choose to ignore.

And there was this group of men in the church calling themselves a prayer-power group – the leader once told me they had 'a good track record', as if it was like a footy-tipping contest.

Anyway, I gave it all away. Now, to my own surprise, I've joined this Christian meditation group my wife has been going to. It couldn't be less like a prayer meeting. I find it really helpful, actually. It's not about asking anyone for anything – it's about stilling the mind and being open to the spirit. I like that word 'open' – I think that's the key to spirituality, actually. Openness. By the way, no one asks you to define what 'spirit' you're open to – we all have our own ideas about that, I guess. But the orientation is Christian – there's no question about that – and the woman who leads the group often reads something from the Bible or some other source – she calls them her 'wisdom books' – before we start the session. The readings are always about love, one way or another. The leader says we're training ourselves to be more loving.

I always come away thinking that's what prayer really is, or should be. It's a spiritual experience, no question, but I wouldn't call it a religious one.'—*Lee*

'My father was desperately ill, and we were all praying for him. And then I suddenly realised – there's nothing there. It became really clear that we were all expressing what we felt and how badly we wanted our father to recover, but no one was listening. That was the moment when it dawned on me that I was really an atheist. Actually, 'agnostic' would be fairer. I'm still very open to the spirit of goodwill in the world – I just don't think you can pray to it. I express my gratitude in other ways.'—*Raf*

As we have seen in chapter 2, when meditation is specifically focused on the development of a kind and loving disposition towards others, it may well achieve the desired result. For many people of faith, prayer is just like that.

Medical miracles

Seen through the eye of faith, apparently miraculous recoveries from serious illness can seem like signs of divine intervention, especially if they were accompanied by earnest prayer. Yet those same recoveries can seem to non-believers or agnostics like the kind of thing that does sometimes happen – the result of spontaneous remission of a disease, skilful surgical and medical care, or the effects of a drug therapy that works better on some patients than others. And there's always the placebo effect to be taken into account: faith is a powerful if unpredictable phenomenon.

If we were to regard 'miraculous' recoveries in response to prayer as a sign of the existence of a caring, intervening God, then logically we would be obliged to regard the lack of recovery in response to prayer as a sign either of the non-existence of such a God, or of God's heartlessness in particular cases. You can't have it both ways.

Still, the idea that apparently miraculous recoveries have some divine provenance is very persistent. In his 1985 book *How Can We Know?*, the British writer A.N. Wilson describes the apparent restoration of sight in a baby born blind, shortly after the child's eyes were anointed by a priest of the Church of England: 'The Moorfields Eye Hospital in London declared that there was nothing which could be done to restore the child's sight since its optic nerves were dead. But, immediately after the anointing, the child was found to have perfect sight.'

While noting that stories of such healings can be heard in all kinds of churches, Wilson, a Christian, cautions us against claiming miracles as an argument in favour of religion. Today, we would probably conclude that the Moorfields diagnosis was simply wrong, given that modern scanning technology was not then available. Nevertheless, Wilson suggests it would be 'unhistorical and unscientific' not to recognise that, at the very least, there are unexplained phenomena in our midst, 'things which admit of no rational explanation'. Indeed there are, and those processes may one day be better understood, or they may not. Since they occur with remarkable frequency in all cultures and throughout history, it is hardly sensible to brand them as supernatural: they are clearly natural, even if mysterious.

Bella and Penny clash over the cure of a friend's cancer

Wild Thyme has been the scene of some of Bella and Penny's most intimate exchanges – most of them loving and supportive, some of them heated. One Saturday morning, the conversation turned to a mutual friend, Robyn, who had recently celebrated the tenth anniversary of her recovery from ovarian cancer.

'I know you're not a believer, Pen, and I admit I'm wavering myself, but Robyn's recovery is one for the record books, don't you think?'

Penny looked puzzled. 'The record books on what? Ovarian oncology? I agree it was a brilliant result, and I've heard Robyn give her oncologist and surgeon full credit. But what's that got to do with whether I'm a believer or not?'

'Robyn herself says her recovery was the result of her family and friends praying for her. Plus her own faith.'

'Does she now?' said Penny, looking sceptical. 'I've never actually heard her say that – perhaps it depends who she's talking to. I had a conversation with her and a couple of women in our book club who had been oncology nurses, and everyone – including Robyn – seemed to agree she was very lucky the cancer was detected early and that the particular type was amenable to treatment. I'm perfectly happy to acknowledge that faith healing happens, but let's stick to the medical facts in this case, Bel.'

'Well, I can only pass on what I heard Robyn say, out of her own mouth. She thanks God for her recovery, pure and simple. I'm sure she thanks the medical team, too.'

'Too? The medical team who detected it early, removed it and wiped out every trace of it with just the right chemo? Oh, you think she'd acknowledge them, too, do you? Really, Bel!'

Bella hated any conflict with Penny. It didn't happen often, and it was always resolved, but since Penny had left the church, she had become noticeably more aggressive on the subject of faith, and Bella found herself becoming defensive.

'All I can tell you,' Bella said, 'is that Robyn calls it a miracle. Her family thinks the same way. People just seem to accept that it couldn't have happened without all that faith and all that prayer.'

Penny sighed. 'Are you really prepared to believe that all that medical skill would have failed to get the desired result if people had not been praying for Robyn, or if Robyn herself had not been so devout? Really?'

'I'm sorry, Pen, I'm just telling you what Robyn said. I don't know any of the medical details, but I do remember at the time people were saying "miracle" rather a lot.'

'Yes, well, "miracle" is rather overused in all kinds of situations – from underdogs winning football games to kids passing exams they hadn't worked for.'

'Be serious, Pen. This was a pretty dramatic outcome.'

'Dramatic, yes. I'll grant you that. Just don't tell me when the whole force of modern medicine produces a brilliant result that there's anything supernatural about it. Credit where it's due – that's all I'm saying.'

'Fair enough,' said Bella. 'But what would you say if a woman was told by her doctor that he couldn't do anything more for her and she should go home and put her affairs in order, and then her family and friends prayed her back to health?'

'Purely hypothetical, Bel. And I cringe when you say things like "prayed her back to health" as if there were no other explanation. No such thing as natural remissions? No such thing as the immune system doing its thing? Anyway, let's drop it.'

A middle-aged man sitting at the next table folded up his newspaper and rose to leave. He hesitated for a moment and then leant over Bella's shoulder and said very quietly, 'I apologise for intruding, but I couldn't help overhearing part of your conversation. I thought you might like to know that my wife died of ovarian cancer last month. Her doctor did tell her he could do no more for her. He did tell her to go home and put her affairs in order. And I can tell you this: I prayed myself to a standstill, and so did her sister, and so did our daughter.'

'I'm so sorry,' said Bella.

The man smiled a faint smile and went to the counter to pay.

Primitive 'signs'

The burgeoning branch of Christianity called Pentecostalism (appearing in Australia in many guises, ranging from Hillsong to Assemblies of God) includes some churches that are devoted to the regular production of tangible 'signs' – events and experiences that occur during church services – that are taken to be proof of God's existence. In such services, people stimulated by music, and by a large and enthusiastic congregation and emotional appeals from a preacher, may swoon, moan, weep or 'speak in tongues' – a form of babbled, non-lexical speech sometimes called 'glossolalia'.

Such speech is supposed to be a sign of the Holy Spirit descending on the speaker – a reference to the New Testament passage where, after the death of Jesus, a group of disciples meeting on the Jewish day of Pentecost were said to have spoken in other languages as a sign that the Holy Spirit had visited them to compensate for the loss of Jesus. In that account, it was claimed that the onlookers, who included 'Jews from every nation', all understood what was being said in their own native language. That is not the case in the modern Pentecostal setting: the primitive cries of the 'speaker in tongues' need to be interpreted for the audience by a person claiming to be qualified to do so.

In *Fire From Heaven* (1994), the US theologian Harvey Cox suggested that the growing appeal of Pentecostalism is due to a 'primitive spirituality' that bypasses the need for creeds and ceremonies and allows people to recover what he calls 'primal speech, primal piety, and a primal hope' that is invested in a radically new world order. Cox also notes that Pentecostalism chimes with the trend for modern seekers after faith to want an *experience* of God rather than a set of doctrines to believe in.

For Cox, 'the unexpected reappearance of primal spirituality in our time tells us a lot about who we human beings are . . . In an age that has found exclusively secular explanations of life wanting, but is also wary of dogmas and institutions, the unforeseen eruption of this spiritual lava reminds us that somewhere deep within us we all carry a *homo religiosus*.'

Cox does not regard the Pentecostalists' experience as proof of the existence of God, but he does see the phenomenon of Pentecostalism itself as a kind of counterpoint to Western secularism; a sign that our yearning for some form of religious faith or religious expression is powerful and possibly innate.

Ecstatic experiences

Closely related to the 'primitive signs' are the ecstatic experiences which people sometimes interpret as an encounter with God. Such experiences can be induced in many ways, and not only for religious or spiritual purposes: Adolf Hitler's Nazi rallies in prewar Germany were classic cases of the careful manipulation and excitation of crowds in ways that sometimes evoked feelings of ecstasy, and the hysteria of ecstatic teenagers at rock concerts is commonplace.

Snake-handling by certain religious cults has been a reliable source of 'spiritual' ecstasy for some people (documented in detail in William Sargant's 1957 classic, *Battle for the Mind*). Chanting, singing, hand-clapping and listening to stirring music can do it, as can well-orchestrated religious crusades where people eager for inspiration or religious conversion gather in large numbers to hear charismatic speakers. Strobe lighting and other special effects can induce the same ecstatic feelings in some people, and hallucinogenic drugs are a very reliable stimulator: 'magic mushrooms' have been a crucial ingredient in the practices of many primitive religions.

In *Everyday Ecstasy* (1980), the British writer and broadcaster Marghanita Laski examined the social effects of ecstatic experiences and questioned whether such experiences require a religious explanation. She was particularly interested in the power of music, art and the beauty of the natural world to evoke feelings of ecstasy, and she found that people who were uplifted and inspired in secular settings appeared to be experiencing essentially the same responses as those in explicitly religious settings. There was one important difference, though: Laski could find no evidence that the uplift created by such experiences persisted, or led to a more benign or compassionate attitude to others. As we shall see, *participatory* forms of ecstasy are more likely to be life-changing than those in which we are mere spectators to the beauty of art, music or nature. Visiting the opera or an art gallery might feel wonderful, but there appears to be no evidence to suggest that such sensations make us better people.

An article by Ray McBride in *The Psychologist* (2014) reviewed both Laski's work and US psychologist Abraham Maslow's parallel work on 'peak experiences'. McBride describes ecstasy as 'surrendering to an unusual experience involving one or more of the following: intense joyful sensations, euphoria, rapture, elation; feelings of unity and oneness with one's environment; altered or detached perception of space and time; a sense of profundity and release from mundane reality; an ineffable yet rational experience'.

More than a century ago, William James in *The Varieties of Religious Experience* (1902) noted the striking similarities between spiritual and psychotic experiences, and he described how 'cognitive labeling of physiological sensations influences one's experience of emotions'. In other words, the way we interpret an ecstatic experience is likely to be influenced by what we were looking for or what we were told to expect.

Ecstatic experiences that go beyond mere spectatorship are often associated with a sense of heightened spiritual insight. Recent research into the effects of psychedelic drugs on the relief of anxiety in terminally ill patients is producing hard evidence to support the view that drug-induced 'trips' may produce outcomes that are directly comparable to religious ecstasy. In 'The Trip Treatment' (2015), Michael Pollan describes the work of US scientists at New York and Johns Hopkins universities, where experimentation with psilocybin (the active ingredient in 'magic mushrooms') is yielding encouraging results. According to Pollan, some of the scientists undertaking this work can scarcely contain their excitement about its potential applications.

People taking part in the clinical trial of psilocybin typically experience the classic hallucinogenic trip associated with the widespread use of LSD in the 1960s. They report extraordinary journeys through time and space, glimpses of their own approaching death, visually confronting their cancer in ways that reduce its emotional power over them, 'looking into the face of God' and a sense of the oneness of all humanity. 'God is everywhere,' concluded one subject after an experimental session with the drug. Love, peace and joy feature prominently in the reported after-effects of these experiences – effects which appear to persist over time.

Though the project has no religious connotations, many of the effects of psilocybin are reminiscent of religiously induced ecstatic experiences, and 'spiritual' is a term often used by the subjects themselves in trying to put their experience into words. Typically, anxiety about disease and fear of death either diminish or disappear altogether.

The mechanism by which all this happens is still poorly understood, but Pollan quotes a UK neuroscientist, Robin Carhart-Harris, who believes that the psychedelic experience may help people to relax the grip of an overbearing ego and the rigid, habitual thinking it enforces. Carhart-Harris suggests we pay a high price for the achievement of 'order and ego' in the adult mind: 'We give up our emotional ability, our ability to be open to surprises, our ability to think flexibly, and our ability to value nature.' As Pollan puts it: 'The sovereign ego can become a despot', with depression a prime example of this, when 'the self turns on itself and uncontrollable introspection gradually shades out reality'.

What does all this tell us? It suggests that the effects of *participatory* ecstatic experiences are often beneficial and long-lasting but that, since such experiences are relatively easy to induce (for example, by drug use), they are an unreliable basis for belief or non-belief in the existence of God.

The sense of 'God's will'

Some believers will offer, as proof of God's existence, their own powerful sense of 'calling' or the conviction that they have had God's will revealed to them.

In general, such claims do not appear to differ much from other people's accounts of a non-religious sense of conviction: the feeling of being utterly sure of what they should do. Would the believer say that such convictions are evidence of God working in those non-believers, even though they themselves make no such claim? Perhaps it is simply the case that all of us are sometimes gripped by a sense of certainty about what we should do next: *I must dedicate my life to the relief of suffering. This is the person I should marry. I must throw in my job and see what happens.* Such convictions are part of the normal processes of cognition and attitude formation, and they often lead people to claim that they are acting in response to what feels like an external force, beyond their control.

It is not uncommon for people with no religious faith at all to account for their actions as if they were 'driven' to do something, or felt 'compelled' or 'swept away' – rather like 'falling' in love – as though some higher purpose was involved, destined by forces greater than themselves.

> ‘I grew up in a very open-minded household, with strong Christian influence, via the Quakers, but also with a mother who was very committed to yoga. So we always had the example of that spiritual dimension to life from two different perspectives. When I came across a book on Zen, I felt that was really me. I started meditating and it felt like the most natural thing in the world. But it was another twenty years before I encountered Tibetan Buddhism, and that happened because I woke up one morning with the absolutely overwhelming certainty that I must go to Tibet. It was like a voice in my head telling me to go. So I did. I went there and I embraced Tibetan Buddhism and it has taken me in a new direction and led me into a deeper sense of inner stability. I'm not sure how to put it – I can face reality more fearlessly than before. I've learnt how to explore inner reality.’—*Nick*

One of the consequences of such convictions – especially when they are attributed to God's will – is that individuals may accept less personal responsibility for their actions than they otherwise might. One of my friends speaks of her irritation at 'Christians telling you they are doing God's will, as if it's nothing to do with them. Buddhists have to take more responsibility for the consequences of their actions!'

In 2015, Burundi's president, Pierre Nkurunziza, announced that he would run for a third term, even though the country's constitution forbids it. Philip Gourevitch, writing for the *New Yorker* (2015), reported that Burundi's economy was in tatters, its independent press had been silenced, dozens of people had been killed by police and many more had been beaten and terrorised by the youth wing of the president's party. More than 100,000 people had fled the country. With his eyes on that third term, though, Nkurunziza seemed unfazed by all this; according to Gourevitch, 'he says he is in touch with God, and does as God wishes'.

Sometimes, 'the will of God' seems to be used as little more than a pious smokescreen for 'what I really want to do'. I felt 'called' to go to India might mean nothing very different from 'I badly wanted to go to India', or 'I was consumed by curiosity about India', or 'I had a burning passion to save the souls of non-Christian Indians', or 'I've always thought of India as the most exotic place on earth, and I wanted to see it for myself'.

Social pressure to conform to the expectations of a particular group can also generate a sense of vocation. In *Family Romance* (2007), the British writer John Lanchester describes the intense family and cultural pressure in Ireland that had led his own mother to enter a convent twice – once, disastrously, at the age of sixteen and then again at the age of twenty-four, 'to general rejoicing and cries of relief all round'. (After fourteen years, she left the second order and subsequently met and married Lanchester's father.)

This is not to denigrate anyone's sincere sense of vocation, but simply to point out that a conviction so powerful that it feels like a 'call' does not necessarily imply that there is an *external* agent doing the calling.

I once watched, horrified, as the US televangelist Benny Hinn, appealing for money, called on the members of his global TV audience to 'pick up the phone and just give what God is telling you to give'. Perhaps people did feel as if God was telling them to give; perhaps they felt pressured by Hinn's powers of persuasion; perhaps giving made them feel that they were doing a good deed by contributing to a worthwhile cause. But whether any of them actually heard a voice within urging them to send ten dollars, or a thousand, to the Hinn project, who knows?

People do sometimes 'hear voices', as Oliver Sacks reminds us. Auditory hallucinations are as real, as convincing, as any other kind, and woefully inadequate as a proof of God's existence. But if your disposition is to believe that it's God's voice you are hearing, it would not be surprising if you felt compelled to do what the voice was telling you to do. If your disposition was *not* to assume it was the voice of God, then the voice might be ascribed to a devil, a friend, a critic or a mysterious inner presence that seems to have more insight than you do ... or you might simply realise you were hallucinating and seek treatment from a neurologist.

The biblical evidence

It's true that reading the Bible may convince someone of the existence of God, but that is a very different thing from proof. The foundation writings of any religion, sect or political movement cannot logically be used to justify the validity of that religion, sect or movement. Since the entire Bible is *about* God and every word of it *assumes* God's existence, it can hardly be wheeled up as evidence for the existence of God.

When it comes to the interpretation of the Bible, it's all in the point of view. If you regard the Bible as the inspired, inerrant word of God, then you'll approach it rather differently – and attach different levels of significance to its contents – from those who see it as a culturally and symbolically rich collection of books written by myriad and mostly unidentified human authors over almost two thousand years. (The way those books came to be given biblical status is itself a complicated story of ecclesiastical politics and competing points of view among scholars. So were the compilers as inspired as the authors?)

The New Testament obviously has a central role for Christians, and it has been the sourcebook for the most spectacularly successful religious phenomenon in history, in terms of numbers and geographical reach. Although many Christians would stop short of regarding the Bible as being literally true in the way some other document might be judged for its historical accuracy, they would typically regard it as true in the metaphorical sense, accepting the 'inner meanings' of its stories as valid and valuable.

> 'I grew up with Bible stories. They were part of the family. But we never imagined they were supposed to be literally true. It was all about the inner meaning, the metaphorical meaning – just like for Greek myths and other stories, even fairy tales, that have powerful lessons to teach us. So we were very impressed by the resurrection, but it was always presented as a story about the endless cycle of life and death.'—*Nick*

People searching for the *inner* meaning of Bible stories would not, typically, be too fussed by historical inaccuracies or inconsistencies. Variations in the different Gospel accounts of a woman breaking an alabaster box of ointment over the feet of Jesus intrigued Ben Wanderhope, a character in Peter De Vries's 1961 novel, *The Blood of the Lamb*: 'It stands in one Gospel that it happened in the home of a Pharisee in a city called Nain and that "a woman who was a sinner" poured it on his feet. In another it was in Bethany in the home of Simon the leper and that the woman poured it on his head. John says the woman was Mary and that Lazarus was at the table, which it's pretty funny the other writers didn't mention if it's true. One place you read Judas Iscariot objected to the waste, another that all the disciples did.' Perplexed by all that, Wanderhope – a lapsed Calvinist – concludes that the Bible couldn't be infallible.

Those seeking the truth *in* Bible stories, rather than the truth *of* the stories, would be inclined to overlook inconsistencies (or actual fabrications) in the details and focus on the broad thrust, which was that the New Testament writers were devoted to the idea of promoting Jesus not only as the promised Messiah but as the Son of God. Many of the stories that grew up around Jesus after his death by crucifixion were part of the process of deifying him in the eyes of his followers, so that needs to be taken into account when interpreting these writings. Sympathetic readers may choose, for example, to disregard the fact that only Luke locates the birth of Jesus in Bethlehem, rather than Nazareth (apparently to fit in with a prophecy made in the Old Testament book of Daniel). If you're on board with the basic thrust of the message, such things may be regarded as nothing more than quirky footnotes to the larger story.

Interpretation is everything. We will inevitably interpret the Bible in ways that fit with our existing view of the world, of religion, and of God. An entire community of scholars has been occupied over centuries, trying to determine the 'meaning' of this or that passage of scripture, and this process has been swept by as many fashions and fads as any other academic pursuit.

In any case, the business of understanding and assessing the Bible is subject to what I regard as the most basic 'law' of communication, whether of the written or spoken word: *It's not what the message does to the audience, but what the audience does with the message, that determines the outcome* (Mackay, 1994).

To quote A.N. Wilson again:

> The purposes of the Gospels were, of course, to instruct the faithful, to provide illustrations of preconceived religious ideas about Jesus. They are not objective, still less biographical, accounts, and to extract from them any 'objective' saying or truth about some putative 'historical Jesus' has been a task which has always ended in failure. We only have the Jesus in whom the evangelists believed, and in whom Paul believed.

The moral argument

When Nietzsche declared that 'God is dead', part of what he meant, as we saw in chapter 6, was that in a secular age of moral relativism, the idea of an absolute and objective morality emanating from God had lost its force.

But not for everyone. Many believers today still regard their moral code as religious in origin, sometimes attributing its authorship to God, via the reported teachings of Jesus or some more prescriptive biblical passages such as the Ten Commandments. The extraordinary claim is even made by some Christians that if they did not have their Christian faith as an anchor for their morality, it would be a case of 'anything goes', as if it is only the constraints imposed on them by their Christian faith that save them from a life of moral recklessness or nihilism.

Belief or Nonbelief (1997) is a series of remarkably cordial exchanges between the Italian novelist-scholar (and non-believer) Umberto Eco and the Roman Catholic Archbishop of Milan, Cardinal Carlo Maria Martini. In one of their conversations, Martini poses the question: What is the foundation for creating an ethical system if a person cannot call on 'metaphysical principles, transcendental values or even universally valid *categorical imperatives*'? ('Categorical imperatives' is a reference to the philosophical theories of the eighteenth-century German philosopher Immanuel Kant, who thought that the existence of certain moral absolutes, discerned by the conscience of any rational person, were evidence of the existence of God.) Martini found it difficult to imagine how a commitment to such moral ideals as altruism, sincerity, justice and forgiveness could be sustained 'in any and every given circumstance' when their value is not founded either on absolute principles or on faith in a personal God.

Eco's reply, in essence, was that our moral sense grows out of our encounters with each other; it is a social phenomenon that doesn't rely on absolute principles at all. 'As we are taught by the most secular of the social sciences,' he wrote, 'it is the other, his gaze, that defines us and determines us.' In other words, we are social creatures whose moral values and behaviour are determined by the social setting – the culture, the era – we find ourselves in. Our moral development is an integral part of our social development: we acquire our moral sense from the experience of gradually learning how to get along with other people, especially people who are different from us. As we come to understand the crucial role of communities in human life, we learn to take other people's needs, rights and wellbeing into account, and, with any luck, to acquire the wisdom to be respectful of their point of view. There's some self-interest in all that, too: we know we couldn't thrive – physically or emotionally – without the support of the communities we belong to.

There is no necessary place for an entity called 'God' in that process of social, emotional, moral and spiritual development, though our moral formation may well be influenced by Christian and other religious teachings. If we were to think of God as the spirit of loving-kindness – or, more generally, the spirit of goodness – then it would be possible to argue that the fostering of this spirit will encourage us to treat others with kindness and respect, which is the essence of morality. While morality is a secular phenomenon, religion can shape and even enrich it, just as, in the wrong hands, religion can be used to distort and pervert morality.

In *The Moral Sense* (1993), James Wilson reminds us that even Voltaire, though famously anti-Christian himself, believed that the moral values of the Christian religion were valuable as a discipline for the masses: 'I want my attorney, my tailor, my servants, even my wife to believe in God,' Voltaire wrote, because 'then I shall be robbed and cuckolded less often.'

(Before we too vigorously mock Voltaire for his hypocrisy, we might note that his attitude differs only slightly from the avowed secularists who choose to send their children to church schools that they assume will be run by dedicated teachers with a 'vocation' for teaching, or line up for the superior care they expect from hospitals and charities run by religious organisations.)

The fact that the ancient Chinese, Egyptians and Greeks came to roughly the same moral conclusions as modern Christians and believers in other religions, or even non-religious humanists, proves only that if communities are to survive and prosper, we must learn to treat other people the way we ourselves would like to be treated – the so-called Golden Rule. Versions of that rule can be found in the Old and New Testaments, but that does not make it the exclusive province of Judaism or Christianity, any more than Socrates's rendition of it made it the exclusive province of Athenians. We need only acknowledge that, as human communities evolve, a certain amount of selflessness turns out to be an essential ingredient in cooperative living.

So we end this chapter where we began. The result of trawling through these well-worn attempts at proving the existence of God is entirely predictable. Theists will have been confirmed in their conviction that faith is never about proof, or it wouldn't be faith. Atheists will have had their beliefs reinforced – though, in fact, there's no comfort for atheists here: if something can't be proven, that means it can't be disproven either. If you're going to commit yourself in either direction, you'll need to take a leap of faith.

And agnostics? Watching theists and atheists – and theists of different persuasions – endlessly wrangle over an untestable proposition, agnostics may wonder why the matter needs to be settled at all.

In fact, this might be the point at which categories like 'atheist' and 'theist' collapse into pointlessness. What atheist is going to deny the existence and value of the spirit of loving-kindness in the world, and what theist is going to exclude *God is spirit/God is love* from their working definition of God? There seems to be a lot of common ground, right there.

The central message from the mystics of every age is that we are at our best – whole, or even 'godly' – when we surrender to the spiritual imperatives of love and goodness, and adapt ourselves to the way of life entailed by that surrender.

The question to be explored in the following chapter is whether the development of a heightened sense of spirituality and an associated commitment to a life of loving-kindness is aided or impeded by subscribing to a specific set of religious beliefs.

8

Beyond belief

Late in her life, in the midst of a robust discussion with me about religion, my mother declared: 'I think I know what I believe.' It was a remark that became famous in the family, and I was reminded of it recently when I had lunch with two friends, both lifelong churchgoers, who confessed that the older they become, the less sure they are of what they believe. They were also discovering that this didn't seem to matter much: as their beliefs became less distinct, their faith remained strong.

I don't think this was purely a function of age. Where once the ticking of 'belief boxes' – inerrancy of the Bible, creation, virgin birth, divinity of Jesus, resurrection, trinity, miracles – might have been thought fundamental to Christian faith, that situation is rapidly changing, just as Western culture is changing.

The twentieth century was a battleground not only for warring armies of unprecedented might and power, but also for ideas. As we have seen, 'the Age of Anxiety' became a popular label for the times, but that was a description of an effect: the *cause* was that we were living in an age of heightened uncertainty, discontinuity and unpredictability. Uncertainty has always been part of human existence, but now it seemed that *nothing* was certain, the pace of change was increasing and the foundations of our very way of life were being shaken by economic, social, cultural, political and technological upheavals. Everything was up for grabs, from the role of women in society to the Left and Right of traditional politics and, courtesy of the information technology revolution, we even began rethinking notions of identity, privacy and the way humans communicate. Every cherished belief – about gender, class, race, religion, power – was subjected to new scrutiny. Our view of human nature itself was challenged by the fresh horrors of concentration camps, gulags, weapons of mass destruction – and, at the other end of the spectrum, by the outbreak of unbridled consumption and materialism stimulated by the postwar economic boom. On top of all that, we were being forced to acknowledge the fragility of the ecosystem of the planet we live on.

In many ways, Sigmund Freud and Albert Einstein were intellectual symbols of the age: their thrilling theoretical adventures, though poorly understood by most of us, suited the emerging spirit of the times, with its emphasis on *subjectivity* and *relativity* – the twin central themes of postmodernism. Yet Freud's speculative stories about goings-on in the unconscious mind and the grandeur of Einstein's General Theory of Relativity have both been challenged: Freud has been widely discredited for alleged professional misconduct and dishonesty (Webster, 1995), and one of the central tenets of Einstein's General Theory of Relativity – that nothing can travel faster than the speed of light – has already been contested (though not disproved) by nuclear scientists working with the Large Hadron Collider. *Moving right along* could well be the catchcry of the age.

The hallmarks of late-twentieth-century postmodernism were the freedom to choose our own 'realities', to distrust theory, to reinterpret the past and to incorporate uncertainty into our world view. In *Reality Isn't What It Used to Be* (1990),

Walter Truett Anderson described the postmodern world as a place where we could no longer live 'by the innocent belief that there are no alternatives'. The internet has since pushed that idea to a new level: all the alternatives in the world are laid out for us at the click of a mouse.

This became the era of keep-your-options-open, hang loose, wait-and-see; a time when young people's favourite question became, 'What else is there?' It was the age where 'believing is seeing' challenged 'seeing is believing' as the basis for intellectual enquiry; where my experience trumped your theory (even if you were my teacher); where conviction yielded to scepticism; where open-mindedness became a cardinal virtue and 'political correctness' our way of scouring the cultural landscape for any traces of outmoded prejudice.

Things, in short, seemed less black and white than they once were.

As part of that general upheaval, some reshaping of the religious landscape was inevitable. One sign of it was the explosion of *choice* – about what to believe, about whether or not to attend church at all and about which kind of church, or church substitute, to attend. Switching became easier; drifting away less stigmatised. Claiming to be an atheist became almost fashionable, though that often turned out to be a declaration of scepticism or agnosticism, or a statement of disillusionment with institutional religion, rather than fully committed atheism. There was a new freedom in the air about whether to abandon religious dogma in favour of a less doctrinaire spirituality, and whether to embrace a more subjective, intimate, internal view of God. There was also a greater willingness to accept that 'my way' is not the only pathway to God or spiritual enlightenment or wisdom. *Doubt* acquired a new respectability; we were learning to live with uncertainty on a heroic scale.

There was a predictable backlash. Not everyone enjoys the freedom to explore hypotheses that are subject to constant revision in the light of new experience and so, in the field of religion, protectors of the old way rose up against the perceived trendiness or shallowness of New Age spirituality; in politics, against the Blair/Clinton 'third way'; in the literary academy, against deconstructionism; in philosophy, against the proposition that 'there is no truth, only interpretation'.

But the cultural genie was out of the bottle and the post-postmodern Western world (if that's what we're now in) is marked by a general increase in scepticism that shows up, for example, in declining respect for institutions of all kinds – from the church to political parties, universities, business corporations, the mass media and trade unions. Even the institutions of marriage and the family are the subject of more open-minded, more sceptical, more flexible attitudes, aided by developments at the frontiers of biomedical research. We are witnessing the increasing democratisation of education, a growing incoherence in political discourse, more freedom in sexual attitudes and behaviour, less stable marriages, less commitment to the stay-at-home care of children, less loyalty to employers and careers, more dependence on technology-based modes of communication, more adventurous consumerism in everything from food to fashion.

In the US, early signs are emerging of one possible consequence of all this: a declining level of emotional connectedness (or 'attachment') among a generation of young adults raised with less parental involvement and more non-family child care than any previous generation, and with an enthusiasm for social media use bordering on dependence. Recent research points to a decline in secure attachments among young adults, an increase in insecure attachments and a rising level of self-esteem linked to a more dismissive attitude towards others, combined with less civic orientation, including less engagement with politics and environmental issues. (See, for example, 'Generational differences in young adults . . .' (2012) by Twenge et al. and 'Changes in adult attachment styles . . .' (2014) by Konrath et al.)

As part of this general dynamism, an increasing diversity in the expression of religious and spiritual impulses should hardly surprise us. In contemporary religion, as in most areas of life, there is no single trend: there are multiple, and sometimes contradictory, trends, each expressing a different response to the Age of Uncertainty.

Fundamentalism remains strong, but that's partly because, as Harvey Cox has noted in *Fire From Heaven* (1994), evangelical churches typically form such powerful subcultures that their members tend to stick, regardless of shifts in mainstream culture. Variations on the theme of 'SBNR' are proliferating, both formally and informally. A gradual increase in the number of declared atheists is being outstripped by the rapidly growing interest in spirituality and mysticism in settings as diverse as Buddhist 'mindfulness' retreats and Pentecostal church services.

The search for meaning goes on, but it is no longer such a single-minded search for certainty. In the new spirit of more open enquiry, there's an expanding place for legitimate doubt, even among those who identify as Christian, about the value of beliefs that once seemed sacrosanct – virgin birth and resurrection, in particular – and a greater reluctance to toe any church's doctrinal line without question. There's wider acceptance of the idea that interpretation is *always* called for when trying to understand any text (from the Bible to Woody Allen's latest film) and that nothing should be taken at face value.

The difference between faith and belief

'Have faith,' we sometimes say, when we might mean 'Relax' or 'Be patient' or 'Don't lose heart'. One of my neighbours has faith in her dog to find its way home when it wanders off. Teachers have faith in some pupils to perform to the best of their ability. We have (often misplaced) faith in leaders to behave with integrity and in the best interests of those they serve.

In the spiritual context, we generally think of faith as an investment in something larger than ourselves – my god, my religion, my family, the essential goodness of humanity, the integrity of 'the universe' in the mystical rather than the cosmic sense. Faith is a way of looking at the world ('the eye of faith' described in chapter 7). It is sometimes an act of surrender or acceptance, an admission of some degree of uncertainty, insecurity, helplessness or inadequacy. Faith is about trust in someone or something to strengthen me, inspire me, protect me or 'ground' me by adding a sense of meaning and purpose to my life.

'Belief', by contrast, is a decision to accept some proposition presented as factual, on the basis that it is probably true, even if not yet proven. I might believe you when you tell me you've turned off the stove. I might believe a political aspirant when she tells me she is determined to respond to the needs of the marginalised members of our society. I might believe weather forecasters when they assure me there's a 90 percent chance of rain tomorrow.

Admittedly, there's a degree of word-mongering in this distinction. Some people use 'faith' and 'belief' almost interchangeably: 'I believe in God' is sometimes intended to convey roughly the same idea as 'I have faith in God', but there is a subtle difference, even there: belief seems static; faith more dynamic. A politician's defiant declaration that 'I believe in Australia!' might sound like mindless, tub-thumping nationalism. 'I have faith in Australia', by contrast, might seem more nuanced, implying a hopeful rather than arrogant trust in the values or the resilience of the Australian people, and possibly a conviction that this is a well-intentioned society that embraces such noble ideals as egalitarianism, justice, fairness, tolerance and compassion.

In trying to understand the complex role of religion in society, the distinction between faith and belief is useful, since most religious tension is about belief, not faith. Sunni and Shiah Muslims disagree violently, not about their faith in Allah, but about who they believe was the rightful successor to the prophet Mohammed following his death in 632. Christian Protestants and Roman Catholics don't appear to disagree over central questions of Christian faith, but they disagree passionately and sometimes violently over matters of doctrine, practice and institutional arrangements – including such things as the status of the Pope, the concept of a celibate priesthood, the idea of praying to the Virgin Mary, and the Roman Catholic Church's refusal of communion to practising homosexuals and divorced persons (a position that strikes non-Catholics, and many Catholics, as distinctly un-Christ-like). Liberal and Evangelical Protestants disagree over such things as the inerrancy of scripture, the place of women in the church, the use of incense in rituals or, indeed, the place of ritual itself in Christian worship. They may even accuse each other of different versions of idolatry: 'Your use of icons amounts to idolatry'; '*Your* attitude to the Bible is idolatrous'. Yet they would all claim to have faith in the same God and to be disciples of the same Jesus.

People will place their faith in whichever idea of God they choose to embrace as *their* God. Whether or not they also happen to believe various propositions put forward by various branches of the institutional church at various points in its history is a separate question entirely – though, in the past, rejection of some doctrines would have counted as heresy, regardless of a person's underlying faith, and might have been punishable by death. (The celebrated modern Australian case of Peter Cameron, the principal of St Andrew's College in the University of Sydney, tried and convicted as a heretic by Sydney Presbyterians for attacking fundamentalism and daring to advocate the ordination of women, resulted only in dismissal, not execution.)

Historically, it was taken for granted that religious faith entailed a set of generally agreed doctrinal beliefs. Today, people are prepared to reject propositions that seem implausible, unreasonable or unnecessary without feeling as if that obliges them to abandon

Christianity holus-bolus. Many Christians feel free to decide which doctrines of the church are better thought of as myths, legends or metaphors without rejecting the basic teachings of Jesus and without diminishing their faith in God, whatever meaning they may attach to that idea.

Faith is fluid, imaginative, sustaining and constantly evolving as we mature and learn from our experience. Beliefs, by contrast, are typically more rigid, limiting and prescriptive. (The prescription is very occasionally changed in response to deliberations by church leaders: for centuries, Roman Catholics were asked to believe in 'limbo' as a place where infants went if they died before they could be baptised, but that idea has been scrapped, and Catholics are now asked *not* to believe in it.)

At every point in the examination of beliefs associated with religious faith, we can ask ourselves the same three questions I raised in chapter 5:

Does it make sense?

Does it point to a better world?

Does it matter?

If you answer 'no' to any of those questions in relation to a particular belief, you might well regard that as sufficient grounds for *not* believing it, at least in a literal way.

The 'meaning' of the resurrection

Take the case of the resurrection of Jesus. Christians who regard that as the sine qua non of their faith like to quote Paul's letter to the Corinthians: 'If Christ has not been raised, your faith is futile and you are still in your sins.' Yet many fully committed Christians don't believe in the resurrection as a literal, physical, historical fact.

The historical record makes it clear that Jesus lived, taught, attracted a large band of followers, offended both the Jewish religious establishment and the Roman political hierarchy, and was executed by crucifixion. None of that strains our credulity. But his followers came to believe that he had been, quite literally, the son of God, and so the stories of his birth, life and death were gradually embellished in ways that would give credence to this claim. By the time the four Gospels were written – in the period between forty and ninety years after the events they describe – the stories many people now regard as myths had been incorporated into the narrative as if they were part of the historical record. It's not hard to work out which they are: they are the things that offend your reason by seeming physically impossible.

Even so, the first Gospel to be written, Mark (written at least twenty years before Matthew and Luke, and thirty years before John), makes no mention of the resurrection. A section was added to the end of Mark's Gospel by a different writer, long after the original was written, presumably to concur with the subsequent versions of Matthew, Luke and John. This is not particularly alarming; as many historians, theologians and commentators have remarked, the Gospel-writers set out to persuade, not merely to describe: they were evangelists, not historians – let alone journalists.

The resurrection presents serious difficulties to a person trying to reconcile Christian faith with reason. Quite apart from the physical impossibility of a dead body coming back to life, Oliver Sacks, in *Hallucinations* (2012), provides us with enough material for us to be deeply sceptical about the so-called post-resurrection appearances of Jesus. And, as British Bible scholar Hugh Schonfield pointed out in *The Passover Plot* (1965), in two of the most dramatic accounts of those 'appearances', the disciples appear to have convinced themselves that some other person was, in fact, Jesus. In one case, several disciples are fishing in a boat on Lake Galilee when they are addressed by a man on the shore. 'It is the Master,' declares one of the disciples, but John's Gospel unequivocally states that 'the disciples did not know it was Jesus' – presumably because it wasn't. In another case, disciples on the road to Emmaus were joined in conversation about the crucifixion by a stranger whom they later decided must have been Jesus, though, astonishingly, they had not recognised him at the time. Such accounts hardly qualify as evidence.

And yet, the resurrection remains a central feature of the Christian story, and the basis for the greatest Christian festival of the year: Easter. The mythical power of the resurrection story is so great, and it lends itself to so many possible interpretations, it's no wonder people continue to be drawn to its metaphorical possibilities, even when they don't believe it was an historical event.

> 'The resurrection? I'm a big believer in it. I absolutely love the idea of it. Love it! I don't care whether it happened literally or not. Anything is possible. Things happen that no scientists can explain. But that's not really the point – that's just a mystery of faith. It's the deep symbolism of it that I love. The idea of God proving himself in that way. And I love what it stands for: there's always a second chance, even for wayward children – a chance to try again. It's like the afterlife, in a way. It's a beautiful thing to think about, whether it's going to happen or not. You just don't know where the spirit goes – that's another mystery of faith. But I am inspired by the idea of the afterlife, in the same way as I'm inspired by the resurrection. Maybe it's just a story, but it's a beautiful story and it feels better to believe than not believe, at least for me.' —*Marija*

For people like Marija, the resurrection stands for the idea that we need never feel defeated; that fresh starts are always possible. For others, it works as a metaphor for the endless cycle of life, death and regeneration in the natural world. For still others, it symbolises hope and renewal – a counterpoint to the sense of shock and outrage that Christians feel whenever they contemplate the possibility that such a good man could be put to death in such a brutal and humiliating way. For many Christians, it is a story about the continuing influence of Jesus and his teachings, and how the Jesus movement was unstoppable, even by the crucifixion of its leader.

> ‘A group of us go to church at Easter. Easter Sunday, that is – not Good Friday, that's way too grim. The music is always beautiful and they have processions and things – it's all quite grand, really. It's not as if any of us believe that Jesus really did rise from the dead, but the whole thing is just so upbeat and positive, you can't resist it. But you do have to wonder why serious Christians regard the resurrection as the big deal, as if it's more important than Jesus's life and teachings.
>
> We were taught at school about this thing called 'the atonement' – the idea of his death being, like, a punishment for the sins of the rest of us, but I always thought that sounded desperately unfair! When I started doing anthropology at uni, I also thought it was a pretty blatant steal from the primitive idea of scapegoats and blood sacrifices. Urgh! The other thing was, would a loving God really require a violent death as a trade-off for human frailty?
>
> So, yeah, we go, but, as you can see, we don't really buy into it. Although one of my girlfriends always says, 'You never know.'’ — *Vanessa*

Vanessa's view of the atonement is supported by retired Anglican dean of Perth John Shepherd, who, in an unpublished paper (2015), declared:

> I don't believe Jesus literally and physically rose from the dead, or that the post-resurrection appearances are literally true [and]

> I don't believe in a God who was so angry at human sin that somehow someone had to pay a fee, or a ransom, or some kind of blood money in order to restore God's equilibrium. I don't believe in a vengeful God who needed satisfaction before He would look favourably on the human race. So I don't believe in the idea that Christ died for our sins. I think this idea was imposed in order to justify, or attribute some kind of reason as to why on earth Jesus would die that way.

In *A Short History of Myth*, Karen Armstrong observes that, through history, the most powerful and enduring myths are those that address our existential fears, particularly related to death, and those that point to divinity as an aspect of humanity. The resurrection myth scores strongly on both counts.

Biblical scholar and historian John Dominic Crossan, in his 1994 biography of Jesus, concluded that even the Gospel accounts of Jesus being buried by his friends rather than his executioners are 'totally fictional and unhistorical'. He acknowledges that the Easter story, like the Nativity story, is 'engraved on our imagination as factual history rather than fictional mythology', but he has concluded that the resurrection story worked as a kind of 'compression' of the events that occurred after the death of Jesus. It was a symbolic representation of the fact that, far from being destroyed, the influence of the Jesus movement continued to gather momentum.

The chorus of an Alaskan miners' song contains these words: 'We rise again in the faces of our children.' There's yet another picture of resurrection: our children carry on the values, the faith, the *life* we give them. The spirit and influence of any life continues, for good or ill, through the lives of all those we have touched. And that is certainly the way Christians see Jesus of Nazareth: he continues to 'rise' in the lives of those who follow his teachings and choose to call themselves his disciples.

Many of us can accept all that in good faith, just as we can be moved and inspired by J.S. Bach's *St Matthew Passion* or by a stirring Easter hymn, without needing belief in a literal, bodily resurrection.

'Does anyone really believe in the virgin birth?'

Some metaphorical interpretation of the resurrection myth is easy enough for most of us to grasp, but the idea that Jesus was mystically, spermlessly conceived by 'the Holy Spirit' and born to a virginal mother is another challenge entirely. The story can be interpreted in many ways: my favourite is Joseph Campbell's, described in chapter 1, where virgin birth symbolises the awakening of spiritual insight – 'the birth of compassion in the heart'. Such interpretations, based on the discernment of inner meaning, are offensive to those who stand in the conservative Christian tradition that regards the virgin birth as the 'proof' of the divinity of Jesus (human mother, divine father). Yet this is the doctrine of the church most likely to strain people's credulity to breaking point: 'If they expect me to believe that, literally, then I'm out of here. In fact, I seriously doubt if *anyone* really believes it.' Notwithstanding that rationalist's view, the truth is that millions of intelligent, well-educated people throughout Christian history have indeed believed it.

People who once believed in the virgin birth and no longer do, and those who have never believed it, typically raise the same set of objections that reveal their scepticism about the value of the story, even as myth, or their tendency to ridicule it as the ultimate example of irrational faith:

> 'If Jesus had not been conceived in the normal way, he wouldn't have been be a biological human at all, and therefore his teachings would be irrelevant to us – it would be like Earthlings trying to take flying lessons from Superman.'

> 'What would Mary and Joseph have told Jesus when it came to the "where-do-babies-come from" conversation?'

> 'If Jesus had been miraculously conceived, wouldn't he have mentioned it?'

> 'It wasn't exactly an original idea.' (The ancient Greeks believed Perseus was the product of the union between the god Zeus and Danai, a human virgin, and the Dead Sea Scrolls have a story about Noah's mother being impregnated by an angel.)

> 'This was just part of the spin about Jesus created by two of the Gospel writers, Matthew and Luke (whose accounts were very different, by the way), designed to make him appear divine. It was common in ancient history for the stories of the birth and early life of heroes to be recast, 'back-filled', in ways that made them seem special or even miraculous.'

Some people think the Roman Catholic Church, in particular, has shamelessly promoted the idea of a virginal Madonna (even declaring that Mary was herself 'immaculately' conceived) to make sexual intercourse seem dirty – certainly less pure than celibacy – and they therefore associate the virgin birth with a generally unhealthy attitude to sex. Some believe the word translated as 'virgin' should have been rendered as 'young woman'. Others simply dismiss the whole thing as too strange to contemplate: 'It would do your head in if you tried to imagine it.'

And yet, every Christmas, we sing the carols and tell the stories as if the virgin birth is integral, or even essential. Viewed rationally, the entire story is fanciful: Luke, famous for his poetic imagination, located the birth in Bethlehem, apparently to line up with an Old Testament prophecy. He is the only one who created an apparently fictitious census, told us the romantic story of Jesus being born in a manger because there was 'no room in the inn', and produced angels announcing the birth of Jesus to simple shepherds tending their sheep on a chilly night. Matthew gave us none of that, but did provide the star and the three wise men – all part of the charm of the accepted Christmas legend, rich with the potent symbolism that has inspired artists, poets, composers and carol-singers through the ages, but hardly to be regarded as an historical account.

If you need your religion to be based on a spectacularly supernatural premise, then virgin birth, like bodily resurrection, would be hard to beat. But if, in the spirit of this book, you are asking yourself, 'What difference would it make to my life – or to my respect for Christian values – if I did or did not believe in the virgin birth?', then I suspect the honest answer would be: *No difference at all.*

Would the teachings of Jesus seem less interesting, significant or relevant if he were *not* supposed to be the result of a supernatural conception? Would they seem to have more – or less – power if their author were the offspring of a mystical, non-sexual union between a human woman and a divine spirit? Up to you, of course; for me, the whole edifice of Christianity would crumble if the idea of a *literal* virgin birth were to be regarded as its crucial foundation.

Making sense of miracles

'How could anyone seriously believe in miracles?'—*Jesse*

'I believe in miracles – absolutely.'—*Marija*

Those comments from two of my respondents capture one of the many fascinating contradictions between different people's views of the world. In this case, it's the contrast between those who are determinedly rationalist and those who are open to mystery; those who want answers to all their questions and those who don't need everything to be explained, at least not in rational terms. Within the second group, there are the strong believers in miracles 'because the Bible tells me so' and those of more mystical inclination, who simply love the idea that there are unexplained phenomena in the world; that anything is possible.

If we took the rational position, we'd say, unequivocally, that a man can't walk on water, feed thousands of people with five loaves of bread and a couple of fish, or turn water into wine at a wedding feast to compensate for someone's inadequate catering arrangements. So, if you're not a believer in the literal truth of miracles, is there any value in the stories that describe Jesus doing these, and similar, things?

At the time of Jesus's life and ministry, wandering healers, shamans and magicians were commonplace though, unlike him, they mostly did it for the money. And, as we saw in chapter 2, there's nothing supernatural about so-called faith healing. But many of the miracles described in the Gospels go well beyond that.

Between them, the four Gospel writers report thirty-five miracles performed by Jesus, comprising three cases of raising people from the dead, twenty-three miracles of healing (ranging from a haemorrhaging woman to a man with a withered hand) and nine demonstrations of power over nature. Only the most literal-minded fundamentalist or the dreamiest mystic would accept that all of this actually happened as written. So what's the point of the stories?

Once again, it's all a matter of interpretation, and Christians raised on the Old Testament as well as the New are accustomed to exploring the inner meanings of apparently outlandish but brilliantly symbolic legends: Moses parting the waters of the Red Sea, for instance, or the voice of God coming out of a burning bush that was never consumed, or Noah loading two of every species into his ark, or God speaking from an erupting volcano to lay down the law to Moses, starting with the famous Ten Commandments, but then going on and on . . . and on (chapters 20–40 of the book of Exodus, and the entire book of Leviticus), including the presentation of tablets containing the law.

As young children, we might have believed such things really happened but, as we grew up, most of us came to see them as myths or legends laden with moral and cultural significance, rather like the Greek myths of Jason and the Argonauts, or Orpheus in the Underworld.

For all but the most literal-minded, most of the Gospel miracles come into the same category. The Old Testament stories were clearly designed to show the power and might of Yahweh, the God of the Jews; the Gospel miracles were similarly designed to show the power and might of Jesus, after his followers had decided that he was not simply the Jewish Messiah but the actual Son of God.

Interpreting the miracles is a highly personal matter: we will each make our own sense (or no sense) of them. You could, for example, think of the feeding of the five thousand (Mark 6: 35–44) as a metaphor for the 'multiplier effect' of loving-kindness: the more you behave in a loving way, the more that positive influence compounds, represented metaphorically by the multiplying loaves and fishes.

The walking-on-water story (Matthew 14: 25–31) is a not-very-subtle metaphor for the idea that we need faith to sustain and support us, and when we lose our nerve, as Peter did, we sink. It's in the same metaphorical category as 'faith can move mountains'.

And the water-into-wine myth, reported exclusively in John's Gospel (chapter 2: 1–11)? I haven't a clue. I've never been able to discern any inner meaning in that one. Some scholars suggest it should be regarded purely as a kind of curtain-raiser – an announcement that Jesus's ministry would be characterised by remarkable deeds. Assuming Matthew, Mark and Luke were aware of the story, they may have been wise to leave it alone. (It's hard not to be amused, though, by conservative theologians who, being opposed to the use of alcohol, tell us that Jesus would actually have turned the water into grape juice – still impressive, in its way, but not quite as miraculous as producing large jars of the fully fermented real thing.)

Another miracle – stilling the storm on a lake (Luke 8: 22–25) – can be read as a warning against becoming too agitated about any events, including the weather, that lie beyond our control. Its inner meaning may simply be that acceptance is the pathway to peace of mind, or stillness.

In these and other cases, the challenge is not to believe the unbelievable, but to make whatever sense you can of the metaphorical meaning represented by the story – just as you do when you read other myths and legends, ancient and modern. If you were to take such stories at face value, you'd be plunged into the realm of the supernatural, and how would that be relevant to your life in the natural world?

What did Jesus himself actually teach?

Like Socrates, Jesus never wrote anything down (except once, enigmatically, on the ground with his finger, but there's no record of what he wrote). At least Socrates had Plato, his pupil, on hand to record what he had said, but there are no eyewitness accounts of what Jesus said or did, though some non-biblical historians, such as the first-century scholar Josephus, confirm the broad outlines of his life and death. For the details of Jesus's central teachings, delivered via parables and the famous Sermon on the Mount, we are left with three of the four well-meaning but somewhat unreliable evangelists. The parables are reported only in the Gospels of Matthew, Mark and Luke; the Sermon on the Mount is exclusive to Matthew.

While the miracles are incredible stories *about* Jesus that don't make much sense until you interpret them, the accounts of his explicit teachings – the parables and the Sermon on the Mount – are somewhat easier to grasp.

There are forty reported parables. Although the disciples sometimes complained that Jesus was talking in riddles, most of the parables seem fairly straightforward, even if their message is not so easy to apply – a problem we'll address in the final chapter. Taken together, though, the parables and the Sermon on the Mount express some consistent themes. They are suffused with messages about the spirit of loving-kindness: good can triumph over evil and love over hate; kindness is the currency of human virtue; forgiveness has healing power; prejudice and judgemental attitudes are destructive; goodness demands vigilance; messages about the spiritual life only make sense to people in pursuit of a spiritual life and will remain meaningless to others.

To put some flesh on those bones, here's a quick summary of three of the best-known parables: The Prodigal Son, The Good Samaritan and The Ten Bridesmaids (also known as The Wise and Foolish Virgins).

The Prodigal Son (Luke 15: 11–32) is the story of a wayward son who takes his inheritance and deserts his family to go off and make his fortune. It does not go well. He squanders his inheritance in dissolute living, one thing leads to another, and he eventually decides to return home and throw himself on his father's mercy. His father, seeing his son approach, orders the best robe to be put on him and a feast to be held in his honour. Brushing away his son's abject apologies, the father says, 'This son of mine was dead and is alive again; he was lost and is found.' The older brother comes in from the field, discovers the celebrations in full swing, and is mightily displeased, feeling that his own loyalty and hard work have gone unrewarded. His father says to him, 'You are always with me and all that is mine is yours.'

While it would be nice to think the father might have previously acknowledged the loyalty and hard work of his elder son, the main point of the story lies in its demonstration of the healing power of forgiveness and the requirement to forgive even in circumstances where that would not come easily. It also offers a salutary picture of waywardness (the younger son) and self-righteousness (the older son). Notice, though, that the elder son will still inherit his father's property; in spite of his father's forgiveness, the younger son will have to bear the consequences of having squandered his share.

The Good Samaritan (Luke 10: 30–37) is a disturbing tale of prejudice, social class, neighbourliness and forgiveness, told in response to the question asked of Jesus, 'Who is my neighbour?' A man, generally assumed to be a Jew, was travelling from Jerusalem to Jericho when he was robbed, beaten and left for dead. A priest and a Levite (a person with special religious status) each came upon him, and both passed by on the other side of the road. Then a Samaritan saw him and was moved with pity. He treated the man's wounds and took him to an inn, cared for him overnight and then left him in the care of the innkeeper, whom he paid. The answer to the question 'Which was the neighbour?' was obvious, leading to the famous remark attributed to Jesus: 'Go and do likewise.'

The sting in the tail of that story concerns the rather narrow Jewish understanding of 'neighbour' – someone near you, someone you have had dealings with, someone within your social circle who is your social equal – and the inferior social status of Samaritans, who were regarded by the Jews as little better than the hated Romans. So the story was not only about kindness and compassion, but also about radically broadening the definition of 'neighbour'.

The Ten Bridesmaids (Matthew 25: 1–13) were tending oil lamps, waiting for the arrival of the bridegroom. Five of them had come equipped with flasks of spare oil and five had not. The bridegroom was delayed and the bridesmaids fell asleep. When the cry finally went up that the bridegroom was approaching, the unprepared bridesmaids realised they had run out of oil. They requested some from the smart group who refused, on the grounds that their own lamps would then go out. The oil-less five then went off to a dealer to buy more oil. While they were away, the groom arrived, the wise ones were ushered in to the wedding feast, the door was locked and the foolish five were excluded.

There's more to this one than 'be prepared', though that's clearly part of its message. It's also about patience, commitment and devotion to duty; about being fully focused, vigilant, and open to uncertainty and unpredictability. While some conservative scholars have interpreted this parable as being about preparing for the second coming of Christ, Eckhart Tolle, in *The Power of Now* (2004), takes the interpretation up a notch by suggesting that the oil symbolises consciousness, the bridegroom represents the 'Now' and the wedding feast stands for enlightenment. He therefore sees it as a parable about the possibility of living in a heightened state of consciousness.

The Sermon on the Mount refers to a long passage in Matthew's Gospel (chapters 5, 6 and 7) in which Jesus retreats to a mountain to escape from the crowd following him, and there explains his world view to his disciples, laying out for them the code of conduct he expects of them – the code that has come to be regarded as the definitive statement of Christian values.

It begins with the so-called Beatitudes, in which Jesus offers comfort to the 'poor in spirit', those who mourn, the meek, the spiritually hungry, the merciful, the pure in heart, the peacemakers and those who are persecuted for their faith. In each case, he makes the paradoxical point that you will be rewarded for not seeking a reward: the merciful will receive mercy, the meek will inherit the earth, the pure in heart will see God, and so on.

Jesus then warns against being judgemental or taking revenge, and makes his famously counterintuitive remark about 'turning the other cheek' if someone strikes you (a teaching also attributed to the legendary Chinese philosopher Lao Tzu). He encourages his followers, instead, to 'love your enemies and pray for them that persecute you', making the point that there is no particular challenge in loving those who also love you. He offers some advice on prayer, specifying that it should be done in private, and warns against trying to serve two masters – God/spirituality and materialism/wealth. He reiterates the Golden Rule: 'In everything, do to others as you would have them do to you.'

Some of the remarks attributed to Jesus seem at odds with the main thrust of his teachings: 'I have not come to bring peace but a sword', for instance, and 'I have come to set a man against his father and a daughter against her mother', to say nothing of the extraordinary outburst when he curses a defenceless fig tree for failing to bear fruit. Such remarks led one of my respondents to say: 'I spent the Christmas holidays rereading the Gospels, and I've decided Jesus wasn't a very nice man.'

The Gospel accounts portray Jesus as being bitterly opposed to dogmatic religious belief: his relentless attacks on the 'scribes and Pharisees' (legal experts) for their intransigence and their prescriptive interpretation of Jewish law suggests that he would have been uncomfortable among today's fundamentalists, with their own characteristic intransigence and their similarly prescriptive interpretation of the Bible.

But if you focus on the teachings themselves, two things may strike you. The first is that none of it was about the pursuit of personal happiness. The satisfactions offered or implied are all, at best, by-products of the good life. The emphasis is on serving others and responding to their needs in the spirit of loving-kindness, the strong implication being that the pursuit of self-serving goals, like wealth or status, will be counterproductive.

The second striking thing is that none of the explicit teachings of Jesus, in the parables or in that sermon, called on his disciples to *believe* anything. He was not prescribing doctrine or dogma for some hypothetical institutional church that might in the future have been established in his name. His teachings were *all* about how best to live: the consistent emphasis was on loving action, not belief. According to Jesus, the life of virtue – the life of goodness – is powered by faith in something greater than ourselves (love, actually), not by dogma.

Perhaps it is only when we get beyond the rigidities and limitations of belief that we can encounter the imaginative possibilities of faith.

The afterlife

If you're looking for the ultimate example of our willingness to believe in untestable propositions, look no further than the afterlife.

Unlike 'God', about which we have vastly different ideas, we are all pretty clear about what we mean when we say 'the afterlife': it implies that after the body dies, the soul survives – to dwell in some spiritual realm, or to be reincarnated in another form.

The afterlife strikes many people as no more than a projection of our great wish that our life should not end and, in the case of reincarnation, our desire to be given an infinite number of 'second chances' to sort out the business of living well. For some people, though, it's a serious, solid expectation based on a firm belief.

Since this is the one thing about human existence we can never test, let alone prove, we are free to believe whatever we choose without fear of contradiction, since no one else knows either. And yet, as with most other beliefs, our beliefs in the existence, nature and purpose of an afterlife are capable of dividing us from each other, sometimes bitterly. Here's a selection of comments about the afterlife I've personally encountered:

> 'I can't believe this is all there is.'
> 'When I die, I rot.'
> 'I would like to think that people will be rewarded – or punished – for the way they lived their life on earth.'

> 'The body dies, but the soul survives.'
>
> 'I have no trouble imagining how the world was before I arrived on the scene, and I have no trouble imagining how it will be when I leave the scene.'
>
> 'I have every confidence in the idea of heaven. I know when I get there, I'll see my heavenly Father, and I'll see my earthly father again, too – I'm looking forward to it.'
>
> 'If this is all there is, it's a pretty feeble effort, don't you think? It's enough to make me believe in reincarnation.'
>
> 'Actually, I've stopped thinking about it – I've just let it go. I'll be a Christian till the day I die, but after that – well, that's one thing I don't think about any more. It really doesn't matter. What will be, will be.'
>
> 'I just wake up every day and think: I don't need an afterlife – this life is bloody amazing. I'm going to make the most of it while I'm here.'
>
> 'After seeing the death of my father, I don't need to be convinced about the afterlife. He had been in hospital for weeks, in such a bad state, we thought the end would be dreadful. But it was quite the reverse. On the day he died, my mother and I went to see him. What a transformation! All the lines in his face were gone – he was giving us the thumbs-up and telling us how happy he was. He had had a dream in which he was convinced he had been given a glimpse of what was to come, and he couldn't wait to get there. An hour later he died with a smile on his face.'

Contrast that last description with Vladimir Nabokov's view of life and death, articulated in *Speak, Memory* (1967): 'The cradle rocks above an abyss, and common sense tells us that our existence is but a brief crack of light between two eternities of darkness.'

Take your pick.

It's hardly surprising that people who feel oppressed, dispossessed, marginalised or defeated would pin their faith on an afterlife where all rights could be wronged, all burdens lifted and all cares washed away. Many of the traditional songs of the African-American slaves are based on that central theme, and that wasn't a matter of belief so much as faith: they *needed* there to be an afterlife – *yearned* for one – to compensate for the rotten hand dealt them in this life.

Blaise Pascal's wager (mentioned in chapter 5) proposes that since we can't possibly know whether or not there is an afterlife, we have everything to gain and nothing to lose by living as if there *is* one, whereas we have nothing to gain and everything to lose by living as if there *isn't*. But that's a cowardly wager, born not of faith but fear of oblivion at best or damnation at worst.

The popular view that the afterlife is a place of judgement, and therefore a reason for living virtuously, is fraught with moral difficulty: if you live well in order to obtain a reward for your virtue, then you have missed the entire point of virtue and it's arguable whether you have behaved virtuously at all. Virtue says we should do the right thing because it's the right thing to do, even if there is *no* reward. Otherwise it simply becomes another act of self-centredness: 'It may look as if I'm acting kindly for your benefit, but it's actually for my benefit – my kindness to you secures my passport to heaven.'

That tension between our moral selves and our selfish selves is one of the themes we are about to explore in the final chapter.

9

Love is enough

Each of us has our own way of looking at the world. One of the recurring themes of this book has been that 'the eye of faith' sees things that more sceptical people might miss, while sceptics see things that are hidden from the faithful. It's all in the point of view, a matter of interpretation; how could it be otherwise?

Which makes our intolerance of each other's points of view seem rather absurd. We are all living in the same world; we are all trying to make sense of life as it unfolds; we are mostly doing our best to live a good life according to the values we have inherited and those we have acquired through experience. To mock people's religious faith would be as insensitive and unproductive as mocking their ethnic or cultural heritage, especially since most people adopt the religion of the family they were born into. Religion has protected the sanity of millions of people; its comforts and consolations – theological, social and emotional – have relieved countless generations of their existential anxiety and encouraged them to live noble, rather than merely moral, lives. It has saved them from despair and given them hope.

Faith makes us whole. Not religious faith, necessarily, and certainly not any one particular variety of religious faith. But, as we have seen at several points in the book, faith in something larger than ourselves is vital for our mental health, our wholeness. Yet we also need to learn to live with some mystery – some sense of awe and wonder – to remind us of the impossibility of getting answers to all the questions we'd like to ask, and to equip us for dealing with life's inherent uncertainties.

A recurring theme of the book has been that dogmatic beliefs are often the greatest stumbling block to peace and harmony in the world. The very fact that such beliefs are untestable makes people cling to them more ferociously, and often reduces their capacity for empathy towards those who don't share all their beliefs: *How can you possibly call yourself a Christian when you don't believe in the bodily resurrection of Jesus?* To which another sort of Christian might reply: *How can you possibly call yourself a Christian when you're so prescriptive and judgemental?*

Common ground is the thing we need. Each person will accept or reject the messages of this or that religion; each person will accept or reject the idea that Reason alone can save us; each person will accept or reject propositions about the afterlife, just as each of us will privately attach our own meaning to our own life. The question is, what can we *all* put our faith in?

In this final chapter, I want to explore the idea that faith in the power of loving-kindness might be one thing that can unite us – or, at least, soften the hard edges of our differences.

I have suggested that we each have our own unique way of seeing the world. It's also true that each of us is capable of looking at the world in several ways according to the circumstances we find ourselves in – almost as if we think with different 'minds' in different situations. For example, we engage our 'rational mind' to concentrate on the facts before us; our 'professional mind' to assess things in the light of our specialised knowledge as a nurse, carpenter, teacher, gardener, banker, baker etc.; our 'romantic mind' when our hormones are alerting us to the possibility of sexual attraction; our 'aesthetic mind' when we are responding to a work of art. When we're indecisive, we say we're 'in two minds'.

Beneath those multiple surface variations are three universal minds, coexisting within all of us. They represent three radically different ways of seeing the world: the *moral* mind, the *self-absorbed* mind and the *compassionate* mind.

The moral mind

Marcus Aurelius, emperor of Rome from 161–180 CE, wrote: 'Since you are an integral part of a social system, let every act of yours contribute to the harmonisation of social life. Any action that is not related directly or remotely to this social aim disturbs your life and destroys your unity.'

That is our default position. That is normal for us. That is the way social beings operate. It's the state of being that ensures the survival and health of the communities we depend on for *our* survival and health. And the moral mind is the resource we need for living in a world we share with others.

At the heart of the moral mind is the ancient precept known as the Golden Rule: *Treat other people the way you would like them to treat you*. Or, as Confucius put it nearly three thousand years ago: *Never do to others what you would not like them to do to you*.

There is nothing remarkable about this: virtually every religious and philosophical tradition on earth promotes the same idea. You don't have to *believe* in the Golden Rule, you need only acknowledge that it makes perfect sense, which is why it's the most widely accepted of all rules of good living.

So why do we make such a fuss about altruism? Why are we surprised when someone helps an elderly person across a busy road, jumps off a jetty to rescue a swimmer in trouble or does some shopping for a sick neighbour, without needing to be asked or expecting to be thanked, let alone rewarded? When questioned, the people who do these things always say 'anyone would have done it' and they are absolutely right. The really weird thing for social beings would be *not* to help someone in trouble or distress.

In her book of essays *When I Was a Child I Read Books* (2012), Pulitzer Prize-winning novelist Marilynne Robinson mentions a study conducted at the London School of Economics whose author, the evolutionary psychologist Satoshi Kanazawa, asserted that 'it is unnatural for humans to be concerned about strangers'. In response, Robinson noted drily that 'all of us can think of a thousand examples that argue against this conclusion'. And so we can.

The truth is that we are village people, and the moral mind is both an expression and a reminder of that. In *A Cooperative Species* (2011), Samuel Bowles and Herbert Gintis argue that we do not behave altruistically because it will somehow benefit us in the long run (by feeling good about ourselves, for instance, or looking good to others) but simply because we are genetically programmed to behave like that. The Rockefeller University's neurobiologist Donald Pfaff agrees: 'We are hardwired to follow the Golden Rule' (2007).

Seen in that light, doing the right thing is no big deal. Doing the *wrong* thing by your fellow humans is a big deal. Respecting someone else's property is utterly normal for members of a species like ours; *not* respecting someone else's property is abnormal. Being sensitive to other people's feelings goes with the territory; *not* being sensitive to other people's feelings suggests you are a suitable case for treatment.

Unfortunately, life teaches us that the Golden Rule isn't put into practice as universally as we might wish; not everyone treats us as we would like to be treated. Sometimes people treat us badly because they, in turn, were treated badly by someone else, or because they're having a rough day, or because their moral mind is dysfunctional for some other reason (such as the influence of growing up in a household of grasping materialists). That's why we create laws: to ensure that we act in accordance with the dictates of the moral mind in circumstances where we might be tempted not to. We need laws to control the speed at which we drive, because we may otherwise drive too fast in order to meet a deadline, or simply for a thrill, thereby putting other people at risk. We need laws to guard against insider trading on the stock market, because we know it's easier for people to behave badly – to resist the dictates of the moral mind – when there is no visible, personally identifiable victim of their bad behaviour. We need laws that protect people against damage to their property and person, and laws that require us to pay our fair share of tax (not merely to fund services provided by government but also as a way of ensuring that poor people are not unduly disadvantaged by their poverty nor rich people unduly privileged by their wealth). Sometimes, we are even forced to enact so-called *educative* laws designed to remind us of the fundamental values that underpin a civil society – for example, laws that insist on equality of opportunity, that prohibit discrimination on the basis of gender, sexual preference, ethnicity, race, religion or ability, and that uphold the right to freedom of speech (within limits) and of assembly.

We need such laws because the moral mind is not our *only* mind: we are frequently tempted to brush aside the messages it sends us in favour of the highly seductive, highly competitive messages of self-interest. Think of the laws of the land as a bulwark against rampant selfishness.

But, to draw on yet another metaphor, the law is the floor, not the ceiling. Our moral mind demands far more of us than mere obedience to the law; morality trumps legality. The moral mind is the seat of the conscience. It frames our view of the world in ways that encourage us to behave ethically, not just legally. The moral life – the life committed to the pursuit of goodness – is a life lived for others. That idea shouldn't surprise you; isn't it obvious that a community only thrives if we are sensitive to each other's needs, sometimes at the expense of our own? In a society truly grounded in the Golden Rule, others would be as sensitive to our needs as we are to theirs: an expectation of *mutuality* and *reciprocity* lies at the heart of every moral code.

Laws are not the only bulwark that protects the moral mind, and this is where, for some people, religion comes in. As we saw in chapter 3, one of the reasons why people attend church is to be exposed to messages that encourage them to keep to 'the straight and narrow'. As many wise people have pointed out, we improve our chances of moral fitness when we align ourselves with people and messages that reinforce our desire to pursue goodness as a way of life. There's a practical tip along these lines in the New Testament: 'Whatever is true, whatever is honorable, whatever is just, whatever is pure, whatever is pleasing, whatever is commendable, if there is any excellence and if there is anything worthy of praise, think about these things' (Philippians 4:8).

It goes without saying that the development of the moral mind depends on more than thinking noble thoughts about goodness. If the moral muscle is not to atrophy, we will need to act on our understanding of what constitutes goodness by developing the habit of behaving respectfully towards everyone we encounter (including strangers and people clearly unlike us), by becoming more responsive to the needs of the disadvantaged and marginalised, and by finding time to listen to people who need our undivided attention. Hypothetical concern for other people's wellbeing is a good start; finding practical ways of expressing that concern is the essential next step if we are to discharge our responsibility as social beings.

The pressure to conform to the standards of a morally sensitive group of friends and associates can be a powerful reinforcement of the moral mind. Since most religions have moral teachings at their heart, the experience of belonging to a church or other faith community can heighten a person's moral sensitivity. But those potentially beneficial effects will be swamped if messages about love and kindness are contradicted by bigotry, prejudice and a judgemental or superior attitude towards non-believers. (And, it must be said, a superior attitude – 'we have *the* answer'; 'we are the Chosen People'; 'ours is the One True Way' – has been a recurring problem for people of all religious faiths. Such super-confidence doesn't do much for the sense of humility that is fundamental to the practice of loving-kindness.)

We may well be, as neuroscientists suggest, genetically programmed to follow the dictates of the moral mind, but we still need to develop the skills that bring those predispositions to fruition. As usual, it's nature *plus* nurture that determines what will become of us. From an early age, we need to learn the practical lessons of morality through the experience of living with others – in the family, in the playground, in the classroom, on the sporting field. Even if we were not programmed to cooperate, it would gradually dawn on us that the system can only work if we take each other's rights, needs and wellbeing into account.

People from all walks of life demonstrate, every day, that altruistic, self-sacrificial, 'good' behaviour comes naturally to us, whether that behaviour is in response to the needs of family, friends, work colleagues, neighbours or total strangers. The self-sacrifice is most obvious – and virtually taken for granted – in the actions of parents of special-needs children, and in spouses or offspring who faithfully visit a demented partner or parent without even the reward of being recognised, let alone appreciated. It's less obvious in those who have had to learn to live with personal disappointment (in their work, their marriage, their kids) and still go on supporting and encouraging the people who have let them down. And how do we account for the many thousands of people in our society who, every day, take meals, books or the gift of conversation to the housebound, who patrol surf beaches or coach slow readers at a local school, who help a frail and bewildered person across a busy street or give someone a bus fare because they've lost their wallet . . . when all the people they help are strangers to them?

The point about those who live a morally praiseworthy life under difficult conditions, including conditions of relentless tedium, is that they are *typical* of the members of this species.

How odd it would be to turn your back on a terminally ill spouse, or to ignore elderly neighbours who need occasional help with shopping or transport or odd jobs around the house, or to give up on kids who've disappointed you once too often. Such behaviour is so unusual for us it's the stuff of gossip and social disapproval.

Although I have suggested that the moral mind is our 'default' mind, we all know from experience that the moral mind is not a closed system, impervious to influences from our social, cultural and economic environment – including the strident, insistent appeal of self-interest. (Who hasn't thought 'I don't have time for this' when considering whether or not to perform a kind deed?)

We sometimes feel as if we are too often taken for granted; we sometimes struggle to be heard; we sometimes feel as if our needs are not being taken into account. And so we soon learn to be competitive as well as cooperative. If your experience is that people rarely treat you as you would like to be treated, or that they mock you for your moral sensitivity, this may well wear you down and lead you to challenge the validity of messages coming from your moral mind. (Though it may also suggest you're hanging out with the wrong crowd.) If you harbour resentment against people who have wronged you, you may be tempted to act in a morally reckless way to 'get even'. If you have noticed that ferociously ambitious self-promoters and highly competitive individuals – including some who cut moral corners – not only get away with it, but actually prosper, you might be vulnerable to the provocative messages coming from another mind . . .

The self-absorbed mind

There's a powerful force exerting constant pressure on the moral mind, threatening its stability, integrity and focus by distracting us from its simple message. This competing mind says, 'Yeah, yeah, yeah, I know all that soppy stuff about the Golden Rule and importance of the moral compass, and the need for mutual respect in a civil society, but I also know that, in the end, *it's all about Me*.' In *The Life Plan* (2015), the Australian executive coach Shannah Kennedy spells it out unashamedly: 'The business of *me* is my first and foremost job – everything else comes after that.'

It's all about Me is the central message of the self-absorbed mind. Its primary concern is with *my* wellbeing, *my* happiness, *my* prosperity, *my* comfort, *my* entitlements – even, in a religious context, *my* salvation. Its entire focus is individualistic. *Who am I?*, *How am I?* and *How can I get what I want?* are its three favourite questions. The state of society is of far less interest to the self-absorbed mind than the state of Me, though when things aren't going well for me, it may encourage me to *blame* the state of society.

The self-absorbed mind is the polar opposite of the moral mind. Its orientation is towards the self, not others; its currency is competition, not cooperation; it's all about getting, not giving. Its goal is the feel-good achievement of personal gratification, however that might be achieved and regardless of any impact it might have on the wellbeing of 'losers'.

Religious belief (as opposed to religious faith) can also feed the appetite of the self-absorbed mind. Many religious believers who are convinced of the rightness of their own doctrinal position draw self-indulgent comfort from their feelings of contempt towards those who hold different beliefs. Whereas religious faith tends to encourage kindness, compassion and unity, dogmatic belief tends to beget bigotry, prejudice and division – all welcome grist for the mill of the self-absorbed mind.

Attempts to persuade others to adopt our point of view often spring from motives of genuine concern and compassion, but they are sometimes driven utterly by the self-absorbed mind: 'I want you to see things my way because I know I am right and it annoys me that you don't get it!' (These are the same people who define teamwork as 'everyone doing what I say'.)

If that sounds a bit harsh, let me hasten to acknowledge that the tendency towards self-absorption lurks in all of us, jostling for pride of place in the pantheon of the mind. The messages from the self-absorbed mind come to us drenched in sweet reasonableness: surely we need to protect ourselves from the effects of *other people's* competitive urges, *other people's* untrustworthiness and *other people's* lack of charity. Surely there are times when any of us might think it's perfectly sensible to 'look out for number one' on the grounds that if we don't look after our own interests, no one else will look after them for us. We might even think that exerting a bit of self-interested muscle might gain us more respect from other people. And who hasn't enjoyed the moment of triumph when you can say, 'I'm right and you're wrong'?

It goes without saying that we must be prudent in protecting our own interests and managing our resources – physical, emotional and economic – so we can care for ourselves and those who depend on us. That is consistent with the dictates of the moral mind. But the self-absorbed mind wants us to go further, by making these concerns our all-consuming priority. If we were to surrender to its core message, we would become enmeshed in a raw and brutal contradiction of the very principles that underpin the operation of a civil society.

In chapter 3, we noted the contribution made to the mass movement away from religious faith and practice by the relentless bombardment of propaganda from the merchants of materialism and happiness, promoting individualism and the deeply unchristian idea of personal entitlement. Now we can paint that same picture on a larger canvas: it's not only the teachings of Jesus that are challenged by these twin seducers; they also challenge our respect for the moral mind.

The self-absorbed mind says I'm *entitled* to please myself, regardless of the consequences for others. The self-absorbed mind says the pursuit of wealth, status and power is a perfectly normal agenda for anyone who's serious about 'making it' in this tough, competitive, materialistic society. The self-absorbed mind says personal happiness is my birthright, and I'll achieve it any way I can; pain and suffering are the marks of the loser. This is dangerous territory: the surrender to the self-absorbed mind can lead to egotism, narcissism and worse. At the end of the line is the sociopath – a person so indifferent to the needs of others as to be incapable of empathy.

It will never come to that for most of us, but we are all tempted by the siren song of self-interest. Who hasn't succumbed to two or three of those 'seven deadly sins': wrath, greed, sloth, pride, lust, envy, gluttony? We all like to indulge ourselves. Most of us harbour occasional fantasies of a life of wealth and ease, which is why we enjoy holidays that create the fleeting illusion that we have achieved it. All pretty harmless. The problem arises when we try to ease the inevitable tension between the moral mind and the self-absorbed mind by engineering a gradual drift away from our moral moorings until we eventually hear ourselves utter that revealing cry: 'What's in it for me?'

While some people willingly capitulate to the self-absorbed mind, others become involuntarily trapped in it, scarcely conscious of what's happening to them. Some forms of psychological distress drive us into the clutches of the self-absorbed mind – anxiety and certain types of depression are classic cases in point. Neither the causes nor the treatment of such disorders are simple or straightforward, but one way of understanding the nature of the suffering they inflict on people is to try to imagine what it must feel like when the self-absorbed mind has taken over to the point where escape seems impossible. As we saw in chapter 7, people suffering from anxiety and depression may find themselves in the grip of an overbearing ego – 'the self turning on the self' – to the point where uncontrollable introspection shades out reality.

The social isolation sometimes experienced (or imagined) by people suffering from such disorders is a symptom of their involuntary loss of contact with the moral mind (to say nothing of the compassionate mind). It can be a very frightening experience to feel cut off from the social connections that give us our sense of identity, emotional security and psychological comfort.

In 2011, Godelieva De Troyer, a sixty-four-year-old doctor and the divorced mother of an adult son and daughter, chose to be euthanised by Dr Wim Distelmans, a prominent Belgian advocate of euthanasia. Like 13 percent of Belgians who are euthanised, she did not have a terminal illness. She was suffering from relapsing depression, relieved by a recent romance and then worsened by its collapse. She had described her suffering as unbearable, particularly because of a breakdown in her relationship with her son, the father of her only two grandchildren. According to a detailed report of the case by Rachel Aviv in the *New Yorker* (2015), De Troyer had equivocated about her choice to die, and did not consult her family. On the day of her death, she was driven to the hospital by friends who reported that she was laughing, evidently pleased at the prospect of ending her life.

Defenders of the rising incidence of euthanasia in Belgium (which also has the second-highest suicide rate in Europe) see it, in Aviv's words, as 'an accomplishment of secular humanism' and a potent symbol of the loosening of the Catholic Church's grip on Belgian politics and culture. Aviv quotes Jan Bernheim, an emeritus professor of medicine at the Free University of Brussels, who sees euthanasia as 'part of a philosophy of taking control of one's own existence and improving the objective conditions for happiness ... that goes towards ever more reducing of suffering and maximising of enjoyment'.

Not everyone agrees. Even supporters of euthanasia in the case of painful terminal illness question whether the 'right to die with dignity' is being too easily conflated with 'the right to happiness'. Herman De Dijn, emeritus professor of philosophy at the University of Leuven, said that De Troyen's story sounded like 'utopia realised: everything is neat and clean and terrible'. De Dijn believes that theories about personal autonomy have stiffened into pro-euthanasia ideology: 'Once the law is there,' he says, 'you have people asking new questions. Do I really have a quality of life? Am I not a burden on others?' De Djin believes that 'human dignity should include not only respect for personal choices but also for connectedness to loved ones and society'.

While most people (including me) support voluntary euthanasia in cases of terminal illness involving intolerable pain or distress, could the trend towards more non-terminally ill people seeking access to legal, life-ending procedures perhaps be interpreted as another sign of a cultural shift away from respect for the communal, moral mind (*It's all about us and how we care for each other*) towards the more individualistic, self-absorbed mind (*It's all about me*)? Every case is unique, of course, but when people feel they want to end their life because they are becoming a 'burden to the family' that surely raises some profound questions about the nature of family ties and responsibilities, and about the way we interpret compassion.

While many people interpret increasingly liberal attitudes to euthanasia as a welcome challenge to the political power of established religions, others wonder whether the pendulum may be swinging too far. Marilynne Robinson detects some 'wistfulness and regret for the loss of Christianity' in Europe, and there may be a trace of that in the British novelist and journalist James Meek's observation, made in a 2015 essay in the *London Review of Books*, that 'the cult of romantic love is the chief post-Christian form of religion'. Such a shift was foreshadowed (and dreaded) by George Steiner, the French-born US literary critic, essayist and philosopher. In *Real Presences* (1989), Steiner speculated that 'forgetting the question of God' would become the nub of emerging Western culture, and that references to 'higher things' and to 'the impalpable and mythical' would gradually drain from our language. For Steiner, the twentieth century was 'one of the cruellest and most wasteful of hope in human record', creating an aftermath where forgetting about God would seem, for many people, like the only sensible option.

Steiner's sentiments were echoed, ten years later, by Jack Miles, the Pulitzer Prize-winning author of *God: A Biography.* In his introduction to Jean-François Revel and Matthieu Ricard's *The Monk and the Philosopher* (1999), Miles wrote that 'in the post-Christian West, where the hope of salvation has disappeared almost without remainder into a craving for success, the appeal of Eastern detachment, as an escape from and a repudiation of this craving, may be larger than anything that can be synthesized from Western materials'.

The compassionate mind

Now we have arrived at the heart of the matter. Engagement with the compassionate mind is the goal of every mystic, every person whose religious faith is untrammelled by dogmatic beliefs, everyone who seeks to nurture their spiritual life and everyone who dreams of a better, more peaceful, less divided world. It is the state people variously seek through meditation, yoga, mindfulness, prayer, fasting, contemplation, religious rituals, drug use, pilgrim walks and participation in the creative arts.

The quest for engagement with the compassionate mind may also arise from nothing more esoteric than a bit of calm, rational thought about the best way for humans to live together. In a letter written in 1950, five years before his death, Albert Einstein concluded that 'our task must be to free ourselves by widening our circle of compassion to embrace all living creatures and the whole of nature and its beauty'.

Whereas the moral mind and the self-absorbed mind are always in tension, with the moral mind in constant danger of being dragged down by the weight of self-interest, the compassionate mind operates in a different realm. Its effect on the moral mind is to provide the buoyancy of spiritual enlightenment.

As an example, take the very natural desire for revenge (natural for humans, that is; other animals don't appear to go in for it). The moral mind recognises the authenticity of the desire but cautions us against giving in to it, on the grounds that revenge is a folie à deux in which the avenger descends to the level of the original perpetrator and they end up wrestling in the same moral mud. By contrast, the self-absorbed mind *loves* revenge. 'I'll treat you the way you treated me' is its perverted version of the Golden Rule. Revenge, for the self-absorbed mind, is a perfectly justifiable assertion of my entitlement to the rough justice of reciprocity: that's the subversive message it whispers in our ear when the moral mind is trying to talk sense to us.

And the compassionate mind? Revenge simply isn't in its lexicon, since the motivation for revenge never arises from kindness, compassion or empathy. The compassionate mind, when we engage with it, offers us the most sublime and noble ways of framing our reality; 'divine' does not seem too strong a word to describe it (whether or not you happen to believe in *a* Divinity).

In chapter 8, we caught a glimpse of the Christian version of the compassionate mind in the Sermon on the Mount. The standard it sets is so tough, so demanding, it's no surprise to find it honoured more in the breach than the observance. While some people dismiss the teachings of Jesus as a rehash of stock-standard moral precepts (the Golden Rule certainly comes into that category), the total package far exceeds the demands of the conventional moral mind. Turning the other cheek when someone strikes you? Going 'the extra mile' when someone asks you to travel a mile with them? Loving your enemies and praying for your persecutors? Refraining from judgement of others? Making forgiveness a way of life? Putting anger and hatred in the same moral category as murder?

Even if you feel some of those injunctions are too far-fetched to be taken literally, the underlying idea is clear: compassion, grounded in humility, is the basis of a good life. In the same way as the moral mind can protect us from the madness and overindulgence of the self-absorbed mind, so the compassionate mind (whether arising from a Christian motivation or any other) offers us a radically different approach to the conduct of our lives, to the management of our relationships, and to the way we deal with the crises and traumas of life that might otherwise bring out the worst in us.

The test of whether you are engaging with your compassionate mind is easy enough to apply. If you were a politician, you would embrace the spirit of loving-kindness in your dealings with your political opponents, treating them with respect and restraint, forgiving them their personal frailties and shortcomings, being unflinchingly resistant to the use of slur and innuendo, and confining the heat of debate to policy issues. If you were a religious fundamentalist, the spirit of loving-kindness would be evident in your respectful attitude to liberals or agnostics, as well as atheists and believers in other faiths. And vice versa: if you were a humanist, rationalist, agnostic or atheist, you would maintain a similarly respectful and kind attitude towards religious believers, including fundamentalists, even while strongly disagreeing with their position. If you were the neighbour of a troublesome and rowdy family, you would commit yourself to managing the situation kindly, respectfully and patiently. If you were in the midst of a relationship breakdown, those same qualities would be the hallmarks of your negotiations.

Utopian idealism? Not at all. There are many people on this planet – you probably know some – who regularly engage with their compassionate mind in ways that enrich their life and the lives of those they encounter. They are the very embodiment of human kindness. You see evidence of the compassionate mind in people who listen to you attentively and with empathy and understanding. You see it in the person who doesn't just give directions to a couple of disorientated tourists, but walks with them to their destination. You see it in a medical practitioner who is as interested in hearing your personal story as in checking the results of your blood test or staring at data on a screen. As Yale Medical School's Emeritus Professor Howard Spiro wrote in 'The Practice of Empathy' (2009): 'Empathy is the foundation of patient care and it . . . can be curative or at least helpful for patients with the "existential pain" that comes from the trouble of living.'

You also see evidence of the compassionate mind in people's extraordinary capacity for forgiveness. Following the murder of nine black churchgoers during a Bible study in Charleston, South Carolina, the pastor of St James's African Methodist Episcopal Church in Newark was quoted as saying that the hard part of being a Christian is that 'we must respond to hate with love, and that someday we will have to forgive even the man who killed Reverend Pinckney and eight others' (Frazier, 2015). It can be done; it *is* done, and not only by Christians. Media reports of appalling crimes occasionally include references to the family of the victim having forgiven the perpetrator. In far less traumatic circumstances, most of us have felt a surge of gratitude towards someone who has forgiven us – for rudeness, carelessness or foolishness.

You could lead a good life – even a life of religious devotion – without ever engaging the compassionate mind. Iris Murdoch, a philosopher I admire, was convinced that goodness, rather than love, was the highest ideal for humans. Certainly, the moral mind is a wonderful resource for bolstering our commitment to the principles of justice, fairness, equity, tolerance and social inclusiveness. If we all consistently engaged the moral mind and resisted the self-absorbed mind, the world would undoubtedly be a better place.

But there are always disagreements about what *is* just, what *is* fair, and how to achieve equity and social inclusion. Those are important conversations, but the compassionate mind takes us to a different level. The moral mind, for all its value as a reminder of our responsibility to the communities that sustain us, stops short of that extra ingredient that can transform us from being merely decent, law-abiding citizens into the kind of people who make a significant contribution to the health of the society we live in. In *What's So Amazing about Grace?* (1997), Philip Yancey quotes Mark Twain's reference to people who were 'good in the worst sense of the word' (that is, morally upright but lacking compassion) and the prayer of a girl who asked God to 'make bad people good and good people nice'.

The compassionate mind takes the pursuit of goodness for granted but reframes it so that kindness becomes the currency for all our dealings, especially the difficult ones. The music and poetry of compassion become the soundtrack to our life. Love becomes our primary source of meaning and purpose; our *reason for being.* The effects of engagement with the compassionate mind are potentially far-reaching: when Jesus referred to his disciples as 'the salt of the earth' or 'the light of the world', he was suggesting that those who draw their motivation from the spirit of loving-kindness will exert a disproportionately positive influence on the wider society, as a pinch of salt may season an entire meal.

India's great advocate for freedom, independence and the rights of minorities, Mahatma ('Great Soul') Gandhi, was most widely celebrated for a strategy that has become known in the West as 'passive resistance' in the face of injustice. But Gandhi himself disavowed that label because he thought it implied weakness. The Indian word he used to describe his approach was *satyagraha* and his preferred translation was 'soul force' or 'truth force'. He conceived the strategy as drawing its power from two apparent opposites: fierce autonomy and total compassion. This is how Marilyn Ferguson, writing in *The Aquarian Conspiracy* (1981), summarised Gandhi's approach: 'I will not coerce you. Neither will I be coerced by you. If you behave unjustly, I will not oppose you by violence but by the force of truth ... Seeing my intention, sensing my compassion and my openness to your needs, you will respond in ways I could never manage by threat ... Together we can solve the problem. *It* is our opponent, not each other.'

For many people of faith, the compassionate mind is nurtured through formal contemplation of it, ritual reminders of it and regular celebration of it, and then expressed in the community through charity and 'good works'. As we have seen throughout the book, there are many pathways to this highly desirable state of being. Humanists and those who characterise themselves as SBNRs may find themselves on precisely the same trajectory as Christians. Kindness, compassion, generosity, charity ... these are not the exclusive province of any religious or philosophical tradition; they are simply the qualities found in human beings at their noblest.

The compassionate mind promotes an attitude of acceptance, openness to others, personal warmth, forgiveness, gratitude, connectedness and grace. It also encourages a healthy regard for our own wellbeing, including a willingness to forgive ourselves: 'Be kind to yourself' is part of the larger prescription. Love's work is hard work and we need to stay in good shape, emotionally and spiritually, to get on with it.

Love sustained at this depth and intensity seeks no recognition or reward. Engagement with the compassionate mind is not about acting well in order to lift your spirits or inflate your self-esteem. I've lost count of the books and magazine articles that present charitable action as the secret of personal happiness, as though we act kindly and with compassion to benefit *us.* I once heard a man share with a roomful of people his secret of personal happiness: when he is feeling a bit down, he goes in search of people who need help and that cheers him up every time – a sure cure! I have no doubt it works for him, and the people he helps are the beneficiaries of his quest for something charitable to do, but his aim seems a little off-target, almost like something that might be dreamed up by the self-absorbed mind rather than the natural result of a loving disposition. It strikes me as an exploitation of other people's neediness in the interests of improving your own emotional state. (But maybe I'm wrong: even faux charity is beneficial to its recipients. I just wish that man would behave charitably even when he's feeling good about himself.)

You hear the same kind of argument in the context of morality: you should do the right thing because you'll feel better about yourself if you do, or because you'll be rewarded in some other way. 'Good ethics is good business' is a popular way of expressing this nonsense in the commercial context. In fact, the person with any semblance of moral clarity will do the right thing because it's the right thing to do *and for no other reason.*

In the same way, the loving disposition leads us to treat other people with kindness, compassion and respect because, as human beings, they are entitled to our kindness, compassion and respect. Period.

Is love enough?

In 'Love is Enough', the rustic musings on the sufficiency of romantic love by the English poet William Morris (1834–96), the lovers overcome all adversity ('though the World be a-waning ... Though the sky be too dark for dim eyes to discover / The gold-cups and daisies fair blooming thereunder') because of the intensity and constancy of their love ('their hands shall not tremble, their feet never falter').

Nice try, William. Unfortunately, we know that romantic love does wane and that, sometimes, the belief that 'love is enough' will not carry the lovers much beyond the first bump in the road, even though, like most people in the first flush of romantic love, they will have said 'this thing is bigger than both of us'. But we also know that something transformative happens in many relationships: a different, more enduring kind of love takes over – also, in its way, 'bigger than both of us' – and couples remain committed to each other, decade after decade, through thick and thin. (In Australia, about one-third of contemporary marriages will end, which means two-thirds won't.) So one kind of love is clearly not enough; another kind is needed – at least in the context of long-term relationships.

And in the wider society? Is love enough? Does the compassionate mind have the resources and the resilience to overcome the tug of self-interest and carry us to an elevated plane of existence that transcends mere morality, especially when we are dealing with people beyond our circle of family, friends, neighbours and colleagues?

Religion says 'yes'. Humanism says 'yes'. Secular mysticism says 'yes'. Gandhi's *satyagraha* says 'yes'. People who have experienced magic moments like those described in chapter 4 say 'yes'.

Not everyone aspires to full engagement with the compassionate mind. Some might say 'morality is enough', some might say 'legality is enough', and those in the grip of the self-absorbed mind might say 'my wellbeing is enough' and regard this entire quest as pointless. But for those who seek it, the resource of the compassionate mind is there for the taking. It might require some discipline, and there are plenty of techniques on offer, both secular and religious, to show us how it's done, ranging from meditation (especially loving-kindness meditation) to yoga, church services, spiritual retreats, psychotherapy and many more.

When people develop the habit of compassion, they report a significant shift in their world view. Some call this 'spiritual enlightenment'; some call it 'rebirth'; some call it 'wisdom'. As we saw in chapter 4, many people describe the consequence of such a shift as a vivid sense of being connected with everything. Whatever words are used, the common thread that runs through their responses is a feeling of greater openness to others and a more generous, less judgemental attitude ... most of the time. (Let's be realistic: all of us are capable of losing touch with the compassionate mind occasionally.) Of course, if we were to become smug about reaching that stage of our emotional and spiritual development, the point would be lost and the entire project would collapse. No wonder Simone Weil described humility as the queen of virtues: it is the ultimate driver of compassion.

You will have noticed that none of this has anything to do with specific religious doctrine or dogma. Yet it does entail faith – whether faith in a god, faith in the inherent value of every person, faith in the power of goodness, or faith in some force greater than ourselves.

What kind of 'force greater than ourselves' might attract the faith not only of theists, agnostics, SBNRs, humanists and atheists, but also those for whom all such labels have zero interest or meaning?

Though most of us would cheerfully put our faith in Reason, that could never be the whole story. Beyond the cool, rational dictates of Reason, every healthy society, like every healthy relationship, *also* needs the civilising, humanising power of Love. In all its manifestations, Love is an unequivocally positive social force. Who can deny the awesome power of parental love, or the love that impels us to help a stranger in need or to act kindly and generously towards the marginalised and disadvantaged?

Loving-kindness is my religion said a bumper sticker spotted by my son in Los Angeles. Though I suspect it might have been the work of an SBNR, it could equally have come from a compassionate atheist, a humanist or a Christian. (If Christianity is not a religion of loving-kindness, what is the point of it?)

Love is never quite enough, though, especially if you're interested in righting the world's wrongs. You'll need courage, as well. You'll need imagination. You'll need dreams of a better world that can be translated into concrete proposals for revolutionary action. You'll need faith in a Big Idea, which could well be the spirit of loving-kindness, whether or not you choose to call it 'God'.

In the light of all this, how should we live?

Augustine of Hippo, the fifth-century philosopher, theologian and bishop now known as St Augustine, once said, 'Love God and do what you like', by which he meant that a person who truly loves God will naturally be inclined towards goodness. There's deep wisdom in that if your God is the spirit of loving-kindness (though not if your God is vengeful, judgemental and retributive, or too remote to be relevant to what you do). As Augustine put it: 'Let the root of love be within, of this root can nothing spring but what is good.' That's precisely how the compassionate mind works, carrying us beyond the requirements of the law or morality to a realm where we are driven by our noblest impulses – 'the better angels of our nature' described by US president Abraham Lincoln in his first Inaugural Address in 1861.

Live like that and you can't go wrong. You don't lose the right to criticise, respectfully, points of view that differ from yours, though you do lose the right to attack the person who holds them. You don't lose the right to be assertive, or to refuse to budge on a matter of principle. The big difference is that, when the compassionate mind is fully engaged, the things that typically cause so much stress in our lives – our ambition, our pursuit of personal happiness, our desire for power, wealth or status, our determination always to win or always to be right – come to seem less important than the question of how to respond with grace and kindness to those in need of our support, encouragement, guidance or help.

Marcus Aurelius again: 'If you can find qualities in life better than justice, truth, self-control, and courage, or anything finer than your own mind's contentment in harmonising your actions to the rule of Reason and satisfaction with your own destiny . . . turn to it with all your heart, and enjoy the miracle you have found.'

Those who discover the transformative power of loving-kindness, through engagement with the compassionate mind, may well feel that Marcus Aurelius's 'miracle' has been found.

References

Alexander, Elizabeth, 'Lottery Tickets', *New Yorker*, 9 February 2015

Anderlini, Jamil, 'The rise of Christianity in China,' *Financial Times*, 7 February 2014

Anderson, Walter Truett, *Reality Isn't What It Used to Be*, HarperCollins, San Francisco, 1990

Armstrong, Karen, *A Short History of Myth*, Text Publishing, Melbourne, 2005

Aslan, Reza, *Zealot: The life and times of Jesus of Nazareth*, Allen & Unwin, Sydney, 2013

Aviv, Rachel, 'The Death Treatment', *New Yorker*, 22 June 2015

Baillie, John, *Our Knowledge of God*, 1939, republished by Oxford Paperbacks, London, 1963

Batchelor, Stephen, 'The Agnostic Buddhist', talk delivered at the symposium American Buddhism Today, Rochester Zen Center, Rochester, NY, 22 June 1996

Baumeister, Roy F., Kathleen D. Vohs, Jennifer L. Aaker and Emily N. Garbinsky, 'Some key differences between a happy life and a meaningful life', *Journal of Positive Psychology*, 8 (6), August 2013

Beare, Hedley, *Creating the Future School*, Routledge/Falmer, London and New York, 2001

Bellah, Robert N., Richard Madsen, William M. Sullivan, Ann Swidler and Steven M. Tipton, *The Good Society*, Knopf, New York, 1991

Betjeman, John, *Summoned by Bells*, John Murray, London, 1960

Blackmore, Susan, *The Meme Machine*, Oxford University Press, Oxford, 1999

Bonhoeffer, Dietrich, *Letters and Papers from Prison*, SCM Press, London, 1953

Bouma, Gary, *Australian Soul: Religion and spirituality in the twenty-first century*, Cambridge University Press, Melbourne, 2006

Bowles, Samuel and Herbert Gintis, *A Cooperative Species: Human reciprocity and its evolution*, Princeton University Press, Princeton, NJ, 2011

Bultmann, Rudolf, 'New Testament and Mythology' in Hans Werner Bartsch (ed.), *Kerygma and Myth: A theological debate*, SPCK, London, 1953

Campbell, Joseph with Bill Moyers, *The Power of Myth*, Doubleday, New York, 1988

Carson, James et al., 'Loving-kindness mediation for chronic low back pain', *Journal of Holistic Nursing*, 23 (3), 2005

Costelloe, Rory, 'The art of building community', *VPELA Revue*, Victorian Planning Environmental Law Association, 94, March, 2015

Cowdell, Scott, *A God for This World*, Mowbray, London, 2000

Cox, Harvey, *Fire From Heaven: The rise of Pentecostal spirituality and the reshaping of religion in the twenty-first century*, Addison Wesley Publishing Company, Boston MA, 1994

Crossan, John Dominic, *Jesus: A revolutionary biography*, HarperCollins, New York, 1994

Cupitt, Don, *The Sea of Faith*, BBC Books, London, 1984; republished by Cambridge University Press, Cambridge UK, 1988

Dawkins, Richard, *The God Delusion*, Houghton Mifflin, New York, 2006

De Botton, Alain, *Religion for Atheists: A Non-Believer's Guide to the Uses of Religion,* Hamish Hamilton, London, 2012

Dennett, Daniel, *Breaking the Spell: Religion as a natural phenomenon*, Allen Lane, London, 2006

Dessaix, Robert, *What Days Are For*, Knopf, Sydney, 2014

De Vries, Peter, *The Blood of the Lamb*, Penguin Books, Harmondsworth, Middlesex, 1961

Eckersley, Richard, *Well & Good*, Text Publishing, Melbourne, 2004

Eco, Umberto and Cardinal Carlo Maria Martini, *Belief or Nonbelief: A confrontation*, Continuum, London, 1997

Ferguson, Marilyn, *The Aquarian Conspiracy*, Routledge & Kegan Paul, London, 1981

Forstater, Mark, *Meditations: The spiritual teachings of Marcus Aurelius*, Hodder, Sydney, 2000

Frame, Tom, *Losing My Religion*, University of New South Wales Press, Sydney, 2009

Frankl, Victor, *The Unheard Cry for Meaning*, 1978, republished by Washington Square Press, New York, 1992

Frazier, Ian, 'The Talk of the Town: Newark Postcard', *New Yorker*, 29 June 2015

Fredrickson Barbara L., Michael A. Cohn, Kimberley A. Coffey, Jolynn Pek, Sandra M. Finkel, 'Open hearts build lives: Positive emotions, induced through loving-kindness meditation, build consequential personal resources', *Journal of Personality and Social Psychology*, 95, 2008

Geertz, Clifford, *The Interpretation of Cultures*, Fontana, London, 1973

Gourevitch, Philip, 'The Talk of the Town: Coming to Terms', *New Yorker*, 22 June 2015

Gittins, Ross, *Gittins*, Allen & Unwin, Sydney, 2015

Hall, Stephen S., *Wisdom*, University of Queensland Press, St Lucia, Qld, 2010

Hartshorne, M. Holmes, *The Faith to Doubt*, Prentice-Hall, Englewood Cliffs, NJ, 1963

Hitchens, Christopher, *God Is Not Great: How Religion Poisons Everything,* Twelve Books, New York, 2007

Hofstadter, Douglas R. and Daniel C. Dennett, *The Mind's I: Fantasies and reflections on self and soul*, Basic Books, New York, 1981

Houellebecq, Michel, *Submission,* William Heineman, London, 2015

Hutcherson, Cendi, Emma Seppala and James Gross, 'Loving-kindness meditation increases social connectedness', *Emotion*, 8 (5), 2008

James, William, *Varieties of Religious Experience: A study in human nature*, Longmans, Green & Co, New York, 1902

Jung, C.G., *Psychology and Religion*, Yale University Press, New Haven, Connecticut, 1938

Jung, C.G., *Memories, Dreams, Reflections*, 1961, republished by Fontana, London, 1983

Kabat-Zinn, Jon, *Wherever You Go, There You Are: Mindfulness meditation in everyday life*, 1994, republished by Hyperion, New York, 2005

Kaye, Bruce, *Web of Meaning*, Aquila Press, Sydney, 2000

Kennedy, Shannah, *The Life Plan*, Penguin Books, Melbourne, 2015

Koenig, Harold G., Dana E. King, Verna B. Carson, *Handbook of Religion and Health*, 2nd edn, Oxford University Press, New York, 2012

Konrath, S.H., W.J. Chopik, C.K. Hsing and E. O'Brien, 'Changes in adult attachment styles in American college students over time: A meta-analysis', *Personality and Social Psychology Review*, 18, 2014

Kuhn, T.S., *The Structure of Scientific Revolutions*, University of Chicago Press, Chicago, 1962

Lanchester, John, *Family Romance*, Faber & Faber, London, 2007

Larkin, Philip, 'Church Going' in *The Less Deceived,* The Marvell Press, Hull, 1955

Laski, Marghanita, *Everyday Ecstasy*, Thames and Hudson, London, 1980

Levin, Tanya, *People in Glass Houses: An insider's story of a life in and out of Hillsong*, Black Inc., Melbourne, 2007

Lodge, David, *A Man of Parts*, Vintage, London, 2012

Lohrey, Amanda, *The Short History of Richard Kline,* Black Inc., Melbourne, 2015

Lovelock, James, *The Revenge of Gaia*, Penguin Books, Harmondsworth, Middlesex, 2006

Mackay, Hugh, *Why Don't People Listen?*, 1994, republished in 2013 as a Macmillan ebook

Mackay, Hugh, *Turning Point*, Macmillan, Sydney, 1999

Mackay, Hugh, *Right & Wrong: How to decide for yourself*, Hachette, Sydney, 2004

Mackay, Hugh, 'Watching the Sparrow' in *The Lure of Fundamentalism*, Griffith Review, 73, Griffith University, Meadowbrook, Qld, 2005

Mackay, Hugh, *What Makes Us Tick?*, 2nd edition, Hachette, Sydney, 2013

Mackay, Hugh, *The Good Life*, Macmillan, Sydney, 2013

Mackay, Hugh, *The Art of Belonging*, Macmillan, Sydney, 2014

Manne, Anne, *The Life of I: The new culture of narcissism*, Melbourne University Press, Melbourne, 2014

Marsh, Henry, 'Better not look down . . .' *The Psychologist* (published by the British Psychological Society), 28 (6), 2015

Maslow, Abraham, *Religions, Values and Peak-Experiences*, Ohio State University Press, Columbus, OH, 1964

Mason, A.A., 'A Psychoanalyst looks at a hypnotist: A study of folie à deux', *Psychoanalytic Quarterly*, 63, 1994

McBride, Ray, 'Secular Ecstasies', *The Psychologist* (published by the British Psychological Society), 27 (3), March 2014

McLuhan, Marshall and Quentin Fiore, *The Medium is the Message*, Bantam Books, New York, 1967

Meek, James, 'The Shock of the Pretty', *London Review of Books*, 9 April 2015

Micklethwait, John and Adrian Wooldridge, *God is Back: How the global rise of faith is changing the world*, Allen Lane, London, 2009

Miles, Jack, Foreword to Jean-François Revel and Matthieu Ricard, *The Monk and the Philosopher*, Schocken Books, New York, 1999

Moore, Thomas, *The Care of the Soul*, Piatkus, London, 1992

Murdoch, Iris, *An Unofficial Rose*, Chatto and Windus, London, 1962

Murdoch, Iris, *The Sovereignty of Good*, 1971, republished by Routledge, London, 2001

Nabokov, Vladimir, *Speak, Memory*, Weidenfeld & Nicolson, London, 1967

Nietzsche, Friedrich, *The Gay Science*, 1882, republished by Cambridge University Press, Cambridge UK, 2001

Pfaff, Donald W., *The Neuroscience of Fair Play: Why we (usually) follow the Golden Rule*, Dana Press, New York, 2007

Pollan, Michael, 'The Trip Treatment', *New Yorker*, 9 February 2015

Robinson, John A.T., *Honest to God*, SCM Press, London, 1963

Robinson, Marilynne, *When I Was a Child I Read Books*, Virago, London, 2012

Russell, Bertrand, 'An Outline of Intellectual Rubbish' in *Unpopular Essays*, 1960, republished by Routledge, London, 2009

Russell, Bertrand, 'What I Believe' in *Why I Am Not A Christian*, Unwin Books, London, 1967

Sacks, Oliver, *Hallucinations*, Picador, London, 2012

Sargant, William, *Battle for the Mind*, Pan Books, London, 1957

Schonfield, Hugh, *The Passover Plot*, Hutchinson, London, 1965

Schumacher, E.F., *A Guide for the Perplexed,* Jonathan Cape, London, 1977

Schweitzer, Albert, *My Life and Thought*, 1933, republished by Guild Books, London, 1955

Seligman, Martin, 'Why is there so much depression today? The waxing of the individual and the waning of the commons', in Ingram, R.E. (ed.), *Contemporary Psychological Approaches to Depression: Theory, research and treatment*, Plenum Press, New York, 1990

Shepherd, John, 'Christ is Risen', *Anglican Messenger*, Anglican Diocese of Perth, April 2004

Shepherd, John, 'God's mystery is best left to poets', *The Times,* 11 May 2011

Shepherd, John, 'Am I a Heretic?', unpublished paper, 2015

Slattery, Luke, *Dating Aphrodite*, ABC Books, Sydney, 2005

Spiro, Howard, 'The practice of empathy', *Academic Medicine*, 84 (9), 2009

Spong, John Shelby, *Rescuing the Bible from Fundamentalism*, HarperCollins, New York, 1991

Steiner, George, *Real Presences*, Faber & Faber, London, 1989

Swedenborg, Emanuel, *Doctrine Concerning the Lord*, 1763, republished in *The Divine Revelation of the New Jerusalem*, Houghton Mifflin & Co, New York, 2012

Tacey, David, *Re-enchantment: The new Australian spirituality*, HarperCollins, Sydney, 2000

Tillich, Paul, *The Shaking of the Foundations*, Charles Scribner's Sons, New York, 1948

Tillich, Paul, *The Courage to Be*, Yale University Press, Cambridge, Mass., 1952

Tolle, Eckhart, *The Power of Now*, Hodder Headline, Sydney, 2004

Twenge, J.M., W.K. Campbell and E.C. Freeman, 'Generational differences in young adults' life goals, concern for others, and civic orientation, 1966–2009', *Journal of Personality and Social Psychology*, 102, 2012

Weatherhead, Leslie, *The Christian Agnostic,* Abingdon Press, Nashville, Tenn. 1965

Webb, Val, *In Defence of Doubt*, Chalice Press, St Louis, MO, 1995

Webster, Richard, *Why Freud Was Wrong*, HarperCollins, London, 1995

Weil, Simone, *Gravity and Grace*, 1952, republished by Routledge, London, 1963

Wilson, A.N., *How Can We Know?*, Penguin Books, Harmondsworth, Middlesex, 1985

Wilson, James, *The Moral Sense*, The Free Press, New York, 1993

Wilson, Timothy, *Strangers to Ourselves: Discovering the Adaptive Unconscious,* Harvard University Press, Cambridge, Mass. 2002

Wright, James, 'A Blessing', in *Collected Poems,* Wesleyan University Press, Middletown, CT, 1971

Yancey, Philip, *What's So Amazing about Grace?*, Zondervan, Grand Rapids, MI, 1997

Text acknowledgements

Epigraph on page v and extract on page 203 taken from *The Blood of the Lamb*. Copyright © 1961 by Peter De Vries. Reprinted by permission of Curtis Brown, Ltd.

Extract on page 27 taken from *Breaking the Spell* Daniel C. Dennett (Penguin Books, 2006). Copyright © Daniel C. Dennett, 2006. Reproduced by permission of Penguin Books Ltd.

Extract on page 27 taken from *Handbook of Religion and Health* edited by Harold Koenig, Dana King, and Verna B. Carson (2001). Extract from p.228 from Ch.15 'Understanding religion's effects on mental health' © 2001 by Harold Koenig. Reprinted by permission of Oxford University Press.

Extract on page 30 taken from *Dating Aphrodite: Modern Adventures in the Ancient World* by Luke Slattery, published by ABC Books. Reprinted by permission of HarperCollins Australia.

Extract on pages 32-3 taken from *The Power of Myth* by Joseph Campbell, published by Doubleday. Reprinted by permission of Penguin Random House.

Extract on pages 49 and 115 taken from *Memories, Dreams, Reflections* by C. G. Jung, published by Pantheon Books. Reproduced by permission of Penguin Random House.

Extract on page 58 taken from *An Unofficial Rose* by Iris Murdoch, published by Chatto & Windus. Reproduced by permission of The Random House Group Ltd.

Extract on page 58 taken from 'Summoned by Bells', from *Collected Poems* by John Betjeman © 1955, 1958, 1962, 1964, 1968, 1970, 1979, 1981, 1982, 2001. Reproduced by permission of John Murray, an imprint of Hodder and Stoughton Ltd.

Extracts on pages 66 and 105 from *Well & Good* by Richard Eckersley, first published by Text Publishing, are reprinted by permission of the author. http://www.richardeckersley.com.au/attachments/EckersleyB.pdf

Extract on page 99 taken from *The Light of the World: A Memoir* by Elizabeth Alexander. Copyright 2015 by Elizabeth Alexander. Used by permission of Grand Central Publishing.

Extract on page 100 taken from *The Mind's I* (9780465030910) by Daniel C. Dennett and Douglas R. Hofstadter, copyright © 2000.

Extract on page 106: James Wright. An excerpt from the poem "A Blessing" from *Above the River: The Complete Poems* © 1990 by James Wright. Reprinted by permission of Wesleyan University Press.

Extract on page 112 taken from *Wisdom: From Philosophy to Neuroscience* © University of Queensland Press and Stephen Hall, 2010. Reproduced by permission of University of Queensland Press.

Extract on page 115 from 'Church Going' taken from *The Complete Poems* © Estate of Philip Larkin, published by Faber and Faber Ltd. Reprinted by permission of Faber and Faber Ltd.

Extract on page 127 taken from *The Christian Agnostic* by Leslie Weatherhead. Copyright ©1985 by Abingdon Press. Used by permission. All rights reserved.

Extract on page 139 taken from *The Good Society* by Robert Bellah. Reproduced by permission of the author's estate and Penguin Random House.

Extract on page 164 taken from *Religions, Values, and Peak Experiences* by Abraham Maslow. Reproduced by permission of Ohio State University Press.

Extract on pages 32 and 169 © Karen Armstrong, taken from *A Short History of Myth*, published by The Text Publishing Co Australia.

Extracts on page 196 from *Fire From Heaven: The Rise of Pentecostal Spirituality and the Reshaping of Religion in the 21st Century* by Harvey Cox, copyright © 1995. Reprinted by permission of Da Capo Press, a member of The Perseus Books Group.

Extract on page 205 taken from *Belief and Non-Belief* by Eco and Martini. Reprinted by permission of Arcade Publishing, an imprint of Skyhorse Publishing, Inc.

Extract on page 248 taken from 'Introduction to *The Monk and the Philosopher* by Jean-François Revel and Matthieu Ricard' by Jack Miles. Originally published by Schocken Books. Copyright ©1999 by Jack Miles. Reprinted by permission of Georges Borchardt, Inc., on behalf of the author.

Extract on page 253 taken from *The Aquarian Conspiracy* by Marilyn Ferguson, published by TarcherPerigee. Reproduced by permission of Penguin Publishing Group.

Acknowledgements

My primary debt is to Ingrid Ohlsson, my publisher at Pan Macmillan, who supported the writing of this book with sympathetic guidance, spirited criticism and constant encouragement. She has created a working partnership as close to perfection as I could imagine. Ariane Durkin, senior editor, has been like a gentle shepherd, guiding the book through the complexities of the editorial process with grace and confidence. Kirsty Noffke has brought formidable energy, good humour and imagination to the task of organising promotional events and publicity. Rebecca Hamilton has been assiduous in securing copyright permissions. I am grateful to all of them, and to Cate Paterson, publishing director of Pan Macmillan, for the idea that inspired the cover design, which has been beautifully realised by Daniel New.

I have benefited, once again, from the astute and sensitive editing of Ali Lavau.

The following people have made significant contributions to my thinking about this book – via formal interviews, informal conversations (in some cases over many years), explicit guidance, and criticism of my ideas: Lucy Bainger, Sarah Carbone, Peter Copleston, Keryl Collard, Sarah Driver, Geoffrey Duncan, Pamela Jane Duncan, Richard Eckersley, Mhairi Fraser, Meg Hart, Andrew Hill, Jane Hutcheon, Bruce Kaye, Max Kimber, Sheila Mackay, Robert McLaughlin, Leith Macpherson, Keith Mason, David Morris, Chris Randle, Melanie Randle, Victoria Robinson, Briony Scott, Christina Sexton, John Shepherd, John Vallance, Alexandra Walker, Garry Walter, Julian Wood, Guy Yeomans, Pamela Young, plus three people who wish to remain anonymous and two close friends, Howard Russell and Meredith Ryan, who died long before this book was conceived, but whose influence lives in its pages.

It goes without saying that none of these people should be held responsible for any of the conclusions I have drawn in the book; indeed, some of them may strenuously oppose the direction I have taken. But all of their contributions have enriched my thinking, and I am deeply grateful to them for their generosity and frankness.

Index

Index